Freemasonry

Through the Jaundiced Eye
of a West Virginia Hillbilly

OPHIR E. VELLENOWETH

ISBN-13: 978-0-9844911-0-0 (hardcover)

Dragonfly Press Publishing
http://www.dragonflypresspublishing.com
author@dragonflypresspublishing.com

Originally released in 1992 by Pearson.
Revised and reprinted per author's directive May 2010.

TABLE OF CONTENTS

Ophir E. Vellenoweth was born December 10, 1931 in the old Rudler Building which was constructed by the Steenrod family in 1819 as a road house along the National Road in Wheeling, WV. He was educated at Triadelphia High School and West Liberty State College. He is married to Patti Lou Ulrich of Wheeling, and they are the parents of two daughters and three sons. Their children have blessed them with seven grandchildren. He served in the U. S. Navy during the Korean War, and is now a retired electrical contractor living in Wheeling. Ophir is currently serving as the Bandleader of a big dance band, Buddy O. and the Dancemasters, and a smaller musical group titled "Seventh Avenue." These two outstanding musical organizations can be found at www.buddyodance.com. During high school he was active in track. At its founding, he became a charter member of the Professional Bowling Association. He was the West Virginia State Bowling Champion on ten separate occasions. He served also as a small arms instructor for the NRA and for the U.S. Department of Civilian Defense. He worked as a football color analyst on radio for three years.

As a young man, he became interested in DeMolay, and served the Wheeling Chapter as Master Councilor, and a few years later as Chapter Advisor. He is the most decorated DeMolay in West Virginia holding: four Blue Honor Keys, Representative DeMolay, five Advisor Honor Keys, the Zerubbabel Key, the Chevalier Degree of which he is a Past Commander in the East of the Wheeling Court. He holds the Cross of Honor and the Guild of the Leathren Apron. He is an active Legion of Honor and is past Dean of the Wheeling Preceptory. He is Past District Deputy of the first district in West Virginia, Past State Ritual Advisor and served as Executive Officer of DeMolay in West Virginia for seven years. One of the founders of the West Virginia State DeMolay Foundation, he served as its President for twenty years. He was inducted into the West Virginia DeMolay Hall of Fame in the sports category in 2000. In 1963, during the Centennial celebration of the State of West Virginia, Ophir was named one of West Virginia's sports greats.

Ophir's Masonic activities include: Past Master of Nelson Lodge No. 30, A.F. & A.M.; Past High Priest of Wheeling Union Chapter No. 1, R.A.M.; Past Grand High Priest of the Grand Royal Arch Chapter of West Virginia; Past Commander of Wheeling Commandery No. 1, Knights Templar; Past Grand Commander of the Grand Commandery of Knights Templar in West Virginia; received the Knight Templar Cross from the Grand Encampment; Past Secretary, and Past Treasurer of El Tor Grotto of Wheeling; Life member of Osiris Shrine A.O.N.M.S.; was a 32nd degree member of the Scottish Rite Bodies of Wheeling; Past Excellent Chief of West Virginia Council No. 7, Knight Masons; Past Prior of West Virginia Priory No. 40, KYCH; Past Knight Commander of Mt. Calvary No. XIX, H.R.A.K.T.P.; Past Sovereign , and Charter member of West Virginia Conclave Red Cross of Constantine; Past Governor and founder of Fort Henry York Rite College No. 61, and honored with the Order of Purple Cross; Past Grand Governor of West Virginia for the York Rite Sovereign College of North America and a Regent Emeritus of that organization.

Other publications by Ophir E. Vellenoweth:

Sesquicentennial "History of Wheeling Union Chapter No.1, R.A.M.", 262 pages, hard bound, published by

Printcrafters of Elkins, WV 1977. This book has a place in the Ohio County library, and also in the controlled environment room at Bethany College.

Sesquicentennial "History of Wheeling Commandery No. 1, KT", paperback, published by Printcrafters of Elkins WV, 1988.

"Tales of Teams", furnished one Chapter, published by Reiman Publications, Greendale, WI, 1995.

Columnist for Wheeling News Register - Column on football officiating, 1978 through 1980.

Ophir also worked on radio as a football color man for three years.

"The Artist Behind the Cartouche", published in "Sons of the Desert', by Beni Kedem Shrine Temple, 1991.

Vellenoweth currently has another book in pre-publication entitled "Tales of the Colstops", also to be released in 2010 through Dragonfly Press Publishing.

Freemasonry
Through the Jaundiced Eye
of a West Virginia Hillbilly

Introduction

Knowledge is derived from study, or from experience. Intelligence converges on those who engage in both without arriving at a conclusion that all has been accomplished. Study is not just the assimilation of the written word, but includes observant dedication to correctly interpreting what is viewed by the eye, and heard by the ear.

Experience is not merely evading the Grim Reaper with the passage of time. It constitutes a focused accumulation of correct, as well as, incorrect information, and the subsequent determination of which category each bit of data belongs. The process can be painstaking, and time consuming, but help is available by reviewing information relative to the task at hand. It is not necessary, nor is it productive, to ignore the history of one's pursuit.

Progress comes from building on that which has been accomplished before, and making sensible adjustments to accommodate a current environment. It comes from the intelligent observation that problems are solved only for the moment, and that circumstance, and/or environment can alter the determination.

Much has been written about Masonry, not all favorable. Those who pontificate on a subject of which they have only superficial knowledge do a great disservice to society, for there are those who eagerly look for a controversial view on all subjects with no thought of examining the background of the writer. They revel in the attack upon any institution, or individual, and relish the opportunity for derogatory discourse.

It has been suggested that the better part of valor is to remain silent, and not respond to antagonists. Confrontation only stirs them to continued effort. Certainly this view commands respect, and is not to be discounted without consideration. However, sitting back in a rapture of grandiloquent silence furnishes a self-indulgent view that the Masonic fraternity is unassailable. An attitude that has furnished interesting chapters in history titled, "The Downfall of the _____." (Fill in the blank)

A realization that the world is not unanimous in its admiration of Masonic objectives or positions, no matter how lofty, must not dull the enthusiasm, diminish the determination to persist in our endeavor, or weaken our resolve. When physically attacked, the response must be immediate and determined, or the conclusion may not be acceptable. However, when the attack is verbal, it is imperative that an immediate and determined self-examination be undertaken before rising up in defiance. That examination must be made in a cold and detached manner rather than from a biased point of view, or the determination will be flawed.

There is no quick fix in modern society for every conceived ill, no matter the quarter in which it resides. In so many cases, a new problem faces us before we have an opportunity to focus on the previous one. Present day communication is both a blessing and a dilemma. The bombardment of news crowds the mind with a plethora of problems that may distract the observer from problems that are very close. The magnitude of information available on a daily basis overwhelms one with more data than can be considered, or handled. Intelligence reaches the heights when what is not known is realized, and that which is known remains under constant scrutiny.

What has here been assembled is the result of both study and experience. It is a collection of several examples of recording that which struck the conscience from something witnessed, or thoughts germinated from a word, a phrase, or an event.

One can only hope to stir the thought processes of those interested enough to follow along. If a few readers are stirred to personal examination and reasoned discussion, then the purpose of this exercise will have been accomplished.

Chapter I
The Condition of the Craft

D aylight breaks upon the earth and things come to life. Animals awake, stretch, and begin the day's task of securing food to sustain the body. Flora and fauna instinctively reach for the sunlight to secure the warmth and nourishment essential to their very being. Dawn brings a perceived promise that all things will survive; that nothing has changed during the night; and that anticipation of the emerging day provides a renewed opportunity for assimilation of nature's bounty.

However, during the day many will become the hunted. Some animals prey upon one another, and the life and death struggle is a never-ending one. Some flora and fauna are devoured to sustain life that is then snuffed out by those who in turn fall victim. Survival is uppermost in the scheme of all things, as the death of some prolongs the life of others.

Most species have developed diverse means of deceiving their enemies in order to grasp an advantage in the eternal battle. If they are successful only to a limited extent, then both survive. There are creatures that move only by night in an effort to evade enemies, but their foes have learned to also move in the dark. This play and counter-play has been going on since the beginning of time, and on many occasions various species, faced with a new and unsuspected enemy was unable to adjust and became extinct.

At some time man made his appearance upon the stage. Subsequently, he was attacked by disease, misfortune, calamity, and himself. Physiologically, he is no better than the animals in his quest for survival, except for the great advantage of a superior intellect, and an opposed thumb.

Intelligence changes the perspective and the objectives. Man was not satisfied to spend all his time searching for sustenance. He determined that controlling the movements of his prey, and growing vegetation that pleased his palate, would keep food readily at hand, and make the task of feeding the body quicker and easier. This provided time for him to pursue other objectives. Those who were more successful in these endeavors were envied by the less fortunate. Innovative ideas and good fortune generated productivity for many, and hard work and dedication was the formula for the success of others. However, some were not as fortunate, and man developed into the haves, and the have-nots. There were those who were not disposed to either hard work, or innovative ideas. They, along with the have-nots, whose status was not necessarily a result of an aversion to work, but rather from circumstance, endeavored to find other ways to elevate their situation and what they discovered was force.

Man learned that force comes from power, and power comes from control. The desire for power led in two directions. Those who were able to obtain the resources for physical power, and thereby control, found that they must be constantly on their guard. There is no patent or protection to prevent the other fellow from obtaining more power than you have; consequently, the drive for an ever-increasing amount of power became relentless.

But what of those who lacked the necessary attributes to engage in physical aggression?

They learned there was another avenue open to them. Just as success may be derived either by innovative ideas and good fortune, or by hard work and determination; so it can be taken away by two different methods.

Power over men's minds became another avenue of elevating one's situation. Some were trapped in an environment not to their liking, and so they attempted to convince others that the present system was wrong, not to their liking, and needed to be changed. When those in authority would not cooperate because they were fearful that submission to change would erode their control, efforts were made to replace the established authority. If such an attempt failed, the malcontents broke off and established their own nascent group in whatever form that might take. History is replete with these occurrences, and many have led to a complete change in the mindset of man.

Discontent changes man's view as he searches for relief from his situation. Often his perspective is narrowed because he does not take the time to research how he arrived at his present condition, and fails to accurately define a direction that gives some promise of success. Historically, he fails to recognize the dangers ahead, and remains with the status quo until he is mired in difficulties that may be impossible to correct. In the dark we know not what is ahead, nor do we know what we touch. In the light of day, we feel that all is revealed, but we are mistaken. Much cannot be recognized even in the brightest light, and there is much that cannot be seen. We know not what is over the horizon unless we have been there; and even so, we may mistake the horizon viewed, and our location, for another. Even what is near is often not seen. What is behind the rock, or the bush? What is hidden under the bark of the tree, or the hole that is in the trunk? What microscopic organism is being borne in the air, and what is in the mind of our companion, or our enemy? In the light of day we see, but are to some extent, blind.

If the brilliant rays of the sun are likened to Truth, in that under their concentration all can be seen; then man is not privileged to walk in the sunlight and thus be cognizant of all Truths. It would be more appropriate to say that he walks in the moonlight whose rays permit limited vision, and in the dim light he often mistakes what he sees. All too often he does not correctly understand, or interpret correctly, and is misguided by the shadows and the perceptions. Man is grossly deceived by a great unshakeable belief that he walks in the light of day and is all-knowing.

Ask any worker about the company where he works, and he can tell you what is wrong, and how the company really should be run. Ask any citizen about his government, and he can enlighten you on how to rectify its perceived faults.

Those not in power are self-appointed experts on the errors and abuses of those who are in power. A classic dilemma develops when those not in power are placed in positions of authority. They must suffer from instant stupidity, as they are soon the ones being accused of error and abuse. The answer here lies in the fact that no one accomplishes goals in the same manner. While there may be similarities, and certain general outlines that are followed, nonetheless, each operates according to his own personality, and his own talents. What must be determined is the final result, given the circumstances and the limitations determined by influencing factors.

What is the Truth? If it could be found in all matters, then as each problem arose it would be solved correctly with no need to revisit the issue. This ideal state is premised on the theory that relative conditions never change surrounding a consideration, and that Truth never changes. If such a status existed in the real physical and political world, there would have been no need for many of our government agencies.

The Founding Fathers did not create a Federal Aviation Administration, nor a Federal Communications Commission, for obvious reasons; but they are certainly appropriate in modern times. All can think of myriad examples of new issues and changing conditions which necessitated the development of new Truths.

If Truth is considered as one entity, then it changes as parts are added to accommodate new, and changing conditions; or Truth is changed in that it is expanded to include circumstances never previously encountered.

Man symbolically walks in the light of the Moon, and thereby lives in partial ignorance. Only those who recognize this fact become great, and live in history. President Abraham Lincoln was an excellent example of a man who followed this tenet. His cabinet was not made up of "yes men" who bowed and scraped at the altar of the Presidency. Nor did Lincoln dictate to them, He presented the problem, sat back, and listened to the debate between the men he selected because of their diverse views and agendas. From the debate he was able to see all sides, hear all arguments, and with an open mind come to a rational and productive solution, taking the best from all that he had heard. More importantly, he was able to determine whether the problem presented was a real problem at all.

As man searches for the Truth, what are his prospects? As he has in the past, he will determine the Truth, only to find out later that he was, at best, only partially right. He will eventually learn the great Truths of life, but only after he has passed through the Valley of Shadows; and then, he will be unable to com-

20

municate those Truths to his fellow human beings who continue to live, and act out their mortal lives.

All groups, or societies, down through the ages have established some sort of religious tradition and system of belief; but they have never come together on common ground. Indeed, many have broken away from their religious community over some point, and established their own religious culture; and once split, there has been very little tolerance between groups. Most likely there have been more killed because of religious belief and dogma, or non-belief, than for any other reason.

Those who have slaughtered in the name of religion did so in fear of, or to obtain, power and control. If all men are different, then there is no solution. However, if all men are created equal, then why should it be so difficult to come to common ground and live together in harmony? The answer is because man is inherently envious and jealous by nature. He cannot stand to see success in another unless his own success is considered superior, and even then, he fears the success of others will lead to further advances which will eventually undermine his own position.

Predominantly, man tries to distance himself from others by putting them down. This appears to be an easier road to superiority than hard work. What cannot be accomplished through dedicated effort might be obtained through disparagement. Only those who recognize this fact, and come to terms with it, ultimately become truly successful, in the sense that the world is better off for their having been a part of it.

Animals are territorial, but they are not prone to respect the territory of others. Hence, conflicts arise and the strongest prevail. Through the ages man has exhibited this same behavior. He expects his territory

21

to be respected, but has no respect for the territory of others; and so, he has participated in conflict and struggle through the centuries. Man seemingly never learns the important lesson that respect for his territory is limited by the extent to which he respects the territory of others. He seems determined to prove that while those who went before could not prevail by certain behavior, he is smarter and will succeed where others could not.

Isn't it strange that man has been able to expand his knowledge and understanding from walking on the Earth with a club in his hand, to computers, jet planes, and walking on the Moon; but during all those centuries he has not been able to extend his ability toward amicable accommodation with one another? Perhaps the answer lies in the fact that man perceives advancement in technology as a path to power and control, and that his objectives are promoted and deep seated in his desire to be preeminent.

Governments legislate safety regulations for automobiles, prescriptions, work place, and a myriad of other health saving items. Laws are passed to protect man from robbery, murder, con games, and other dangers. It appears to this writer that these functions of governments are only made necessary by the lack of progress in the human species' ability to respect, tolerate, and be charitable to one another.

Keeping what has been previously said in mind; let us now examine the Condition of the Craft. Masonry teaches no creeds, espouses no causes other than charity, and preaches no doctrines or agendas other than a tolerance for your fellow man. Masonry is based on all men symbolically meeting on the level, irrespective of their station in life. Thus it appears that the world would do well to take note of Freemasonry and the Masonic teachings, and that Freemasonry can provide a great service by spreading its basic tenets. An examination of Freemasons and their service to society verifies this statement.

In the separation of the Thirteen Colonies from Great Britain, the influence of Freemasonry was one of leadership and unity in a reasoned cause. It has been written that Sam Adams "recruited" Paul Revere for the Symbolic Lodge because of his stance regarding the relations between England and the Colonies. Once a member of the Lodge, he was taken into the confidence of Adams, Dr. Joseph Warren, and others of the "inner circle". Does this infer that Freemasonry was behind the move for independence? Of course not! But a big majority of the leaders for independence were coincidentally, Masons, and they felt most comfortable with those who had knelt at the altar and taken upon themselves the Masonic obligations.

Brother George Washington's staff was not totally Masonic, but nearly so. Did he lean toward Freemasons as members of his staff? We'll never know, but the circumstantial evidence might lead one to think so. However, there may be a dichotomy here in that perhaps it was merely a matter of men of education and social standing gravitating toward the Masonic Fraternity, so that the selection of leaders were predominantly Freemasons as a matter of natural course, rather than a specific desire to restrict the selection to members of the Craft.

Many signers of the Declaration of Independence, and the Constitution were indisputably Masons, and others were thought to be Freemasons, albeit no documented proof exists in some cases.

In Nazi Germany, none of the leaders were Freemasons. In fact, Masonic leaders in Germany were on the list for extermination, and a list of known Masonic leaders in other countries were also listed for extermination. Masonic Halls were pillaged and all documents burned. Indeed, a vigorous effort was made to suppress and exterminate Masons and Freemasonry in Germany. Freemasons in fear of their lives wore none of the traditional visible evidence of being members of the Craft in Nazi Germany, and adopted the device of wearing a little blue Forget-Me-Not pin in their lapel as a means to recognize each other. This writer is privileged to have one of those little lapel pins worn by some unknown member of the Craft during the years of World War II.

Since a vigorous effort was made to suppress and exterminate Masons and Freemasonry in Nazi Germany, and in any country the Nazis controlled, it must have been thought that Masonry contained the type of people that were to be feared by a totalitarian regime.

Hence, for those who would advance the condition of mankind toward a more cohesive and successful society, Freemasonry appears to be a valuable ally. However, to those who would subjugate and control for their own benefit, and those who would attempt mental control of society to establish devious aims, Masons and Freemasonry are an anathema.

Historical statistics show that following any large conflict such as the Revolution, the Civil War, World War I, World War II, there is a great influx of men seeking Freemasonry. Membership goes up dramatically, activities expand, and the Craft experiences great success.

History also demonstrates that the further such major conflicts recede into the past, interest in Masonry wanes, membership declines, activities disappear,

24

and the Craft experiences some concern over its status. Personal experiences in the Navy brought to light the fact that being thrown together with people previously unknown gives rise to a concern regarding who can be trusted. My observation indicated that members of the Masonic Fraternity readily accepted each other as trustworthy. With that awareness, it became obvious to me that Masons could enjoy an immediate acceptance among their own, wherever they might be, and no matter the circumstance.

Given the thought that man should be striving toward a more peaceful and respectful society, and that Freemasonry has exhibited over a long period of time its efforts in that direction, the condition of Freemasonry being a viable asset to society is germane and secure.

In further examining the Condition of the Craft, we must investigate its present ability to function successfully given today's environment, today's distractions, and today's competition.

Every effort demands manpower, to some extent, and Freemasonry is no exception. If membership rolls reach zero, then Freemasonry will remain only as an historical phenomenon, and its ability to assist in the struggle to create a better society will vanish.

Is it necessary for all men to be Freemasons? No, it is only necessary that enough men be attracted to the Craft so that there is a cross section of all the skills necessary for the Craft to function properly. On the other hand, the more men that are attracted to Freemasonry, perhaps the closer we may be coming to the objectives of society.

If the membership roles are adequate, the next consideration is whether the membership is actively engaged in the activities of the Craft. Are they merely names on a piece of paper that pay their dues, wear a pin or ring, and never attend Lodge meetings, or provide any sort of support other than monetary?

If membership roles are adequate, and attendance at meetings of the Craft are well attended, is there a pool of good officer material from which the members can choose those who will provide leadership?

The answers to these questions cannot be correctly answered in response to the overall general question stating the condition of the Craft. They must be researched in each locale. Each area realizes different problems of population, average age, and competition for the attention of the citizenry. Additionally, there is the question of the appendant bodies such as the York Rite, the Scottish Rite, Grotto, Shrine, and others. If the Craft Lodges are not functioning as they should then all bodies experience difficulties; however, it is possible for Craft Lodges to be vibrant and healthy, and one or more of the appendant groups to be realizing deterioration.

Over the years, there have been many outstanding Masonic scholars, but despite their extensive knowledge, like all men, they mostly have walked in the moonlight of Truth and perception of their world. Their standing derives from a constant pursuit of Truth, and a search through the dim light to achieve a better understanding. Constant study and search brings them closer to the Truth, or at least to a better perception of where the Truth lies, but their quest is not completed until emergence from the Valley of Shadows.

While the contribution of many Masonic scholars is of great value to the Craft, it would not appear that many have successfully analyzed, and successfully communicated the causes of, and solutions to the fluctuation of interest in the Craft. Occasionally we are privileged to see a paper presented by some good Brother, who expresses his concerns and makes some valid suggestions. Very often these suggestions have to do with the general structure of Freemasonry. What is here stressed is that each member of the Craft needs to examine his own position and that of the Masonic Organizations to which he belongs. If he feels there are issues of concern, he needs to instigate reasoned discussion on his concerns.

The Condition of the Craft is also relative to its stature in the community. An examination of history provides many instances of the Craft exhibiting its teachings before the public. Masonic funeral parades were the norm for a prominent Mason in the past. A study of old minutes will exhibit the fact that civil suits between Brethren were not tolerated. The two parties were called in, and the matter settled in a Masonic setting, rather than in a Civil Court. Unbecoming behavior was addressed, and the guilty party made to understand that such would not be tolerated. To be expelled from the Craft was a black mark that haunted the recipient not only among the Craft, but also in the community as a whole. Any Brother whose conduct is not exemplary should be counseled, and at one time that was the case, but no longer. Hence, by reason of such occurrences, the public's perception of the Craft suffers. At what point does society become indifferent to Freemasonry and its continued existence?

At present, more than one religious group either downplays Freemasonry, or objects strenuously to it. Perhaps that's not all bad. As long as those exist who struggle against the Craft, then a perception remains that Freemasonry is potentially of some force and influence in society.

There are only two ways Freemasonry can be relieved from an adverse spotlight. One is when membership declines to where we can no longer meet, or competent officer material cannot be found. The other is where society learns that in Masonry lies the architecture of the Brotherhood of Man under the Fatherhood of God.

A legitimate question regarding the Condition of the Craft is whether Masonry can survive with all the organizational divisions, and diverse fraternal activity? Without the Craft Lodges there is no Masonry. So the viability of that institution must be considered first. Beyond that, it is merely a question of how many Masonic organizations a community can support. A small village cannot support a complete York Rite, a complete Scottish Rite, a Grotto, a Shrine, a Tall Cedars, an Eastern Star, and so on, but it can support a Craft Lodge.

However, the big city can support all these, and more, without difficulty. One can belong to everything, but he cannot be active in all without perhaps permitting other obligations to suffer.

While our main concern is the Craft Lodge, we cannot overlook the other valuable Masonic organizations in our discussion. Their success can add much to the mix of recognition of Masonry's value to society. The exemplary charity work of the Shrine comes to mind. Certainly that body does not hide its light under a bushel, and is recognized and respected for the work it does by society; however, the Shrine depends on the membership of the Craft Lodges for its prospects. The connection between the Shrine and Masonry is not clearly understood by all of our citizens. Some think all Masons are Shriners, and others are not aware that any connection exists.

At issue in regard to the Shrine is the suggestion that has been made on more than one occasion that the Shrine remove the prerequisites, and accept whomever might desire to petition, whether a Mason or not. Unfortunately the Shrine has removed part of its prerequisites. One no longer must be a member of either the York, or Scottish, Rite in order to petition the Shrine. One must be a Master Mason and a member in good standing of a Craft Lodge in order to petition the Shrine. This brings the Shrine into a direct confrontation with the Grotto, which has been an excellent organization for many years, and also does outstanding charity work. The prerequisites for both these groups is now the same. It was supposed that changing the prerequisites to the Shrine would create a large influx of new members...Well, how's that working out for ya!

It has been said that perception is Truth. Perception is only Truth to the perceiver. It is not necessarily the real Truth. However, perception will open doors and command the attentive ear. It has been only on rare occasion that a truly well planned, ongoing, program of membership is seen in these appendant organizations. Mostly there are just a few who seem adept at securing petitions, and the Masonic Body depends on that select group for replenishment of membership. Sometimes time erases the ability of the few, and petitioners become sparse in numbers. Hence, the perception that there are adequate numbers seeking membership in any particular Masonic organization may be faulty. In researching the Condition of the Craft as it relates to any of the myriad organizations, the perception of the various groups must be researched both within and without the Craft to assure the perceptions are correct.

29

Man is different than the animal because of his intellect. The animal is often unable to determine that a new enemy is in the offing; hence, the animal is unable to adapt, and extinction becomes a distinct possibility. Man, with his intelligence should be able to sense that a new enemy approaches, or that there has been some change manifested in his old enemies. In the dim moonlight of his perception, he may mislabel, or misinterpret, but he should be alert to potential danger and attempt to make due preparation. In this dim moonlight he must determine the extent of the danger and attempt to make due preparation.

In this dim moonlight he must determine the extent of the danger he faces which often encompasses trail and error. He looks, he listens, and he makes his best guess. Should he find that he is mistaken, then he must be alert and ready to change again to meet whatever challenge he believes faces him. There is a potential for self-inflicted wounds in the scenario however.

To determine that a problem exists and be mistaken is tantamount to shooting one's self in the foot. Very few things are more destructive over the long run that to be expending vast amounts of time and resources on a problem that doesn't exist. The results are the depletion of reserves that should have been devoted to other objectives, plus the bottoming out of morale, as it is gradually discovered that a dead end road is being traversed in attempting to solve a problem that in reality does not exist. Man is impatient with projects that never exhibit any progress, and is prone to abandon those who persist in an apparent unrewarding effort. What effort could be more doomed to failure than attempting to solve a problem that is not there. Perhaps the Rev. Paige Chagnois of Richmond, Virginia, said it best, "Stop looking for downstream solutions to upstream dilemmas".

One of the most difficult problems in society is correctly identifying problems. Once correctly identified, the solution should be simple. Just try something that makes sense, and have the open minded intelligence to recognize whether it is working or not. If it isn't working, then try something else. Eventually the correct solution will be found.

If research and reasoned discussion determine that there are concerns in your Masonic community regarding membership, officers, finances, and community stature, the solutions may very well lie not in one change, or approach, but in several.

If Freemasons are faced with a new enemy... that enemy is themselves! Today there is much competition for everyone's time and resources. The days of yesteryear when citizens were looking for some way to spend their free time, and lacking today's transportation, technology, and level of income, ventured not far from home, are gone never to return. Masonry must, like the endangered animal, either adjust, or face the possibility of extinction.

In this light, there is no aspect of Masonry that should be sacrosanct from examination and study. During the exercise of such examination and study, we walk in the metaphorical moonlight, and must be judicious about what we perceive, and keenly alert so that we do not make self-defeating mistakes.

Let us now examine the benchmarks which might give us further insight as to whether the Craft needs to make some self-examination.

In the Twentieth century the United States had eighteen men serve as President. Of the first nine, six were Masons. Of the last nine, one was a Mason, but he was not elected to the Presidency, nor the Vice Presidency. What this means to the writer is that men with the qualities of leadership are not being attracted to the Craft in the numbers they once were.

During the Twentieth century the population of the United States nearly quadrupled, but Masonry has not come anywhere close to that figure. In fact, in many areas familiar to this writer, there are fewer Masons today than there were in 1900. The determination is here again obvious that men are not being attracted to the Craft in the numbers they once were.

Dr. Curt Chezem, editor of "The Oregon Scottish Rite Freemason, reported the following numbers in his January 1996 issue:

1) 1958 was the last year for Masonic membership growth in the United Stated.
2) The yearly decline in membership is approximately 3.5% nationwide.
3) 85% of Masons in 1988 indicated that they had not attended a Blue Lodge function in the past three years.
4) The average age of Masons in the United States is approximately 68 years.

This writer requests that you go back and reread the statistics just recounted, and ponder them for a few minutes. A continuation of the above legislates that each year it will become more difficult to find leadership among the Craft as the pool is shrinking. Hence, much like the snowball going downhill, each year the recognized difficulties not only grow, but grow exponentially.

At the beginning of the Twentieth Century, the Craft Lodge and its members were visible to the public through references in newspapers, public parades, and visible activity. Members were assigned to aide and assist the widows and children of deceased brethren. This may not be true in some areas today. This tends to indicate an unplanned withdrawal from public view which might not be in the best interest of the Craft.

What is being here suggested in regard to the Condition of the Craft?

First, that each member of the Craft should examine his Masonic environment. Is he a regular Lodge attendee? Does his Lodge have any difficulty filling officer's stations with quality officer material? Is the fraternity a well-known and respected part of the community? Does the membership experience a full calendar of Masonic activity? Is there a thirst among the young men of the community for membership in the Lodge? Are Lodge finances in keeping with economic overview vis a vis today and fifty years ago?

If the answer to any of these questions is negative, then it would be well to gather and discuss the issues. Again, we must be reminded that we should not seek to correct problems that do not exist, but if it is determined that there is reason for concern then we must seek solutions and change, carefully and judiciously.

The Masonic institution has weathered the test of time, and proven itself on the anvil of history. No, if there are problem issues, they lie in the brethren. We have been challenged by the competition for the time and attention of the citizenry. It is imperative that we not whine about how things have changed, but rather that we accept the challenge and begin addressing issues and problems that face the Craft today.

What is the Condition of the Craft?

We are at a point of self-examination. We are at a point of reviewing every aspect of our operation to make sure we are meeting the competition head on.

We are at a point of great necessity for thorough research, reasoned discourse, careful examination, and individual involvement.

Overwhelming circumstantial evidence indicates that inattention to the issues dictates that the Craft is in the final throes of dissolution. However, of great importance, is the opinion that if a willingness can be found among the Craft to step forward and address the issues in an intelligent, and appropriate manner, then the Craft is on the verge of a resurgence of service to mankind at an unprecedented level.

To the reader: Following our discussion on the Condition of the Craft, we here address the matter further in terms of its possible demise.

Chapter II
Prognosis on the Condition of the Craft

"Death is a subject that treats of no levity when mentioned by mortal man." The conscious mind rebels when the subject is thrust upon us, and the tender senses tend to barricade us from its reality. Life is precious to the owner; but as it applies to the rest of the world, he reflects upon it only as it impacts his own well-being.

Self-sacrifice for the sake of the common good has been lionized throughout history as the most admirable of deeds, while self-preservation at the cost of others has been vilified, deemed unworthy, and at times labeled treasonous.

Very few are faced with the choice between martyr and coward where the consequences are to live, or not to live; but all are faced with the proposition where finances, time, or popularity are involved. Given the choice of sacrificing one's life for the benefit of others may be influenced by thoughts of historical approval, and thereby a sort of immortality; but when the sacrifice is money, time, or popularity, no such lofty pedestal presents itself. Indeed, in the latter case, no doubt the result will be at best, approval by some, and disapproval by others. At the worst, it is ignored.

Society has established standards regulating conduct by its members in an attempt to prevent one from taking advantage of another. As time passes, and

35

conditions change, those standards, and the penalties for not observing them change. Legislative government exists on the national, state, and local levels to review and revise those standards. All phases of the media devote most of their news time to reporting the violation of the standards of society. Society does not, however, legislate against sacrifice for the common good. We are free to exercise this noble enterprise each and every time the opportunity presents itself. We are also free to judge on a case-by-case basis whether we shall engage ourselves, or not. Indeed, there are no established standards to judge whether an action is a sacrifice for the common good, or whether the participant has an agenda unknown to others. While society will decide whether an action is worthy of being placed in the category of self-sacrifice for the common good, or whether the event falls in the realm of self-serving, it cannot take away, nor add to the self-satisfaction of the contributor.

While many standards change over time, and some vary in accordance with the judgment of each individual, there are a great many not so ephemeral. Standards in nature are absolute and finite. Remove enough heat and water freezes...add enough, and it boils. There is no deviation from this rule. What springs into life will eventually wither and die, if not obliterated first by some cataclysmic event. Nothing is immune, not you, not this writer, not the birds or the animals, not the plants or the trees, not even the Earth on which we live, or the Sun which gives us light and heat, are immune. But as standards apply to man and his actions, they are stretched and bent to the whims of the moment as man decides on what level he will apply the standard to himself.

There are few that would not state that man

should be truthful and honest. All would agree on the loftiness of these virtues, and the desirability of being labeled by society as possessing these two ideals. And yet, how many can truly lay claim to them? Most with whom you come in contact in life claim to be honest and truthful…but are there really any who can justly make that claim? The answers to these last questions depend on the standard. If one sets the standard of truth as complete and unvarnished, no matter the circumstance, then those who fit the standard will be extremely scarce. Most have shaded the truth at some time or other in order to save the feelings of another.

For a nickel or dime, a person will most likely observe the standard of honesty, but will he do so for a thousand, or a million dollars? Yes, many will observe the standard of honesty that is absolute as long as money is concerned. But suppose the consequence of honesty and truthfulness involves the matter of one's personal safety? That well might put the matter in a different light. To raise the stakes even higher, let us suppose the matter involved the safety of one's family.

A man may be truthful when he will be acclaimed for doing so, but will he distort the truth in order to put himself in a better light, or to promote his own welfare? Absolute truth and honestly are goals which are seldom reached. Indeed, life presents situations where deviation from the absolute standard is in the best interest of society, as well as one's own personal relationships.

Honesty and truthfulness are standards, and as such are absolute and finite. Unfortunately, they come in degrees in actual practice. Difficulties arise when individuals err in choosing to alter these two standards to their personal benefit when it is merely self-serving, rather than in the best interest of society, or one's associates. While these standards, by their very nature, can become confused in their application, they are absolute and finite in their definition.

Life and death are standards not arbitrarily defined. The question is when do they begin, and when do they end. A great issue in today's society is when does human life begin. Attempts to legislate the matter meet with great disapproval from those on the other side of the stated determination, or definition. The boundary is perhaps unclear, but there is a point at which all agree that life exists. When the consensus arrives, the debate disappears; and life, of whatever quality, exists by any and all standards.

At the other end, we again reach a boundary somewhat hazy and in question. Flora and fauna that appear dead sometimes respond to proper care and become beautiful and viable again. Even men and women have appeared, and been pronounced dead; but miraculously live long and full lives after such declaration. Stories of ghosts and goblins have been fueled by the unfortunate circumstances of people presumed dead, being buried prematurely many years ago.

Both life and death are standards absolute, even though their boundaries may be unclear and in question. However, there is another consideration - that transitory state in between. It is said there are three stages, to wit: birth, life, and death. That is to say that between birth and death exists a state referred to as living; however, in all too many cases that state is more correctly referred to as dying. Dying can be that waste of energy used to hasten the grim specter of dissolution by focusing one's attention on the inevitable. Many agree that perhaps the ideal death is to pass into the Valley of Shadows in an instant rather than suffer the cruelty of lingering in pain and anxiety. Certainly there are those to whom this unfortunate circumstance becomes a reality; but there are many who enroll themselves in discomfort, fear, and a morbid anticipation, unnecessarily.

Living is that state of existence whereby continuance is preserved by active engagement in sustenance, procreation, and a devoted involvement in the well being that surrounds that life. It further connotes a dedicated cooperative effort in promoting the quality of that life, as well as preserving and advancing the environment in which that life exists.

Dying, most assuredly, reflects a surrender of will, a detachment from those standards and dedications which are necessary to survival. Death occurs in an instant, and is inevitable; but dying is a long and painful process that in many cases can be avoided.

What is the Prognosis on the Condition of the Craft? The answer is not simple in that it cannot be answered with a brief word or two.

First, let us examine the big picture. Unquestionably, Freemasonry was born; however, much like the debate regarding human life, there is some division on the exact moment the phenomena occurred. That question is of no importance to our discussion, as the debate surrounds dates and events long passed. Whatever one's position on the origins of Freemasonry, we can all agree that it is here, and it is now.

Second, we must decide whether Masonry is dead. Of course it is not dead. Freemasonry continues over the world with continued meetings, candidates, and philanthropic work. The fraternity cannot be adjudged dead while all its functions are active and operating.

The question of whether Masonry is dying well might be another matter.

In the days of operative Masonry, the apprentice was patiently and steadfastly trained in the skills of the art that he might be able to contribute to the general welfare of society, as well as provide a quality of life for himself and family. The learning was not only the practice of dexterity of the hands, but just as importantly, the advancement of knowledge that assured the future of the Craft as a productive society, both for itself, and for the world at large.

A time arrived when it was beneficial to the Craft to accept those who did not, and would not, be working on magnificent physical structures. Their involvement was speculative, and coursed toward the construction of one's life and mind, so that they would assume the proportions of a philosophical glorious edifice to be admired and emulated by all the world.

Where before, the Craft built great structures within which to learn and teach the laws of man and of God; it now applied that same science to constructing the standards and inter-relationship, which would motivate man to a better quality of life within and without the Craft of Freemasonry.

History is rife with societies, kingdoms, countries, and religions that have come and gone, but the Craft remains steadfast in its landmarks and its ideals. Language, music, dress, modes of transportation, and all the physical things of life are in a constant flux of change. Change in those physical things simply means that some die, and others are born. We should not say, however, that all things are dead, never to return, because some of them have, and some of them will.

The minds, emotions, and basic stimuli of man have not changed in all his history. He still thirsts for Truth; he still longs for peace and security; he remains desirous of knowledge and understanding; and he still yearns for respect from his fellow man.

Therefore, the Prognosis for the Condition of the Craft is excellent as regards the desire and need for such an institution among men. The Craft has not changed; it has not lost its ability to contribute to the well being of men, nor to the harmony of society. However, Freemasonry survives only through the efforts of the Craftsmen. Its life and viability are in direct proportion to the intelligent effort of each generation to supply those basic nutrients that guarantee its continuance.

In the archives of the Wheeling, West Virginia Newspaper are several interesting items referring to Freemasonry. Items that appeared on the front page of the paper with no hesitancy to mention the involvement of Freemasonry. Three of those items will be here recounted, but not quoted.

In the early nineteenth century a pirate ship captured a vessel in the Caribbean, rifled the ship of its valuables, and was disposing of all those aboard so there would be no witnesses. In desperation, one of the passengers made himself known as a Freemason. He was so recognized by the Pirates, and the Mason was put ashore on the east coast of Florida, safe, unharmed, and the only survivor of the captured vessel.

In 1825, General Marquis De Lafayette traveled from France to New Orleans. He then began a trip through the United States by way of boat up the Mississippi, into the Ohio, and eventually to Pittsburgh. From there he traveled by stagecoach to Washington, D. C. Partway through the trip, he arrived at the wharf in Wheeling, West Virginia (then Virginia) where he was met by Morgan Nelson as "representative of both the City of Wheeling and the Masonic Fraternity." The paper reported that after being received at the wharf by Morgan Nelson on behalf of the City of Wheeling, and the local Masons, Nelson then escorted the General to a Lodge of Freemasons. Following the Lodge meeting he was escorted to the home of Colonel Shepherd at Shepherd's Hall to enjoy an evening of music and dancing.

Chroniclers of our Civil War report an officer serving on a Union vessel on the Mississippi being killed in battle. The officer was a Freemason, and members of the ship's crew signaled the Confederates on shore, and under a flag of truce, a Masonic Lodge was convened by Confederate soldiers, and the Brother was given a proper Masonic burial on shore, attended by the Masonic members of the Union vessel.

The volumes of history are resplendent with such stories of the high esteem in which Freemasons were held by the world at large.

It is also recorded that Adolf Hitler feared the influence of the Craft, and set out to exterminate the Masons along with those of the Jewish faith. The list of Masons to be executed even contained the names of Brothers, resident of other countries, including the United States and England. The Craft was admired and respected as above reproach by good men, and was feared by evil ones.

By the example of its members, a favorable impression of the Craft was extant to the point that young men aspired to become Masons because of the respect in which the institution was held, and perhaps also because of their respect and admiration for some member that had touched their lives.

Over the years Masonry did not tolerate a deviation from the standards it set. Conduct within and without the Lodge room were not categorized. A search of minutes of the Craft dating back to mid, or early nineteenth century will confirm these statements. Brethren would be assigned to travel by horseback many miles to discuss the behavior of a Brother, and to admonish him that his minor lapse in conduct would not be tolerated. Brothers were assigned to look after the widows and children of deceased members for a number of years with authority to draw on the funds of the Lodge when necessary to assist. They assured themselves weekly that there was sufficient food and shelter, and that the children were being properly educated.

In considering the Prognosis on the Condition of the Craft, the question arises whether Masons have surrendered their will, detached themselves to some extent from Masonic standards, and are no longer dedicated to those activities necessary to the success of the institution?

Is the Craft actively engaged in the Masonic education of its members which is so vitally necessary to its continued existence? Does it carry itself with the dignity and strict adherence to is established standards that spark the admiration necessary to be placed in its deserved position in the community? Are its members still dedicated to that cooperative effort of promoting the quality of life, as well as the preservation and advancement of the environment in which it lives?

From the youngest Entered Apprentice to the oldest Master Mason, whatever their lot in public life from the menial laborer to the highest of public servants, the standards expected of a Brother are the same. The admiration and respect by the world at large is to be the same for both. They are, should be, and must remain on the level.

While governments change laws because of societal change, the moral laws of interpersonal relationship must not be changed or amended.

History of law in every older town in our country contains regulations regarding the removal and disposition of material from one's outhouse. Any such regulation today is useless, and humorous. There are a myriad of such examples, all just as useless, and humorous. None of them are relevant, or provide a better quality of life for the citizen. However, those matters that relate to the manner in which we treat and respond to each other have not changed, and are just as important yesterday, today, and tomorrow.

Each of us appreciates being treated with respect. Each appreciates his thoughts and opinions being considered. Each desires not to be ignored, or demeaned. Each wishes for an equal opportunity to live in peace, prosperity, and happiness. These basics have not, nor are they likely to change. Hence, the basic tenets of Freemasonry are just as viable today as they have been since the origination of the Craft. It is not unique for man to be offered that which he desires as a cover for some unseen, but devious purpose. Masonry has never been used in that manner, and its very intricate design prohibits such an exercise, and therein lies one of several attributes that has kept it influential and desirable over the many years.

Is Masonry dead? Certainly not, but dying might be a possibility. If it is dying, it is from a lack of attention, a compromise with the standards, and a lack of devotion and love amongst its members. Freemasons can only foster that respect and admiration in the world which they give to each other.

Masonry by its very nature requires a certain amount of self-sacrifice of time and talent. It also demands strict adherence to its standards, if it is to continue into the distant future undiminished. To be a

Mason tried and true is a lifelong endeavor. It is a voluntary effort that consists of that self-sacrifice necessary to the common good, and while not likely to place one on the pedestal of martyrdom, the sacrifice assures the quality of life of a valued institution, and inspires the intrinsic thought that we will live respected and die regretted.

No, Masonry is far from dead, and the prognosis must be determined by each individual examining himself, and the condition of the Craft in his area, to decide the future of this valuable institution within his purview.

For centuries institutions have sought man's time, money, dedication, and attention. Some were successful for a while, others lasted a long time, some have had their ups and downs, but continue to exist, and some of today's viable institutions will go to bed anticipating the morrow, but will not see the sun rise. What is the determining factor in the continuation of any enterprise, no matter how exalted, no matter how worthy? The answer may simply be the willingness to compete, to constantly be aware of the danger of complacency, never to compromise basic principles or values, and an abiding determination to be the best. If there are enough hearts filled with the determination to be the best, the prognosis of the Craft is excellent!

To the reader: Now let us begin examining areas of operation that have the ability to impact the Craft.

Chapter III
Expulsions, Demits, and Suspensions

L oss of membership through expulsion is a matter of serious import. Its occurrence has the ability to alter the perspective in which the Craft is viewed both by members, and by those who, one way or another, become aware of the action even though not members of the Craft.

Perhaps the first consideration by the Craft is whether the investigation and subsequent use of the ballot box was properly accomplished. A question that might arise is whether the former Brother was properly investigated, or whether the investigating committee simply took a cursory look at the petitioner, and made a favorable report without research and inquiry. Would it not be proper to call a meeting of the investigating committee to review their report on the petitioner who has now been expelled by the Craft? Would not a review be proper to determine whether the Brother in question had questionable traits before being accepted; or whether he had succumbed to unacceptable actions attributable to temptation not previously encountered? The issue being here raised is the thought that the expulsion of a member should be more than just that single action. Perhaps it raises a question of self-examination to make certain the Craft has not permitted procedures to become slipshod.

At the same time, there is the thought that the actions of some are overlooked rather than go through the procedures of expulsion. It is here suggested that overlooking the examination of possible Masonic offenses might very well be extremely detrimental to the Craft. Being compassionate is an admirable trait, but it is an individual attribute, and not one to be associated with an organization that prides itself on moral character.

It is appropriate to consider what amount to collective individual actions as being the expansion of individual concerns and sympathy, to the point of compromising the Craft. In those instances where the question is out, the view must be taken in proper response to the law, as well as the image of the Craft.

As an example: This writer was aware of the circumstances surrounding a Brother who was not just a card carrying member of the Craft, but an officer in a Masonic body. The Brother committed a grievous Masonic offense…one in violation of his obligations. Rather than a trial and expulsion, which would have been appropriate under Masonic law, the body in question asked the offender to simply quit showing up for meetings, and the matter would be kept quiet. The result was that the offender showed up three years later in a class of candidates of another Masonic body. A few of those who were aware of the situation not only took notice, but were noticeably absent as time passed, and two previously active members demitted. The members of the first Masonic body did not execute their duties properly. They diminished themselves in the eyes of others. They inadvertently created an untenable situation in another body, and deprived the Craft of further constructive effort from members of that other body. It cannot be too strongly stated that the Craft must not refuse proper consideration to petitioners because of some petty pique, or because of some business differences; neither can it overlook, nor condone, violation of obligations by members.

There is another area of concern when an expulsion becomes necessary. Did the Craft, in some manner, let the Brother down? It would seem that once a petitioner has taken upon himself Masonic obligations, we could assume that he has been well versed in what is expected in regard to behavior. The Craft might very well feel the new member has been properly instructed, suitable lessons learned, and that he will henceforth completely understand Masonry and its concepts. The first mistake is the mindset that the degrees are teaching valuable lessons in the same manner that the student is taught in school. Education consists of learning about that which was not previously known, or only known in the abstract. Masonic degrees are a revelation of the manner in which the petitioner was investigated. It is a confirmation to the petitioner that he has not been found wanting in the stature Masonry expects from its members. While the degrees are informative to some extent; the moral lessons exhibited are a reminder to the candidate that he has been accepted under these guidelines, and he is not to deviate from them in the future, or he will no longer be accepted in the Masonic Society.

Expulsions are sad in that they exhibit an error, or a failure, on the part of the Craft. At the same time, the stature of the Craft is maintained when it recognizes a member is no longer acceptable because of an improper action. It diminishes itself when it seeks to hide the same. Further, it very well may damage itself by withdrawing from an unpleasant, but appropriate task.

Expulsions might be likened, in a sense, to parents losing a child to inappropriate actions. Maybe with more careful supervision, more attention, and more genuine Brotherly love, the event which caused the expulsion might not have occurred. However, when deserved, the Brother must be expelled without hesitation. Masonry is in the business of bringing good men together, and not in the business of rehabilitation. However, when these rare events take place, we need to look inward to see if there is any place where the Brethren might have failed.

Demits are not a major problem, but must not be overlooked, if indeed we are to be concerned about the health and viability of the Craft. It is imperative that the Craft discover the reason behind the request. Perhaps the Brother belongs to a myriad of Masonic Bodies and his financial situation has changed so that he deems it necessary to relieve himself of at least a part of his dues obligations. If we grant the demit with this knowledge, then we are saying, "We want you only as long as you have money!"

Another reason for demit may be a change of location. If this is so, should we not do what we can to assist the Brother in relocating himself Masonically? When we provide no such assistance, even to the point of going along to introduce him in his new location, we are again exhibiting a lack of interest, if we are no longer to realize his dues.

Sometimes a demit is the result of some legitimate grievance that the Brother harbors, and which is unknown. This is perhaps the most debilitating event for the Craft in this category. We have not only lost a member, but have permitted one to be set fraternally adrift with a bad taste from his experience.

It is imperative that we make diligent investigation into any request for a demit. Of course it will be granted, the member being clear of the books; but we

49

cannot maintain a healthy environment Masonically, if we do not make absolutely sure of the reason behind the request, and see that we do what is necessary on behalf of the best interest of the member, as well as what is imperative in the best interest of the Craft.

If it is discovered that the demit evolves from financial considerations, the matter becomes delicate. Many are embarrassed to reveal that their financial condition has deteriorated, and reluctant to admit the same. If this can be determined, surely actions can be taken in some of the Masonic Bodies to relieve the Brother. Some Masonic Bodies have addressed the matter up front by awarding continuing membership without further payment of dues after a certain number of years of continuous membership, or after a certain biological age. Both these programs are to be commended, and should be examined by both Constituent and Supreme Bodies. Every organization has a fiduciary responsibility to its members to assure continuation; however, the Craft is not in the business of accumulating great sums of money, but in the business of accumulating great sums of good men for the benefit of all.

By far the greatest loss of membership in the three categories being here addressed is suspension for the non-payment of dues. Again, the problem may be that the Brother's financial status has changed, and he may not feel comfortable in seeking relief. It is not an easy thing for a man to say that he has fallen on hard times and cannot afford to pay yearly dues any longer. Pride has severed many a good relationship, unnecessarily. We should not be too proud, or self-serving, to find a way to help a Brother without injuring his self-esteem.

Sooner or later, everyone finds it necessary to

examine his financial prospects, vis a vis retirement from his occupation. If his Masonic career has simply been that of a non-active card carrier, and he sees no service or benefit in return for his dues, he may strongly consider letting his membership drop. Mistakenly, the blame is focused on the member for not being active. The true failure is with the organization. Opportunities must be provided and offered. Members must feel welcome and experience genuine interest and warmth of brotherhood. New members must not get the impression that there are cliques and factions extant in the Masonic Body of which he is a member. The atmosphere must be one of harmony and concern for each other.

It has been the experience of this writer that new members are all to often welcomed, and then left to their own devices. If they attend regularly and sit on the sidelines, in time someone will, perhaps, ask them to do something, and get them involved. In all too may cases research into the talent and expertise of the member is non-existent. Many are placed in situations, which make them uncomfortable, or one that is not of interest to them. In those cases, they do a poor job for a time, and then abandon their interest, never to return again. They have been inadvertently run off !

If they are not regular attendees, then they have not been truly welcomed into the fraternity, with all that connotes. Masonry is not a social gathering, although it does engage in social functions from time to time. Masonry endeavors to teach and remind its adherents of great moral truths, but it cannot succeed without students. Public education is benefited by laws and truant officers to ensure attendance; but Masonry must depend on the enthusiasm and thirst of individuals seeking its Truths. That enthusiasm and thirst is usually latent in all right thinking men, but it must be stirred and brought to an intensity by the fraternity itself. If such is not done, resulting in nonattendance by members, then they are prospects for suspension for nonpayment of dues at some time in the future.

The solution to the suspension for nonpayment of dues lies in competition. Many years ago there was very little competition for an individual's time and attention. Radios and television were nonexistent. Transportation was limited and slow. People thirsted for somewhere to go that would perhaps be at least moderately interesting. Their options were few, but Masonry was one of them. The examiner of today's dilemma is quick to cite the competition for attention as the cause of declining interest in fraternal fellowship. In reality, the failure of the Craft to accept the challenge and make the necessary adjustments is the true culprit. Competition should be welcomed as a stimulus to become better, not as an excuse for failure.

A new member may not ever again attend after receiving his work. If so, why did he petition? It is the duty of the membership to investigate. If the person is not attending, then why do we want him as a member? Masonry is an active, and not a passive type of organization. It flourishes on the activity of the membership, both within and without the meetings. Not to become familiar with the talents, abilities, and interests of each member, and put them to use, is again to eventually invite suspension for nonpayment of dues, or a demit. How many jurisdictions have an ongoing viable program of addressing the problem of suspensions? This writer asked all constituent secretaries not to suspend anyone for nonpayment of dues until they sent a list of the Companions, and wait forty-five days before acting. After that, they were to execute the suspension.

Less than half the Secretaries complied with the request. After all, what would the presiding Grand Officer know about their problems? Of those that complied, it was discovered that some constituent bodies had lost track of some of their members, and had no idea how to find them. They felt it was the individual's responsibility to keep them apprised of his location. Perhaps so, but is it in the best interest of the organization to merely say that since we don't know there the member is, and haven't received his dues, we are going to suspend him? Hardly!

With some effort, this writer was able to locate most all of those who had been lost. In a personal letter, it was explained what the organization stood for, and how important it was they be retained as a member… not for the little bit of dues, but as one of our representatives in the community. The results were astounding! Within the forty-five days, the dues were received from 74.7% of the names submitted by the several Secretaries. Further, there were additional Companions who accepted a quiet waver of their dues through myself, rather than applying to the organization for relief. Pride would not permit them to have it read on the floor that they were financially indisposed, and could no longer afford to pay dues.

Success is often the result of work, and for such there is no substitute. When expulsions are indicated, the Craft must not hesitate to see that the law is enforced, but should also make a self-examination to assure all procedures are as they should be. Requests for demits should be investigated to establish reasons for the application. Perhaps there is much to be learned, perhaps the member can be saved, perhaps the Craft will be better for the exercise.

Suspensions simply cannot be accepted without exploring every avenue. Communication with the membership is an absolute must, and cannot be shunted aside by the excuse that it is too expensive. Conversely, it is too expensive not to communicate, and communicate in an interesting and informative manner. Suspensions are the business of all the membership, and everyone who can be of assistance should be brought into the equation. Not to compete is surrendering the field uncontested, and is thereby the major contributory factor for expulsions.

To the reader: Membership is the life blood of any organization. It is imperative that we direct our attention to this subject.

Chapter IV
Membership

Recruiting is a word that is seldom used when discussing the Craft Lodge. There are a few jurisdictions that now permit the practice as a response to declining membership. Most have refrained from this practice although it is not without precedent. The history of solicitation for members will not be here addressed, but if the reader can locate a copy of "History of Freemasonry" by Brother J.W.S. Mitchell, he will find some interesting passages on this topic. Whatever the reader's opinion in the matter is not relevant to this discussion. Whether a jurisdiction permits solicitation. or does not, has no bearing on what will be here addressed.

As time passes nearly everyone has desires, and strives to attain them. It may be a new automobile, a new home, a boat, a hula hoop, a motorcycle, or some other objective. Some of these desires may be filed in the category of fads or whims, but some are far more serious than a mere fad or whim, and persist over a great many years. Some have to do with the attainment of stature in the community, a direct desire to be respected by society.

At one time, the puddlers (the man who decided whether the pour was ready, or if it needed more coke, more heat, or more ore) in the iron mill earned fifteen times the compensation of the other workers. The trade was not only lucrative, but a highly respected one. These puddlers had a Brotherhood, or Fraternity, and it was closed to any except the eldest son of a puddler. In those cases where a puddler had no issue, he could propose a young man of his acquaintance for membership in the Brotherhood., and to be taken under the proposer's wing to learn the puddling trade. Most usually the person proposed was a youngster eight or nine years of age that had been working in the mill. If accepted, the proposed was in line to learn a very lucrative trade by the time he reached the age of eighteen or nineteen. Ancient Masonic Guilds were no different. It was a closed corporation in which it was assumed everyone wanted membership, and if somehow accepted, one would expend every effort to be proficient. The rewards were monetary for member and family, security because of the skill involved, and a certain stature and respect in the community. However, in modern times it cannot be presumed that everyone wants to be a member of the Craft; hence, it becomes necessary to approach membership in a different perspective. Those who are urged, begged, coerced, or solicited for membership are under no self-imposed obligation to be an active part of the whole. Their membership has developed from a response to one type of pressure or another, and therefore cannot be expected to stimulate a vibrant organization.

Therefore, the practice of petitions being submitted based on a favorable impression of the Craft, and a sincere desire to become a part of the whole, creates a common ground between petitioner and existing membership upon which excellent fraternal relations can be constructed.

In the overall view that without the individual pieces the whole cannot exist, we must explore the term recruitment as relates to the Craft Lodge from a different direction. "A favorable impression of the Craft," is the foundation upon which our petitioners seek us out, and it is upon that foundation that our "recruitment" must be built.

Let us explore a recent event to which this scribe was a witness. A regular event at a local golf course is a two-man scramble tournament of nine holes of golf. For those of you not familiar with this type event, the format is as follows: Two golfers are paired (in this case, by lot) and each drives off the tee. The partners select one of the drives as being the best to play, and both hit their next shot from that position . This continues until the hole is completed. There are prizes (sometimes money) for the low scores. This can also be a four man scramble, or even a six man scramble.

It fell the lot of my partner and myself to play in a six-some. This makes the play slow, as usually there are only four playing together. All the rest of the competitors were playing in foursomes. One twosome in our group was playing very well, and reaching the seventh hole, they were two under par. One of them hit his ball on number seven green close enough to have a great chance at another birdie. Because of our slow play, the next two holes in front of us were open. The twosome asked if they could play out and go on to the next tee in order to speed up play. No one objected. They made their birdie and went on to the next tee. We finished our play and arrived at the next tee in time to see the twosome walking up the fairway of a very long par three hole, and we could see that one of them had hit his tee shot on the green, again in position for a very possible birdie. We watched as they made their putt and went on to the final hole. When we reached the final hole, the twosome was on the green, and as it was the last hole, they waited for us to play up.

57

As we reached the green, we heard a competitor who had finished ahead of us ask one of the twosome how they stood. They replied they were four under par. The questioner replied that he could certainly understand that as they had broken away from the six-some and were playing in a twosome.

One member in the twosome, who had been playing with us, became very vocal and upset. He angrily asked the questioner if they were being accused of cheating? The questioner replied that cheating was not a consideration, it was a matter of being assigned to a six-some and then seizing the opportunity to move out in front and play just a twosome which is, of course, much faster.

Unkind words developed. The golfer who had been questioned about his score made a big issue of being accused of cheating. His conduct was unseemly, and not admirable. Playing in a twosome is an advantage, of that there is no doubt. Playing in a six-some is a distinct disadvantage when everyone else is playing a foursome. But it's the luck of the draw when a number of contestants is not divisible by four. This episode was untoward and unnecessary. The twosome should not have left their assigned six-some in order to play by themselves even though there was nothing sinister in that they did. The man made a spectacle of himself by becoming livid at the remark. He made an issue of the event and drew unfavorable attention to himself. The big problem here is that the irate golfer in question was wearing a ball cap with a Scottish Rite emblem on it. This was hardly a fit exhibition to inspire others to become a member of that man's fraternity!

Recruitment of members for Craft Lodge comes from building a favorable impression of us and our fraternity in everything we do and say in every phase of life. Recruitment comes into play in another phase of Craft Lodge operation. Outstanding leadership is essential to the viability of any organization, and the selection of officers in any part of the Masonic Fraternity is critical.

Here we face a dilemma. No one, absolutely no one, should seek Masonic office. The office should seek the Brother. When Brethren seek office, they thereby reveal a private agenda, and the Craft is not well served by private agendas. As membership and attendance have declined, it has been unfortunate to see Brethren openly ask for anyone interested in being an officer to let the present presiding officer know of his desires. This is a terrible, and self-defeating mistake!

Many years ago the good Brother sitting next to me was nominated for Junior Steward in our Craft Lodge. One could feel the seats move as the Brother sat up straight, and was obviously surprised and proud to have been nominated for office. He had been a member no more than a few months, but had impressed everyone with his ability and voice. Then someone else was nominated for the position, who got up and declined,. A third party, and a fourth were nominated, both of whom declined. At this time, the good Brother next to me leaned over and ask me quietly, but with much concern in his voice, "What's wrong with this job?" The Brother was elected, but did not show up to be installed. To my knowledge, he has never set foot in a Craft Lodge since! Obviously, when no one else wanted the job, neither did he!

The abilities necessary to be a good officer are well known,. Those attributes are easily recognizable, and when it comes time to select officers, whether by election, or appointment, the choices should be obvious to everyone. Lack of numbers can make a problem in that the field of known abilities may not indicate anyone suitable for consideration. In that case, the membership must be perused in its entirety to discover that which is needed. The task is not a simple one, but one that should be undertaken with great care and concern. This procedure is vital to our "recruitment" of new members. It is vital that the community looks upon the Masonic leaders as citizens representing the attributes necessary to good leadership, rather than the opposite.

All too often organizations fall into the trap of partisan elections and appointments. The good friend is nominated, or appointed. Not wishing to create an aura of discord, there is no opposition to the individual presented. The error does not lie in seeking harmonious elections,. The error lies in presenting those whose expertise in life does not include the ability to preside and lead. The error lies in considering only those who are regular in their attendance, or only those who, mistakenly have made it known that they have aspirations. The error lies in not outlining the qualities and background needed for the office in question, and searching the membership thoroughly for those who can best serve the Craft.

Whatever the Masonic Body, the search for officer material is vital, and should be undertaken in a serious and careful manner, devoting whatever time necessary to assure the best interests of the Craft are served.

Has anyone ever seen a Brother who is likeable, a regular attendee, a willing worker, but really poor officer material, either elected or appointed to a prestigious office? Have you seen elections, or appointments that put a Brother in line to automatically become vitally important to the organization's operations a few years hence, and it being obvious that the end result will put the good Brother in a position for which he will never be prepared? Have you seen a Brother appointed to a position simply because of the city in which he lived, or simply because he was a personal friend of the right person? Is the Craft well served by this practice? It is a delight to say that not all jurisdictions engage in this practice, but many still do. In so doing, they deprive themselves of some very fine officer material simply because someone lives in the wrong place. There is an obligation to the Craft when it comes to appointing, or electing, officers that transcends acquaintance and/or geography.

Let's move on to the other Masonic Bodies. The discussion regarding selection of officers remains the same, but the subject of solicitation of members is now changed. We are not prohibited in any jurisdiction from asking a Brother to join us in the York Rite, the Scottish Rite, the Grotto, the Shrine, or any other appendant bodies. Any lack of personal familiarity with the Brother has been dispelled. If he was not the right sort of person, then we presume he wouldn't be in good standing in a Craft Lodge.

Let us set up a familiar scenario. The newly elected presiding officer of one of the appendant Masonic Bodies says, "Everyone bring in a petition, and we'll have a good year." Mathematically, he is correct. In substance, he is far afield. There must be an organized program of obtaining new members, and it is the responsibility of the presiding officer to see that such a program is in place, and is working effectively. What's more, it is the responsibility of the presiding officer not to change or interfere with a program that is in place, and working effectively.

First, it must be recognized that an effective

program involves effective marketing, and all the established rules of marketing must be observed, if success is to be reached. Here is a golden opportunity to research the membership looking for someone with background in business administration. No doubt they will have taken some marketing course in school, and can be very helpful in this endeavor.

If we have something of value in our pocket, and never talk about it, or never show it to anyone, who will be interested in it? On the other end of the spectrum, a large corporation can determine how much of the market they will corner by research and a determination of how many dollars must be spent. They will then make a cost effective judgment on how many dollars to spend. To corner a large share of the market may not be cost effective.

Many years ago, it was this writer's opportunity to attend a seminar put on by an appliance distributor in Pittsburgh, Pa. The guest speaker had nothing to do with either the appliance distributor, or the appliance manufacturer. He was a professor from the University of North Carolina, and he was there to talk about marketing.

He began his talk by saying that he had something in his right hand pants pocket, and that he would give a one hundred dollar bill to the person who could correctly guess what was in his pocket. All during his presentation, he would stop and give members of the audience the opportunity to guess what was in his pocket. No one did. It turned out it was some sort of obscure Chinese artifact. During his presentation he held up an empty box he had gotten from a box manufacturer. It was obviously for some new brand of soap powder. He inquired how many in the room used the soap powder. No one responded positively, as no one had ever heard of the brand. He then held up an empty box he had obtained from the same source which was for some new toothpaste. He asked how many use the toothpaste, and again received a total negative response. He then stated that the two manufacturers had determined the cost of promoting both products, and they had decided that it would be cost effective to corner 28% of the market with the toothpaste, and 22% of the market with the soap powder. The soap powder was Tide, and the toothpaste was Crest.

Our organization must be well known, and well respected. The Masonic population must be made aware of the importance of being a member of whatever appendant organization you are promoting. Therefore, an effective membership program must be coupled with an effective program of promoting the image, and the stature of the body.

Of equal importance is the awareness among the Craft of this particular body, how it fits into the Masonic structure, and the objectives it seeks. Yesterday, this scribe was sitting at a table in a local restaurant with a Brother. Another gentleman approached, and I was introduced Masonically. In a few minutes the conversation turned to Masonry, and in the course of the discussion, the Royal Arch Chapter was mentioned. The Brother whom I had just met stated that he had never heard of the Royal Arch Chapter. This Brother was a member of the local Shrine, and been a Mason for several years. Our local Royal Arch Chapter is One Hundred and Eighty Eight years old as of this writing. Success cannot be reached if no one knows we exist.

Let us examine a couple examples of membership efforts. The Grand Commander who preceded this writer got into his car, and traveled to a number of small towns that were remotely located from any constituent Commandery, or Royal Arch Chapter. He made himself acquainted and established good relations with a number of good Brothers around the state. The year he became Grand Commander, he met with these good Brethren at a local restaurant in their town and talked to them about the York Rite, and made them familiar with what could be expected from membership therein. Through his efforts several York Rite classes were held around the state, and with the cooperation of a number of Royal Arch Chapters (we do not have separate Councils in West Virginia)) the Grand Commandery had a gain in membership during his year.

This concept was well thought out, well planned, and successful, It should have been revisited every few years.

Well, we seemed doomed to going back to a loss again the following year - this writer's year. Not so, we had another gain because a new program with a different twist was put together. It so happened that it was my honor to be both a Senior DeMolay, and at the time the Executive Officer in West Virginia With those facts in mind the following program was developed. "On Saturday, March 9, 1980, in Clarksburg, West Virginia, bring your son and be in attendance. The State Line Officers of the Order of DeMolay in West Virginia will confer the degree work on your son, and the Executive Officer of DeMolay in West Virginia will give your son the Flower Talk - all of which you will be able to witness. In the afternoon, the Grand Commandery Officers will confer the Orders of Knighthood upon you, and you will be knighted by the Grand Commander of West Virginia, who gave the Flower Talk to your son." It was made clear that the Grand Master of Masons would be in attendance, the Grand High Priest, the Executive Officer of the Scottish Rite, the Grand Master of the Grand Encampment, the General Grand High Priest, the Governor General of the York Rite Sovereign College, the Grand Master of DeMolay, and several other dignitaries. A big class of candidates was realized in DeMolay, and with the fifty five knighted that day, the Grand Commandery again showed a gain.

Time, planning, and work are the three necessities to a successful membership program. You never know when a new wrinkle will pop up. An investigation of the Laws of the Grand Encampment revealed that if a Companion desires to petition Templary, and there is a Commandery across the state line that is closer than the one in his home state, he can petition across the state line. This discovery was communicated to our constituent Commanderies, and a few more candidates were garnered. It was argued that this point is one of convenience, and not a suitable part of a membership program. A successful membership program consists of locating all prospective candidates, making them aware of who you are, what you stand for, and why they should be a member. Any Brother, who is closer to you than to a Commandery in his own state, is one of your prospective candidates.

In the appendant bodies of Masonry, the pool of eligible candidates is limited by the membership of the Craft Lodges. It is the responsibility of every Brother to establish a favorable impression of the institution, if that pool is to grow. It is not productive to avoid being a part of Craft Lodge activities. Our first obligation is to the construction of a sound and viable edifice of Blue Lodge continuity. Essentially, if we do not take proper care that our foundation is well maintained and strong, we cannot hope that the rest of the structure will survive. The Craft Lodge is the foundation.

Membership in Masonic Bodies has been on the decline nationally for the past several years in terms of numbers. If one only counts numbers, he is led to an inaccurate conclusion vis a vis the decline. If one compares the percentage of population to membership, he arrives at a more accurate, and a more startling conclusion. To cite numbers is not a productive exercise. In truth, a decline in the percentage of the population that are members of the Craft is a more accurate read on the decline in membership. However this eye popping revelation is really of no particular concern. A rather shocking statement that needs explanation.

It being true that a certain level of expertise can be more readily found in a larger number, this being applied to a larger population, Masonry should be better than ever. Not necessarily bigger, but most definitely better. It means that the Craft has a larger pool from which to select. It means that the ritual, the finances, the programs, and the operations should be superior in quality than in the past. It means that Masonry should be an even larger influence on society than in the past. However, all this depends on recruitment by a favorable impression of the institution. If that favorable impression is not extant then while the pool is larger, and therefore most likely more available, the Craft has less access to the pool. It has inadvertently, by lack of attention, severed all connections to that most valuable of resources - membership.

It is the responsibility of each and every member to join in the creation of this favorable impression. Only in that way, and over a long period of time can Craft Lodge membership problems be solved.

As Craft Lodge rolls increase, expanding Masonic edification into the appendant bodies is basic. It constitutes planning and work…work and planning…planning and work - and it starts with the presiding officer. The danger is in the appendant bodies losing interest in the Craft Lodge. It is not for any to say, "They have a problem," for we make the statement about ourselves. There is no "they" in Masonry, only "us."

Yes, there is a way to recruit for the Craft Lodge, no matter in what jurisdiction you reside, and there are many ways to recruit for the other affiliated Masonic Bodies. It takes image, work, and planning - planning, work, and image. There are many pleasurable rewards in life, and most of them are derived from work.

To the reader: In the previous chapter we touched on the role of the presiding officer. In this chapter, we will examine the role of officers in more detail.

Chapter V
Training for, or Training on, the Job

One of life's travails is being thrust into an unanticipated position. Those instances that occur along life's highway that cannot be foreseen are occasionally traumatic, and at the very least, we often have second thoughts about our reaction and our response. If it's a matter of words, we can think of clever retorts, or some sensible response after the fact. If it's an activity, we are caught up in the exercise, and it is only after completion, as we reflect that we regret that which did not come to mind. Such is life. But such manifestations are totally unacceptable when we have ample time to prepare. Given the circumstances well in advance, not to research, investigate, study, and inquire, is inexcusable. And yet, far too many are guilty of just such failings when elected to a position they knew was coming long in advance.

Certainly, as the time draws near, the prospective leader thinks of some ideas, and often jots them down, perhaps even in a formal manner; nonetheless, all too often he is not properly prepared for the task ahead.

His ideas and thoughts, while original in his mind, may be items tried many years before that failed. His plans for change may contradict present posture that took years to develop, and may in reality be a step backward. There is much to be considered in preparation, and the effort should be carefully orchestrated.

In Masonry, ritual is of prime importance. It is that portion of our effort that instrumentally sets the Craft apart from other organizations. It must be presented in an excellent and professional manner. There is no acceptance of "that's good enough." The ritual presentation absolutely must "be the very best it can be."

Jurisprudence sets the limits within which we operate. Man long ago discovered that it was necessary to establish a code of laws in every facet of life upon which the majority will agree, and to which the minority must conform, or suffer such penalty as the majority has adjudged appropriate for violation. These codes not only apply to behavior, but also are just as important in the matter of communication and understanding.

We are in agreement to count one, two, three, and four. However, if a few decide to count two, four, one, three, then two and two would still be four, but the few would interpret the answer differently from the majority. The majority would view the answer, and envision twice as many items as being counted by the minority. The interpretation put on the answer by the majority would equate the interpretation put on four and four equals three by the minority. How confusing! There must be a Code of Laws in everything we do, otherwise we not only experience chaos, but progress of any kind, in any field, would be slow and difficult. What ever endeavor we attempt, there are rules of one kind or another. And with that last statement another consideration arises. We must stress that it is imperative that one KNOW the rules and regulations, and not just THINK they know.

For many years football officiating occupied a

great deal of my time. The vast number of coaches and players that had a poor knowledge of the rules was always cause for amazement. On the other hand, the coaches who were successful everywhere they went, had an excellent knowledge of the rules, and it appeared they passed this knowledge on to the players.

So, if one does not spend at least a year in concentrated study of Jurisprudence, including the By Laws of the local body, the history of the same, and ask for assistance in this study, then he is doomed to make errors of one type or another. While these errors may only result in lost time, nonetheless, lost time is punitive in nature, in that time is a finite resource.

Finances have caused people to divorce, rob, cheat, kill, and go to war. Surely anything that has evoked such response in the history of man must be taken seriously. Hence, study time is warranted in financial research. Financial planning and budgeting are absolutely essential to the success of any enterprise. It is improper for a presiding officer to infer that these matters are the responsibility of others. Not so! The responsibility is his, and others to whom he refers are his advisors, or helpers. He must make sure that his term will exhibit proper fiduciary responsibility to the members past, present, and future.

Wealth is an unforgiving mistress. It beckons to be sought and conquered, and yet never surrenders itself fully to control. It is a seductress that can lead to destruction, or to security, or to brief exhilaration. Yet, it does not dictate how it will be handled. It willingly bows to the wisdom, the luck, or the stupidity of its pursuer, and constantly teases the stability of society. It is the yardstick by which much is measured, the enabler of much that is good, and yet the bottomless chasm by which much is destroyed. Since some small

70

measure of financial stability cannot be done without, and recognizing the perils, an intelligent approach to fiduciary responsibility is in order.

Whatever financial condition we presently find our organization is the responsibility of those who preceded us. We can make some minor adjustments in order to alleviate a current condition, but we cannot improve the big picture for ourselves. If we are pleased with the present condition, then it behooves us to study the financial management of the past in order to follow along what apparently is a good plan.

On the other hand, if we find that financial matters are not in keeping with the present economy, we must devise a financial plan that will correct the present situation for those who follow.

What are the yardsticks? How much money should an organization have? Well, that is a matter that must be researched and decided. There are no established answers because each situation is different. For example, when I was newly married, early twenties, and children on the way, it was obvious that a car was needed, as well as a home for my family. The wealth was not available to accomplish the purchase of a car and a home. There is no reason to be ashamed of the fact that a young man in his early twenties had not the wherewithal to pay cash for major expenditures. The local banker assisted, and the payments were made. However, while there was no doubt the home purchased would retain value proportionate to the current economy, it was without question the automobile would not only depreciate, but would also deteriorate, and have to be replaced. Would it be foolish not to begin saving money for the purchase of an auto once the loan for the first one was paid? Those who never prepare for the replacement of items that reason indicates will become necessary are the banker's sweetheart!

Suppose that the young man pays $1550.00 for his first car, and when the payments are concluded, is fiscally responsible by opening a savings account to prepare for the next car when it becomes necessary. He reasons that his present car will be worth about $350.00 as a trade in, and that he will therefore need to save $1200.00. Once the $1200.00 is saved, he ceases adding money to the car savings account. We must at least admire the fact the young man is at least making some attempt at fiscal responsibility; however, he has not carried his thinking far enough. What about the impact of inflation on his thinking? Is there a possibility that his family might need a different type of car in the future; perhaps a station wagon, or maybe a four wheel drive vehicle? Once the children start to school, will his wife want to go back to work, and therefore will he need an additional car? There are lots of additional factors the young man must address in regard to this lifelong expense...transportation!

And so, in our organization the research must cover the cost of replacement, the cost of updating, the cost of expansion, the cost of promotion, the cost of assistance to members and their families, the cost of entertainment, and the cost of operations. What's more, preparation must be made for the unknown and the unexpected.

The study and research necessary by an incoming officer in the field of finances is an extensive one, and unless he is an expert economist, no doubt he will need some help and advice.

Most of our organizations have investments that are revenue producing. Those investments were made many years ago when the initiation fees were representative of the economy. Those fees have not maintained parity with inflation; hence, it is no longer possible to add to the investments, and organizations continue to raise the yearly dues in order to pay current expenses. In some cases, study might indicate that the net worth of an organization that has substantial worth in numbers is actually deteriorating financially in real dollars. To put it simply, how many loaves of bread can they buy with their net worth as compared to forty or fifty years ago? If they cannot buy as many, then their condition is deteriorating. If they can only buy the same amount, they are making no progress. A sound financial program is vital to the continuation of any endeavor.

Presiding is more than just banging the gavel. Again, there are rules to be followed. Most generally, Robert's Rules of Order will stand a presiding officer in good stead, and he should make sure he is an expert on their use.

The prospective presiding officer should study the philosophy of handling a meeting, as well as the theories of chairing. Open debate is desirable; however, it must be orderly and prompt without giving the impression of railroading items and decisions, The presiding officer has a difficult task to handle when controversial issues arise. As long as it is a matter of reading the minutes and paying the bills, the task is simple and easy. The difficulty arises when controversial issues are on the floor. The presiding officer must not become caught up in the debate because of his own personal opinion. Should the matter come down to a tie vote, he can then cast the deciding vote, but in the meantime, he must learn to be impartial and fair to both sides. He must not let one side monopolize the debate, nor permit wandering outside the issue. His job is to keep the matter fair, unbiased, and throughout to maintain the dignity of the debate, and the institution. A thorough knowledge of Robert's Rules of Order will be of great value, and some research in the local library in the area of instructions to Supervisors, and/or Management is very important.

Okay, so our prospect is ready to make sure that any ritual presentations are of excellent quality, he has studied the Jurisprudence of the organization and the local By Laws, and gathered an expert group to assist him in financial concerns, and has generated an outstanding financial program…he's ready! Not so fast my friend! What is the agenda for the upcoming term? Are there to be social activities, and do they interfere with other well-attended social functions in the area? Are there specific dates for the introduction of new members? Have adequate means of communication with all members been set up? Has an effective membership program been established as discussed in a previous chapter? Have there been any training programs set up for the other officers to assist them in their preparations to move up? Has there been any inquiry of the membership to see if they have any suggestions regarding operation of the organization? If not, then there is much more work to be done before the prospect is ready for the gavel.

Planning, scheduling, and programming will have a great deal to do with the success of any endeavor. The days when people joined simply to have something to do are gone, and will never return. No longer can you simply open the door and stand back while the crowd rushes in. Today, and in the future, there exists a fierce competition for people's attention, time, and money.

Unfortunately, all too many are more than willing to despair and withdraw. They feel there is no hope, blaming the competition, the times, the TV,. the morals, and myriad of other excuses. Competition will make you better, or will drive you from the field. Someone will win the battle for people's attention, and that someone will be those willing to expend their time, energy, and resources to ensure success.

It is an unusual circumstance that brings someone directly to the gavel. Masonically, this would only happen to someone who has been there before, or who is skipping over only one station in the progressive line. Usually there are at least a few years of service prior to arriving at the presiding chair, and thus ample opportunity to be aware, and to accomplish the necessary preparations.

As in all things, two heads are better than one, and so it would be well for a group of officers to sit down with a group of past presiding officers to review those things constituting necessary preparation. A list could be made assigning each category of study to a year of service in the progressive line. An outline could be made to assist the student in his learning experience, and importantly, each year the student completing that year's study could review and add any new discoveries to the outline. This is not a fresh idea, but one put together by Past General Grand High Priest Winchester of Florida. The outline he prepared for just such an endeavor is an excellent one, and is highly recommended in this quarter.

Of vital importance in this preparation is the study of the organization's history. We are not here interested in the who, what, and when. Nor are we interested in dates and genealogy. A careful study of the history of the particular body that is germane to the issue is imperative, whether it be constituent, or Grand Body. The only manner in which this can be accomplished is by reading, and studying the minutes. Let that be stated one more time! Read and study the minutes of the organization of which you are in line to preside. Should there be any question...not some of the minutes...not part of the minutes...but all of the minutes! What can be learned from the minutes is essential to a productive and knowledgeable presiding officer. So many times someone proposes what they think is a great idea, but it was tried many years ago, and it didn't work. There is no reason to think that we are any smarter than our predecessors, unless some error can be spotted in their application that leads one to believe that approached in a different manner, it can be made to work this time around.

It is also imperative that we learn through the minutes from whence we came. What might seem like a reasonable change in one of our procedures, or one of our organization points might very well take us back to something that was found untenable years ago. If history is not studied, we are doomed to repeat the mistakes of the past, or perhaps return to some unproductive arrangement.

At the same time, the opportunity to restore what was once a viable and successful project of the past can be realized. Some successful event can be revisited, or some organizational point can be restored that was only changed on the whim of someone who had a personal agenda. There is much to be learned from the minutes, and in some cases, it is possible to learn the fine details of some particular occurrence by interviewing someone who was present at the time, Permit me to elaborate on that last point.

Upon my entry into the Grand Commandery line of my state, I was contacted by one of the local Past Grand Commanders who had also been active in the Grand Encampment. This Sir Knight was a very quiet man, but extremely intelligent. He suggested that if it were agreeable, he would be glad to have me visit his home to discuss Templary. This opportunity was seized, and two subsequent calls were made to see if the esteemed Past Grand Commander was available for additional discussions. Never during any of these discussions, each of which lasted two and one half hours to three hours, did he suggest what should, or should not, be done. His entire focus was on recounting events and problems to which he had been privy, the subsequent solutions, and the results of those solutions. I felt like I had obtained a Master's Degree in Templary.

If any part of the preceding rings a bell, then you must discount training on the job. To learn as you go might be an acceptable alternative in those cases where the tenure is of long duration, but we are not facing lifetime assignment. We are attempting to preside for a year or two, or in some cases, three; certainly much too short a period of time to even contemplate learning by trial and error. If we permit such behavior, we suffer the organization to become a school of learning with the presiding officer, the student. New members are students, and are to be brought along to a fuller understanding of the institution. We certainly cannot afford the added burden of educating our presiding officer, only to see him leave office before the learning experience is complete, and his place taken by another student. If the institution is to prosper then we must realize the absolute necessity of installing presiding officers that have done their homework, and are genuinely prepared for the task ahead.

To review our check list again, we expect our new presiding officer to have made proper preparations to see that the ritual work is exhibited in an accurate and impressive manner. Our man, hopefully, has spent much time reviewing and studying the Jurisprudence of the organization including all Rules and Regulations, Constitution, Decisions, Edicts, and By Laws, both Supreme and Subordinate, and has a thorough knowledge of the same.

Before being installed, our new presiding officer has thoroughly acquainted himself with the financial condition of the body; has reviewed the investments; has studied previous budgets, and with the assistance of his officers and the financial committee, has prepared a budget for his term.

Our new prospective officer has absorbed a complete study and familiarization with Robert's Rules of Order, as well as thorough knowledge of any administrative procedures peculiar to the organization.

Our new leader has prepared and planned well in advance for his term in office. He has met with the proper committees to review his programs, and has met with his officers who will be serving with him to obtain their approval and support for his intentions.

Finally, our man has made a thorough study of the history of how the organization he is to head arrived at its present position by reviewing as many of the minutes as time will permit, hopefully all of them. He has availed himself of all the knowledge learned by those who went before by sitting down and talking with past presiding officers.

All too many will say that we cannot expect anyone to take the time to prepare in such a manner. With today's competition for the individual's time, to expect so much would doom us to a rejection of anyone considering accepting a position that eventually might lead to their being the presiding officer. My reply is that you certainly will never get more than you expect; but if you expect too much, and determine not to settle for less, then you will be successful. Granted, you might not be able to have a new presiding officer every year, at least not in the beginning; however, the objective must be kept uppermost in mind. It is not our intent to make sure we have a new presiding officer every term, nor is it our intent to make sure we do not re-elect someone to the post who has served there before. Our intent is to establish the expectations of our presiding officer that will guarantee that he make the proper contribution to the success of our organization. Indeed, in this instance, training on the job mandates at least partial failure; training for the job will most likely bring success.

To the reader: In the previous chapter we discussed the wisdom of an officer preparing to preside. In this chapter we will explore the relationship between leader and retinue.

Chapter VI
Lead, Follow, or Get Out of the Way

Life is full of decisions. What time do I get up tomorrow? What shall I wear? What shall I have for breakfast? What to buy my spouse for our anniversary? Shall I buy a new car, or repair the old one again? Does my daughter really need her own telephone, and what are the ramifications if I don't get her one? On and on it goes, seemingly with no respite... decisions, decisions, decisions!

Some of these dilemmas appear to be minor and insignificant. No matter the resolution, our lives will not be noticeably impacted, nor will the lives of those around us be affected to a large degree. Indeed, by far many day-to-day decisions are made with little thought, and little concern. Many are made without much conscious thought about the matter at hand; in fact, many times they are made relative to what is convenient at the moment. It is often only when a decision appears to have a life impacting result that we tend to give the matter time and consideration.

Do we buy a house? Such a decision will change our budget for many years to come. In addition, we have to consider the upkeep, the time to do the necessary maintenance such as raking leaves, and mowing the grass.

Purchasing a car, deciding to have children, changing jobs, all will impact our lives as well as our finances. Everyone can think of many things to add to the list of decisions, both minor and major. The real question is whether we recognize the importance of those decisions that impact not only our lives, but also the lives of others.

Most of all, matters to be considered will impact not only ourselves, but our families as well, and in that light we need to be careful to move in a direction that seems to be the most sensible, given the best information we can gather. When purchasing a house, we must consider the payments relative to our income, and other obligations. We must also consider the taxes, the utilities, reserve funds for maintenance, as well as the matter of location in regard to work, church, schools, shopping, and other logistic issues. Not to be overlooked are such things as whether the structure is free of vermin, has a dry foundation, and is safe from damage by nearby rotting trees, or unstable hillsides. Homes that appear safe in every way sometimes develop cracks and damage from deep mining underneath. There are many considerations, and much to be studied before making a decision that will impact one's family for many years to come, a fact recognized by all, and given careful study.

All too often we meet a seemingly innocuous situation with a snap judgment that we later regret. We didn't realize the ramifications of our decision, and had no idea that our action would escalate into a problem, or adversely affect someone else. However, time, the great educator, gradually teaches the great lesson of an investigative and intelligent approach to all matters.

In spite of the process of intelligent consideration of matters, we nevertheless fall victim to glossing over considerations that seem all too simple. We are faced with what seems to be a simple matter, head off in a direction not realizing that some time in the future our actions, or lack of them, may very well result in unproductive established procedures. When these matters rear their ugly heads, the over used words that pop are, "That's the way we have always done it."

This brings us to the discussion of our title, "Lead, follow, or get out of the way." The title is not a new one, and is seen on bumper stickers, or on desk plaques. It is a line that bears careful examination. All organizations need leaders. All organizations need followers to assist and implement the procedures, plans, and programs, both new, and existing. What they don't need are those that get in the way of progress by contrary and negative attitude.

Given time, all of us can think of someone who is opposed to change. They are never in favor of anything, opposed to all new ideas, and constrict the expansion of progress by blocking the influx of vibrant new approaches to the solution of issues. Perhaps venturing into uncharted waters they cannot comprehend, unwittingly frightens some of these people.

All too often what a person believes, is that which he does not understand. What is extant has taken time to assimilate, and unconsciously they feel threatened by that which is different. "It has always been done this way." "We are not aware of any problem." "We don't know why you want to change when we are here, we exist, and therefore things cannot be as bad as you say!"

It is also possible that they fear a loss of stature. Not as a result of a carefully considered judgment that any change will diminish their viability in the organization, but merely an undefined discomfort that things are getting away from them. It is human nature to desire a feeling of respect, feel good when needed, and exhilarate in the glow of being important to any process. Many of those who fall into this category are not necessarily recognized as leaders, but have always fallen into the list of followers. Their contribution as members has been exemplary in implementing the programs and procedures of the institution. Their regular attendance has indicated a genuine interest and concern over a long period of time. It may be that they have leadership qualities, unfortunately unrecognized, and overlooked; or it may be that they have been more than satisfied not to be placed in the role of a leader, feeling that leadership carries more responsibility than they are willing to shoulder. Whatever the motivation, or circumstance, that has placed them in the role of follower, the thought of change brings them to their feet to object and create a difficult situation for everyone. In many instances it is merely a matter of not being included in the decision making process. Permit me to cite two examples of this last consideration.

A number of years ago a bowling alley came up for sale in my hometown. I stopped into the business place of a fellow bowler and suggested that we buy the establishment. His immediate reaction was that we certainly didn't have the money to consider such a financial responsibility. I explained to him that it was not my idea for the two of us to buy the place, but that we get all the bowlers together, and that for a few hundred dollars apiece, we could purchase the property, and then run it any way that suited the customers, who would actually be the owners. This rang a bell and he was soon on the phone talking to many of the customers of the bowling alley in question. This writer did the same.

We soon discovered that there was great interest in the idea. We now made our mistake. With this assurance of interest, we got together a group of five who formed the corporation, negotiated the purchase, and completed the transaction. Those matters completed, we set out to sell stock in our new concern. Our error was soon evident. Very few were willing to buy stock in the enterprise. The previous enthusiasm had cooled dramatically. We finally managed to scrape together enough to continue the effort with assistance from a local bank.

What had been overlooked was the interest in being personally involved. The enthusiasm was generated by the glamour of being part of the implementation of a good idea. When that was removed, and the matter became merely investing in the efforts of others, the enthusiasm withered and died. These same people would not hesitate to invest a few dollars in a blue chip stock; but the objective would be to realize a financial return. In purchasing the bowling alley, no one had any delusions about financial profits to stockholders. The enterprise fell more in the area of a cooperative, and in that light they expected to be an integral part of the formation. We had come this far on our own, they had not been included, and we could now get along the best we could.

The second example occurred when it became my honor to serve as Grand Commander of Knights Templar in my state. There were several problems the Grand Officers knew needed to be solved. The problems were not new, and attempts had been made in previous years to address them, with no success.

During the year, all the constituent Commanderies were visited, not as a dignitary, but rather just as a Sir Knight on a visit. This provided the opportunity to chat informally with the Sir Knights around the festive board, and ask then about the issues in question, and gather their opinions. The first question asked was whether they felt the problems needed consideration. After discussion, everyone reached the conclusion that these matters, indeed, needed to be addressed. They were asked what solutions should be attempted. By revisiting, and suggesting solutions that had been gleaned, a consensus was reached during the year. It was then simply a matter of putting these solutions in proper form for presentation, and the membership unanimously passed them at the next Grand Commandery session.

After the Grand Conclave, several of the Past Grand Commanders patted me on the back and stated that they didn't know how I did it, but congratulations. As you can see, I didn't do it! The members did it because they were given the opportunity to be a part of the solution, and were given ample time and opportunity to carefully consider the matter.

In any organization, we do not need those people who block everything proposed. All too often their opposition is created by not being included. They feel that there is an inner circle who decides these things, but who are unable to implement their decision with the affirmative vote of those who seemingly are outside the circle. Unintentionally, a wall of resistance has been artificially created where it is not intended, and one of three scenarios will develop.

First, the organization remains stagnant, as needed corrections cannot be implemented. Matters are dropped for a time, and then revisited, only to find that those who perceive themselves as being on the outside are not about to permit the passage of what they had rejected previously. Further, as there are perhaps new members to whom the matter is new, those who are objecting quickly catch them up to date, and warn that "they" have tried this before. The organization remains, unknowingly, split into two undefined factions.

Second, those in responsible positions trying to implement corrections maneuver the circumstances so that the matter they favor is somehow implemented over the objections. This creates a defined split in the membership, and those who consider themselves as outsiders will find it difficult to be agreeable to even the most innocuous presentation.

Third possibility is the realization that progress comes from inclusion rather than exclusion. An example of inclusion comes to mind that is worth examination. Many years ago it fell my lot to serve as Chapter Advisor of our local DeMolay Chapter, and to be in charge of our Chapter's attendance at the State DeMolay Conclave. Just imagine having two or three hundred high school age young men on a college campus for three or four days!

Among our group was a set of twins who were high school sophomores. They were fine young fellows, but the type that were targets for the butt of every practical joke that the "big shots" could dream up. We no more than arrived, and room assignments concluded, when the twins came to me saying that someone had been in their room, hung a chair out the window, tied their clothes in knots, and sprayed shaving cream on the mirrors. They were told not to worry about it...I would see that it didn't happen again. Now I tried to figure out how I was going to keep my word.

Careful thought led me to believe that I knew who the guilty parties were. There were brothers, one eighteen and one seventeen, who were happy go lucky, and good athletes. Really great kids, and always interested in a good laugh. Of course, I had no proof of their involvement, just a hunch. These brothers were sent for, and asked to meet me in my room. When they arrived, I did not mention what had been reported to me by the twins. I told them that I needed a favor, and solicited their assistance in a very important matter. They quickly agreed to help me in any way they could. It was explained that there was concern regarding the twins. This was their first time away from home, and that it was important the experience be a good one. I didn't want the twins to spend their whole time worrying about being picked on, or being concerned about the practical jokes that might be played on them. It was pointed out that they were young, not athletically inclined, and really not able to protect themselves. I asked the two brothers if they would accept the responsibility to see that no one played any jokes on the twins, or made them feel uncomfortable during the conclave.

The two brothers jumped at the chance to look after the twins, with the agreement that our conversation was not to be made known. The twins had a great time, and by the end of the conclave were more involved with all their peers. In this instance, I felt that I had successfully put the foxes in charge of the hen house. My experience has been that the inclusion up front can often negate negative attitudes. To follow is to recognize the leader's responsibility, and that he deserves, and should welcome your constructive input. To follow is to become involved and realize that success is the result of cooperative and continuous effort. To follow is to accept the consensus when you have made your point, but to be alert to the time when the question needs revisited.

However, to follow is much more than being agreeable. It is much more than asking what you can do to help, and it is much more than carrying out every assignment with attention to detail and a successful conclusion.

To follow is to pay attention to every aspect of the operation for two very specific reasons. A leader needs desperately to be aware of the pulse of his organization. He can only read that pulse if it is communicated to him by followers. Imagine blacking out the windows of your automobile and driving to the local grocery store. You know the way, and you are an expert at handling your vehicle, but without vision, your task is hopeless. A leader's vision comes from the input of his followers. Not just his immediate circle of friends, but from all who take an interest in the progress of the organization.

Following is keeping one's eye open to the road ahead to warn of dangers that the leader may be overlooking. My wife does not drive, but she is a great follower. She keeps me abreast of every consideration ahead as we travel. A leader's success is measured by the comfort of his followers, and their enthusiasm. Without them, he would not be a leader.

Following is also the realization that through some set of circumstances, as yet unseen; the follower may some day be called upon to lead. Hopefully the follower will have ample warning before such an event; however, a follower can learn much by attention to those things that will be of tremendous value to the present leader, and thereby unconsciously prepare himself should the mantle of leadership fall upon him. He will still have much study to undertake, but the do's and don'ts can be learned ahead by proper self-application.

Leading is the remaining category. If proper preparation for leadership has been accomplished, and all the considerations of followers, and the potential road blockers have been properly attended, perhaps the term will be successful. However, if leadership is not receptive to the voice of experience and reason, it bypasses that which very well may be the ultimate piece in the matrix of success.

Being an officer and eventually presiding is a tough study. Most all have grand ideas as to what they will do when they have the chance to preside, and when they are finished, feel they have done a good job. Most likely they have no frame of reference to measure what constitutes a good job. They have made no study of the activities of those who preceded them, nor have they had any discussion with their predecessors about the pitfalls of leading an organization. It is not productive to have an organization that changes officers every year, and end up with one man, one year, rule. Good programs are abandoned in favor of new ones that are again discarded, and there is no continuity in the organization. Appointments are made on the basis of familiarity and friendship rather than an investigation of the knowledge and expertise of potential appointees. Why would a presiding officer start a program if he doesn't have agreement from those who will follow? Why would a presiding officer make an appointment that is unsatisfactory to his successors? Should he not discuss these issues with his junior officers and come to a resolution?

There are many in this world that welcome the opportunity to be the "big cheese," and many of them, if properly prepared will perform admirably. However, there are all too many who are unwilling to get in the vat and be "processed."

Many ponder what they will do when given the chance to preside. They decide on some things they would like to do, and a direction they would like to take. Hence, they make their plans. Where they often fail is by not researching the question of how the organization got where it is. They establish a map of sorts, and some direction for the organization in the blissful ignorance of not knowing they are going backward instead of forward. All too often the organization has been over the same ground before, many years ago. Many ideas thought to be new were thought of a long time ago, and research would point out the reasoning behind not proceeding in the same direction.

Being an officer and presiding over a Masonic Body is not a two or three hour a week task. It takes careful planning, study, research, and asking questions. The best program this writer has ever seen along these lines was developed by Past Grand High Priest Winchester of Florida. He laid out areas to be studied by each officer of a Grand Chapter, and assigned a year to each subject. By the time the officer was elected Grand High Priest, he would be thoroughly prepared for the position.

Let us use a Grand Chapter line of officers, and set up a program. We will assign the subjects of Ritual, Jurisprudence, Finances, History, Constitution, Rules and Regulations, Committees, Constituent Jurisdictions, and Edicts. That is nine subjects for nine officers. At the beginning of the year we assign a subject to each office, and the assignment is to remain with that office over the years. A couple of months before Grand Chapter Convocation, a weekend retreat is held with all the officers in attendance. Each has an opportunity to give a report on his assigned subject with the others taking notes. Three things result from this exercise:

1) Officers become considerably better prepared.

2) The ability to research and learn is heightened.
3) Those who are not willing to devote the time to prepare, or who are really not Grand Officer material are revealed.

The subjects to be studied may vary, or they may be changed from time to time. Perhaps, it might be a consideration to have Past Grand Officers attend on each occasion to give a lecture on one of the areas of concern. However it is put together, the wisdom of doing so should be apparent.

But what if no one can be found who can meet all these requirements? We have a Brother here who is a good administrator, businesslike, and handles a crowd with comfort. The problem is that he is not a good ritualist. He learns the words, but cannot get them across in an interesting manner, or he just cannot learn the words accurately enough. He may be the type of person who can put on an interesting talk, given a subject and his own devices, but has difficulty when required to recite specific passages. What should be done?

When there is no other alternative, for goodness sake, relieve the man of the ritual responsibility! The ritual work must be outstanding, and there can be no compromise. Get the best you have to do the ritual work for candidates. Perhaps you have proficiency requirements, but that is not to say that the Brother cannot learn the work to the best of his ability, and exhibit a reasonable proficiency in the ritual of his office. However, the candidate deserves the best, and it should be seen that he gets it.

However, it very well may be said that there is a trap very easily tripped if we leave the ritual responsibility in the hands of a very few. Time, the Great Equalizer, will leave us without assistance, and he will most likely do it when we least expect. This is a perfect example of solving a problem, and not revisiting the issue. Dividing the responsibilities of office is not necessarily to be avoided, but it must be done judiciously and steps taken to remove the necessity.

No short cuts! No easy outs! No letting Jim do it even though he's not very good. There is too much at stake to sit back and not make every effort to sort through the entire membership to find the best that you can. Very often there is outstanding officer material that never shows up at the meetings,. Maybe the reason is that they have nothing to do!

Leaders may be born, but they can also be developed, and it is the responsibility that the membership "lead" by being diligent in their search for the raw material that can be developed into good leadership. It is the genuine concern of each member to take an active part in this search and development.

Following is leading from the rear. It is being in step, facing forward, and cheerfully accepting the responsibility of the progress of the organization. A leader leads because there are those who follow, but who have in fact, laid out the trail to be followed. They have also joined the leader in removing all those prone to be a problem by obstructing every move, every new idea, and every change. This removal is not the physical removal, but rather the philosophical removal. They have not been escorted to the door, but have been included in the process, made a valuable part of it, and full advantage taken of the expertise and abilities not formerly revealed.

If there are any left that cannot, in good conscience, be a part of the process, and even though included, find it beyond their power to contribute rather than detract, they need to stand aside and get out of the way. There is a danger here, however. It is possible that an atmosphere may be created wherein no one objects to anything. Dialogue must be open, contrary views must be sought, and thoroughly examined. But once this process is completed, and everyone has had fair opportunity to state his position, then…lead, follow, or get out of the way!

To the reader: Let us now examine those items that may have gotten out of focus, and perhaps impact the present condition of the Craft.

Chapter VII
Money Talks

A number of years ago, partners in an appliance store took advantage of an opportunity to purchase a tractor-trailer load of microwave ovens. They were a recognized name brand, full size, full power, and touch pad control. They were all the same model, and amazingly, through a buying group, they paid only $130.00 each for these state of the art, full sized ovens. The partners made careful plans feeling this was a golden opportunity to make some quick bucks, and also to realize a tremendous flow of store traffic which would undoubtedly lead to more sales. Newspaper ads were designed with care, copy for radio spots were developed with expertise, and a TV spot was taped for the local station. The advertising was properly positioned to coincide with delivery of the ovens, and at a price of $169.95, the partners anticipated a great crowd on the Saturday established for the kickoff of this great promotion.

Saturday morning the partners arrived at the store with excitement and anticipation. Much to their chagrin, not one oven was sold, and indeed a week went by with no interest whatsoever in this great sale of quality microwave ovens. What had been anticipated as a golden opportunity had quickly become a horrible albatross to the owners. A warehouse clogged with new microwave ovens, and a manufacturer who would soon expect payment for the shipment, and no customers.

After some sleepless nights the partners, with great apprehension, used the same exact advertising program the following month, except that the price of the ovens was changed to $269.95. They raised the price $100.00, and every oven was sold in three days!

It is difficult to comprehend the preceding true story; but yet, we are all guilty of believing that you can't get something for nothing, and are misled daily be marketing techniques. Every day, in everything we do and see, the mind responds to what the eye sees, and what the ear hears. Is it easier for a person of 49 to get a job than one of 50? Do we pay $1.98 for an item that we might pass over if it was $2.00? How about the big item that costs $1,998.00? Would we hesitate if the price were $2,003.00? To state unequivocally that we only get what we pay for is injurious to our sensibilities. Facts indicate that many times we receive less than what we pay for, and that realization drives us to shop for price, provided the price does not raise our suspicions by being what we consider to be too low.

However, a problem arises in price competition. All too often the mind responds without carefully analyzing what the eye has seen.

For example: In store "A" navel oranges are 25 cents each; and in store "B" they are three for a dollar: but in store "C" they have a whole bag of navel oranges for just $3.50. Who sells the most oranges? Probably store "C" where the whole bag of oranges consists of ten pieces of fruit. Who sells the least oranges? Probably store "A" even though they actually have the best price! Perception is the word that applies, and is the way the mind interprets what the eye has seen. Hence, we need to keep in mind that contrary to a buzz slogan used by many - perception is not necessarily truth.

Previously we mentioned that there is a relationship between what is heard, and how the mind reacts and reasons information from the ear. There is an old story told in response to the statement that figures never lie. Three men went into a hotel and asked to rent a room for one night for the three of them. The clerk charged them $30.00 for the room. Each man gave the clerk $10.00, and received a key for the room. An hour later, it dawned on the clerk that he had overcharged the three men. He called a bellhop, gave him $5.00, and told him to return the money to the three men, as they had been overcharged. On the way up to the room, the bellhop deliberated on how to split the $5.00 between the three men. He finally decided that the easy way would be to pocket two dollars, and give each one of the men a dollar back.

Examining the mathematics the story teller states, "considering the dollar each man got back, the room cost each man $9.00. Three times nine is twenty-seven, plus the two dollars the bellhop pocketed makes a total of twenty-nine, but we started with thirty dollars...What happened to the other dollar?"

A plausible story, and the math seems correct, except that it does not add up properly. The listener has been carefully directed away from the true nature of the math involved even though indirectly touching on the correct focus which is to account for the original thirty dollars. The thirty dollars is easily accounted for by realizing that the clerk has $25.00, the bellhop has $2.00, and each of the three men, $1.00. That accounts for the original thirty dollars. When the storyteller stops with, "What happened to the other dollar," the listener has been presented with a carefully crafted "perception." He has been led down a trail and the proper fork in the path intentionally obscured, while the listener is steered in the wrong direction.

Many years ago, this writer was encouraged to petition the Grotto in my hometown. If sounded great! They had a nice building, an extensive social program, individual units, and a philanthropy. Also, upon initiation, each new member is given a key to the building so that he can enjoy a comfortable room with tables and chairs, nice soft lighting, machines with snacks and beverages, and a big screen TV. any time he chooses, a sort of home away from home. The good Brother was asked for a petition, but after leaving his place of business, it was realized that the cost had not been discussed. It sounded expensive, and it was thought that an adjustment would have to be made in the personal budget to save enough money to take advantage of this opportunity. Returning and inquiring about the cost, the reply was that the fee was $40.00, and the dues were $15.00 per year. What happened? Without any conscious thought, what had seemed like a great opportunity apparently now paled in the subconscious. Well, the petition was not submitted until several years later when my eldest son suggested the two of us petition the Grotto together. It was everything I had been told, and more…and the price had not changed. Keep in mind that in order to petition the Grotto, you only needed to be a Blue Lodge member in good standing. At that time the Shrine required that one be either a Knight Templar, or a thirty-second degree Scottish Rite member. Because of the economics, you would think the Grotto in our town would be much bigger than the Shrine in membership, but the reverse was true, and still is.

In 1977, my home Commandery charged $90.00 to petitioners. This included a $50.00 fee and $40.00 for the Armory fund. Fifty years before, in 1927, the same Commandery was charging $50.00 fee, and it was mandatory that the petitioner purchase a uniform that cost $65.00…something out of place here, something out of balance!

In relation to the weekly income of the average wage earner, Masonry at one time was expensive. Now it is extremely inexpensive, and the question here posed is, "What is the impact of the initiation fee vis a vis the economy, and average income had on membership?

Manufacturer, distributor, and retailer all have a common problem, and a common goal. They have an objective to provide for their family, their investor, and themselves. To accomplish that goal they could easily charge a very high price for their commodity, or their service, one that would absolutely assure them of more than reaching their goals. But would the consumer co-operate? The marketer could quickly, in general terms, arrive at a cost of operation, add a bunch for odds and ends, add a bunch more for hard times and contingencies, and then pile on some more for himself. The end result would no doubt be bankruptcy, as the price would then be beyond the customer's willingness to pay.

Up to this point we have examined two opposite scenarios. One is when the price seems too good to be true; and the other when the price seems way too high for the value received. Let us pursue a little further the question of prices being too high. Luxury items generally carry a high markup, and that contributes to their mystique and desirability. Owning expensive items tends to set one apart from the average. Those who can afford expensive items are envied by the rest. However, the fact that the cost of expensive items restricts the available customer base, it becomes necessary for the markup to be higher in order to offset limited sales. Luxury items tend to set the successful person apart, and in so doing advertise their success to the world at large. In so doing, others are inspired, and resolve to endeavor to emulate that success. Essentially, this is the carrot that makes the economic engine function. Goods that are a necessity must be good quality for a reasonable price. Goods that are considered, at least to some extent , a luxury, will arouse no interest, if the price is too cheap.

At the same time, the factors involved in achieving success must not appear to be utterly unobtainable. While the path to success may be strewn with difficulties, it must not appear to be insurmountable. A balance must be struck so that the determined and willing worker sees opportunity, and yet the goal to the lazy and undedicated is beyond reach.

Since the beginning of time, man has sought to better himself, his family, and his society. He has been, and continues to be successful in this endeavor. On this constant is based invention and economic progress. Those who recognize this and base their endeavors on this principle are the ones most likely to be listed among the successful.

In the beginning, man walked in order to pursue food, shelter, recreation, and communication. He learned about traveling over water by boat, he learned to use beasts of burden to carry himself and his goods. Entrepreneurs developed wagons to carry people and goods, and as time passed they made fancy carriages and harness for the well to do. Man went from oars to sails, and then to steam. However, nothing stands still, and man is never satisfied. His eternal belief is that no matter how good it is, there is probably a better way. Henry Ford hung on to the Model T for too long a time. He made cars available to the common worker, but eventually he had to give in, shut down his factories, and retool in order to make better cars to compete with developing competition. Competition is the fuel that drives success and progress. Ford had a great idea regarding the manufacture of automobiles. His Model T was a quality product at the right price for the wage earner. Henry had it big for a while, but competition caught up while he stood still.

With this lengthy prelude, let us now apply the preceding to the Craft. In the opinion of this student, Masonry has become too cheap monetarily. However, having said that, let it be known that the financial structure of every Masonic Body in the world is unknown to this writer. The statement applies to all the Masonic groups with which he is familiar, but to none others. Henceforth, the author will lump all into the same category, recognizing that there may be exceptions.

How can Masonry possibly maintain its viability when it has permitted its income to be eroded by inflation? Arguments would be that if we raise the price, we would have no candidates. Well, the reply would appropriately be the question, "raise the cost how much?" Certainly the cost can be raised to the point it is prohibitive to most. On the other hand, the point is here made that the cost has been economically eroded to the point it has lost its stature. If each of us was instructed to sit down and make a list of those material things we most desire, is there any question that the most expensive in relation to the economy would be at the top of the list? Does it not then follow that as Masonry becomes less expensive in relation to the economy, it moves down toward the bottom of the list of desirable things?

100

The question is whether the Craft would be in a better position in terms of stature, membership, and finances, had it matched increases in fees with the economy over the years? There are far too many Masonic organizations depending on a return from investments to cover the operational costs without adding anything to the portfolio.

There is a mindset in some quarters to raise the yearly dues and not raise the fees in order to cover increasing overhead, but this raises another point. In 1943, the Building Trades worker made $25.00 per week, and paid $75.00, or three weeks wages as fees when petitioning a Craft Lodge. Today, his grandson, who is also a Building Trades employee makes $700.00 per week, and submits $100.00 with his petition, which is the equivalent of five and three quarters hours in wages! Is the same prestige attached to membership by the grandson as was attached by the grandfather?

Let us apply the numbers to an everyday item. Cars were not available in 1943 for the public, but if we go back to 1940, the grandfather would have considered purchasing a 1940 Willys Overland four door sedan without a heater for $550.00. The writer's father bought one in 1940 for that price. Projecting the cost of the Willys in relation to the increase of petitioning a Craft Lodge, the Willys would sell for $734.00 today. Now think about that! If you went to the car dealer today, and he had a brand new sedan at a price of $734.00, what would you think? You know it couldn't be any good! Just look at the price! $734.00! There is no way this car can be any account if it only costs $734.00! It must be some kind of toy for my kid, or maybe it has no engine?

Surely, an organization that required $75.00 in 1943 from a petitioner cannot be of the same quality if it only requires $100.00 from a petitioner today. While that statement might not be true, it would certainly be reasonable to be thus perceived. If the fee has not advanced in proportion to the economy, then something must have been eliminated, or there must be cuts somewhere. Well, let us examine that theory.

The grandfather, who is now on Social Security, is expected to assist in covering today's economic shortfall with ever increasing dues. Now that he is on Social Security, he pays 2% of one month's income. His grandson is paying 0.8% of a month's income in yearly dues. These figures are based on $3.00 dues in 1943, and $25,00 dues in 1993. Obviously the grandson is getting a break on the dues, and is being subsidized by the return on his grandfather's fees which were invested in 1943.

For the economics to be fair and balanced, and to bring the picture into focus with today's economy, the grandson's fees should be $1050.00, and his dues $36.00 per year; and the grandfather's yearly obligation should be reduced to $12.00 per year when he goes on Social Security.

Some of our Masonic organizations have kept the fees the same for the past fifty years, but have increased the dues to where they are extremely high. The premise is that with the low fee, we can encourage them to petition, and once they are in, we'll have a high yearly dues to cover costs. It is here contended that such a practice is grossly unfair to the older member who paid a much higher fee upon petitioning, relative to his income, and is now billed a high dues fee because the younger member was charged a very low fee considering his income.

In regard to the older members, it is certainly common knowledge that a member can claim hardship and have his dues remitted in his later years, or in fact at any time, but the author wonders how many would rather demit than claim hardship? How many is not known, but you can add my name to the list!

What was an interesting concept used in the 19th century was a rather small yearly dues of $1.25, plus twenty five cents each time a meeting was attended. The twenty five cents helped offset the operating cost of the meetings and, at the same time, there was dues relief for those unable to attend meetings for whatever reason; an idea that perhaps has some merit.

Let us presume that the reader has been prodded into some consideration of the cost of the Craft, but a debate still exists. If we raise the fees, will we still have interested petitioners? If we reduce the dues, will we still be able to cover current expenses? What is the long term projection if no changes are made?

First question: "If we raise the fees, will we still have interested petitioners?"

Reply: How many do you have now? Is there a healthy interest in petitioning your local Craft Lodge? Is your investigating committee busy checking into the background of petitioners? Is the percentage of the eligible population in your area that are Masons the same as it was fifty, or seventy five years ago? Are the candidate classes in the appendant organizations in your area large and enthusiastic? It is here suspected that all of these questions are answered in the negative. If that is the case, then what are you going to lose. In 1977, it was suggested from this quarter that our Commandery of Knights Templar raise its fee from $90.00 to $150.00. When several Sir Knights exhibited fear of such a raise, the question was put as to how many candidates there had been the past couple of years. It was then pointed out that they might as well not get candidates at $150.00 each, as not to get them at $90.00 each. The fee was raised and the Commandery had eleven petitioners during the next calendar year; not because the price was raised, but rather because an organized membership program was put into effect, but the point is that there was no resistance because of the price.

A Craft Lodge, a few years ago, raised their fee from $75.00 to $425.00, and where there had been no interest before, there was considerable interest after the raise in fees.

Our local Grotto raised the fee from $60.00 to $150.00. The raise did not dissuade candidates, but actually there were more petitioners after the raise than there had been before.

If the fees are raised, there will very likely be more interest rather than less: but certainly the effect will not be negative.

Before moving on, we need to clarify just what the fee should be. The answer is very easy. Don't mess with success. Research the history of your organization and find a period in its history when petitioners were plentiful. Compare the fee at that time with the economy, and you will be able to arrive at a number that is correct.

Question 2:"If we reduce the dues, will we still be able to cover current expenses?"

Reply: Well, what is included in current expense? You must first decide what part of the expenses the dues should cover, and how much you feel is appropriate to place in the investments. If nothing is added to the investments each year, they shrink by virtue of inflation. That is to say, each year they will purchase fewer gallons of milk. One thought would be to cover the current expense with the dues, and add the fees to the investments. This is not an easy decision to make, and most importantly needs careful study.

However, it is not a given that dues are to be reduced. The local Royal Arch Chapter has current expense each year consisting of payroll for the Secretary, the Tiler, the rent, and the Stewards, totaling in the neighborhood of $3500.00. The Chapter receives about $420.00 per year in dues. The dues have not been changed since Warren Harding was President! Obviously, the consideration in this instance would not be whether to lower dues, but rather how much to raise them.

Question 3: "What is the long range projection, if no changes are made?"

Reply: That depends. It may be that the Craft in your area has been cognizant of economic changes, and has kept up with the times. If that is the case, and you continue to be responsible, the long range projection is that monetary considerations will not affect the membership roles, nor impact the financial stability of your organization. You may have problems, but this is not one of them. However, if the Craft in your area is still operating on the fees established fifty, or seventy-five years ago, you are, or will be, facing serious financial difficulties. Moreover, you are, or will, suffer a lack of interest in an organization that thinks no more of itself than to price itself at one tenth of its real value. Now, let us suppose that all financial considerations are addressed and corrected. We have carefully examined our present situation, researched our history, and changed both the fees and dues to appropriate amounts in relation to today's economy. Is that the end of the matter? Are we all set now, and can relax and enjoy prosperous and bountiful times? No, I'm afraid not! There are other pressing matters which we will explore in the next chapter.

To the reader: Perhaps the following should have been included in the previous chapter concerning finances.

What follows is affected to some degree by financial ability. We are now going to pursue a tangential issue consistent with the thought that we must reflect on those areas that need to be revisited on a regular basis.

Chapter VIII
Compete or Surrender

Competition most often comes to mind in regard to athletics, whether they are high school, college, professional, or independent in nature. There are those among us who followed and worshiped Lou Gehrig, and marveled at the new rookie, the Yankees, Joe DiMaggio. We followed on a daily basis the batting average of Ted Williams...would he finish the season with a batting average over 400? The Chicago Bears, the Monsters of the Midway, were seen in movie theaters in sports shorts. We marveled at Cornelius Warmerdam's proficiency in the pole vault. Indeed, the sports world was the epitome of competition to all youngsters.

However, to the adults, competition was a more serious matter. One needed to be good at his workaday skills, or he could not get a job, much less hold one. The captains of industry were in constant competition for a share of the economy, and during the thirties, competition between countries became an ever-increasing possibility.

Looking at all those things today, we must be impressed with the increased ability of the athletes. Warmerdam's feats in pole vaulting are matched today by high school athletes. Baseball, football, basketball, and all sports boast of far better athletes than in the "good old days!" No, no one has hit .400 since Williams; however, while the batters are bigger and stronger, so are the pitchers.

Captains of Industry have pushed the economy of the world to unprecedented heights. Everything is bigger, better, stronger, and continuing upward. How did all this happen? Competition! That is the fuel that makes things better. At some point in time, some football coach got the idea that if he could make his players stronger, he could win more games. He put his team on conditioning programs throughout the year, had them lift weights, and used film to show them their mistakes. If one team, and none other had done this, they would have quickly outdistanced their competition. Hence, the other teams had to do the same, and the level of the sport became better, and better.

In the market place, we see the same results,. Some company makes a better product, and others must compete, or close the doors. Some company comes up with a new product, and others must do the same, or fall behind. The competition continues, and society benefits from it, one way or another.

Many years ago this writer was told that the Order of DeMolay was doomed as there was too much competition for the time of teenage boys. What was being said was that the competition had become better, and we are unwilling to compete.

At one time a DeMolay Chapter was easy to start, and easy to make successful. All you had to do was open the door, and let it be known you were there. Those days have long since passed. DeMolay must be more interesting and exciting than the competition!

Competition is here to stay, and those who do not meet it are doomed to oblivion. What's more, the public expects more and more, and the market place is compelled to respond. Examining the minutes and records of Masonic Bodies of the nineteenth century indicates that the Craft today, provides less and less in response. While there are many philanthropies that have been undertaken by the Craft, and commendable work done in these areas, the services to its individual members is not comparable to that provided a hundred and fifty years ago.

Examining old minutes, it is evident that it was unacceptable for members to face each other in a civil court. The contesting parties were called in and the matter settled; and if not, when the matter went to public hearing, at least one of the parties would no longer be a member of the Craft.

This writer is aware of two frivolous suits brought by one member of the Craft against another. In one case, the member sued, asked leaders in his Blue Lodge to examine the matter, but they refused to get involved.

At one time when a member passed away, two or three members would be called on to see to the widow's needs; and if there were any children, they would see that they were provided with support until their schooling was completed. These assignments were not just to make a call or two, but also to provide support, advice, and comfort over a long period of time.

This writer and his wife visited the widow of a Past Master some years back. The lady was so pleased to see us, and to spend an evening together. Her comment was, "you know, your husband spends hours away from home involved in Masonry, and through him you meet lots of wonderful people who you think of as friends. When he passes away, you discover that they were his friends, but not yours!

In the City of Wheeling, during the late nineteenth century, there was a little booklet published every year that fit into your shirt pocket. A Past Grand Master of our Grand Lodge, who was a printer, published it. In that booklet was listed every member of the Craft in the Wheeling area, the various bodies to which he belonged, what type of work he did, and his employer. This information was not just interesting, but for those who preferred to deal with members of the Craft, a ready guide was thus provided. Secretaries of various Masonic Bodies were adequately compensated for their time and effort, Members who provided some service to the Craft from time to time were appropriately compensated, and donations of time and money were not expected. Many Secretaries have not had their compensation raised for fifty years.

The world has changed in many ways, but basic human emotions, desires, and stimuli have not. With the rapid growth of communications and ready made entertainment, there is competition for people's time and attention, It is easy to sit back and moan about how it's all changed. The world is different, and there is a lot of competition for people's time and attention. That statement is not only easy to make, it is the plain unvarnished truth. One may have produced the finest buggies in the world, but no one's interested in one now. One may have made a great Model T Ford, but they are not in demand for transportation now. Two seat biplanes were a thing of wonder, but who wants to fly to Chicago in one now? The need for transportation is still there, but competition has raised the mode of travel over the years to what we enjoy today.

People still cry when they are sad, and laugh when they are happy. They still appreciate genuine concern, and are elevated when others exhibit interest in them. The emotional and psychological targets are still there to excite and involve people, but the approach must be different.

Remember when you were small, and one of your "well-to-do" friends had a birthday party? You were amazed at the magician, but could he hold the attention of young people today? The magician's trade has not disappeared, but it has changed. Today he must make a tiger disappear, or the Statue of Liberty. If these marvelous feats are beyond his capacity, then he has to inject humor into his presentation, or something else that enhances his act.

The Craft has fallen on hard times. Membership declines although the overall population increases. Even the slightest hint that the Craft is now a cheap outfit greatly reduces the stature if once enjoyed. Society has no respect for cheap, but has great admiration for expensive, provided the quality is excellent.

Maybe it's already too late. It seems most are satisfied to sit back and see what happens, and if the Craft succumbs to desuetude, they will simply say, "What a shame, someone should have done something!" If the Craft is worth anything, then it's worth the effort to give some serious and intelligent thought to strengthening it. Perhaps it would be well to follow those two sentences, which in essence make up the bottom line for a Masters in Business Administration:

1) Plan your work, and then execute.
2) Remove the obstacles to productivity.

Chapter IX
Leadership

"You can lead a horse to water, but you can't make him drink" is an old adage, and one that bears investigation in our present circumstance.

It has not been established that the horse is thirsty. This has been an assumption of the trainer hired by the owner of the farm. There is a problem, and from past experience, the trainer decides that water is the commodity that is needed; after all, that was the solution that worked in his other assignments. The trainer communicates to the horse that water will be the answer, and informs the horse that he will lead him to a beautiful glen, drenched with shade ,and awash with glorious wild flowers through which winds a stream of the clearest, coolest water he has ever experienced. While the horse is not so sure that water is the solution, he, nonetheless, is enthusiastic and readily follows the trainer. But part way to their destination the trainer apologizes and leaves, assuring the horse that a new trainer, who is competent, will continue to guide him on his journey. However, the new trainer decides that while he agrees with the premise, the path is not of his choosing, and strikes off on a new path to the clear, cool, water.

The scene is repeated over and over, each time with a new trainer who chooses a new path. To complicate the matter, each path contained an unanticipated obstacle. On the first, a tree had fallen and blocked further progress. On the second, a deep chasm was encountered, and on the third a rocky stretch of ground injured the horse's hooves which were unshod.

When another trainer arrived and started down

the path the first trainer had taken, the horse speaks up and says, "If you want to go that way, you need to take a chain saw with you and allow some extra time for clearing away a tree."

The trainer replies to the horse, "What would a tree be doing in our path. You are just being difficult. Either come along quietly, or I'll get a horse that will."

As the story continues, the horse relates to a subsequent trainer that he will need ropes to build a bridge over a chasm, and receives the same rebuff. He asks yet another trainer to be shod to protect his hooves from the rocky ground, and receives, yet again, another rebuff.

As time passes, at what point does the horse begin to believe that he will never live to see the beautiful shaded glen with the sea of wild flowers, and the winding stream of clear cool water? At what point does the horse begin to believe that this whole exercise is merely a sham, and that the real focus is providing opportunity for the owner of the farm to see in what manner each trainer would attempt to lead the horse to water, and indeed has no interest in the completion of the journey?

Truly, at some point the horse learns the lesson and quits trying to communicate! He swallows his frustration and resigns himself to waiting for that glorious day when he is determined too old to be of any use on the farm, and is put out to pasture. The horse will always wonder, what might have been!

It is agreed that the owner of the farm has the latitude to employ the trainer of his choosing. The horse has the responsibility to trust the judgment of the trainer, whoever he might be, and no matter how many times the trainer might be changed; but history has taught the horse that this next trip will not amount to anything more than all the previous ones, and loses interest, becomes a lackadaisical pawn, and not a productive team member. What is the responsibility of the trainer, and how might he better provide the desperately needed leadership? He must not use the same approach. While the new trainer might be more competent than the last, he must establish recognition and a trust, or he will be doomed to failure. Perhaps he should first investigate the horse's circumstances. He might find out that an Arabian mare is being used to plow fields; a Percheron, or a Suffolk being used as a saddle horse and a Tennessee Walker is pulling hay up into the haymow.

It is entirely possible that the stable is not aware of their attributes, and does not understand why the horses are dissatisfied and uncomfortable with their lives. The perceptive trainer will move the assignments to take advantage of each horse's natural attributes. Would this not be to the owner's advantage? Might there be a new enthusiasm in the stable? The danger is that some may be moved simply for movements sake, when they were really best used in the assignment they had. Perhaps if the horse were given a chance, he would tell the trainer that he is not thirsty, but could really use some hay. Another might be comfortable with his supply of water and hay, but inform the trainer that he desperately needs some oats in his diet. Another might say that the food, the water, and the work are more than satisfactory, but please clean out the stall more often; and yet their needs might be nothing more than a bath, curried, and a pat on the back.

For the moment, let us presume that the trainer has listened to the horses, and in his wisdom has responded to what he has learned. Would he not now have their confidence? Would he not now have established a good relationship? And should the horses not now recognize that the trainer was employed because of his expertise and knowledge, and be ready to embark on the trainer's agenda? Should the trainer decide that the trip to the shaded glen is necessary, should he not listen, and take into account the precious experiences that have been related to him. Should he not listen, and cover all the eventualities by seeing that all the horses were shod in case they run into rocky ground, pack some ropes to make a bridge for any chasm encountered, and carry a chain saw for any tree blocking the way?

Who knows, perhaps a mud slide has covered the rocks, perhaps an earthquake has closed the chasm, and maybe time has rotted the tree across the path, but diligent investigation in history and experience, and an open communication has established the mutual trust and proper preparation that will insure success.

You cannot necessarily lead a horse to water, much less make him drink, without his interest, his desire, his trust, and his cooperation...all of which must be earned!

To the reader: One of the highways to success is teamwork. However, teamwork is not necessarily an easy path to travel. It takes more than a simple declaration that we will establish a team!

Chapter X
Teamwork

In the field of sports, the cry for teamwork is loud and clear. The star of the team, after a particularly successful game, complements his teammates to the media. During practice, the coach stresses teamwork, and now we hear the same emphasis in industry. Employees on the payroll are no longer called employees; they are called team members. Industry has developed a myriad of programs to teach, encourage, and emphasize the necessity of coordinating the efforts of everyone into the big picture…"People, we need to work as a team if we are to compete favorably in the market place!"

What is the idea behind this modern concern about teamwork? In the past there was someone in charge who said, we're going to do it this way, and that was the way it was done. No questions, no discussion, just follow orders and get it done. To stretch the point only slightly, most things were run in a dictatorial style. Occasionally, the man in charge might ask for ideas and input, but the final decision was his. There was no thought of reaching a consensus. Somewhere along the line things have changed.

Today we have more people with good educations that must be respected. History taught us that everyone has something to add to the mix that could very well be important. Communications are almost instantaneous with the advent of television, and the general public is exposed first hand to much that stirs the emotions. Awareness has been raised to a historic level in the world today, and while everyone has always had their ideas, today they want to be heard. Fear is no longer as viable an option for controlling society as it once was. The employee, or team member, is no longer concerned about being fired by his employer. A variety of laws have emboldened the attitude of the employee, and thus changed the workplace forever.

How has the change worked? For those who have recognized the evolution in the workplace, and properly directed their energies, it has worked exceedingly well. But there are some who only do lip service to the new concept, and behind the scenes still operate in a dictatorial manner without a team agenda. Their motto is, "Perception is truth." Their determination is to make it look like everyone is being included, but in reality the end determination has already been decided. If a decision is reached not to their liking, the matter is not pursued. Eventually the question is revisited in the hope of reaching that which is desired; or an explanation is made after an appropriate lapse of time that new information, or circumstances, have prompted those in authority to head off in a different direction than the consensus previously reached.

It is difficult to think of a more precipitous attitude to take than to operate on the discourse of presenting a perception in order to promote one's agenda. Today's society is calloused to flowery speeches and promises. There is a great "perception" that everyone is lying in order to promote his own welfare. Establishing a perception is to plant a seed in the dark. It will not grow until brought into the light of day, and that brightness is the lamp of truth. Society as a whole has adopted a wait and see attitude. It is not about to buy into a perception, only to find that the entire presentation is a myth. Listen, yes: believe and buy in, no! Success only comes to those who operate on the plain unvarnished truth!

Only when it is discovered that faith and dependence can be placed in the individual and his agenda, which comes only after time has proven that the individual is not simply putting up smoke screens, can a progressive and successful program be established.

If society as a whole is becoming a part of the team concept, how does it affect the operation of organizations? Here is a new thought process that needs careful examination as it relates to the success or failure of an organization.

As the world at large becomes more involved in team concepts, it will become more difficult to continue those organizations that operate with a different thrust; and yet at the same time, some of those agencies cannot structurally make a complete transition to the textbook modern team concept. Not all things must be the same, and perhaps there is a middle ground that will be successful to all. This suggestion is not put forth to promote a change in any organization, but only to examine the operation of the team concept, and perhaps from examination, some productive points may be incorporated into an acceptable approach to congenial and productive leadership.

Teams consist of four personalities, as does all society. One is the "leader" who has the answers, and arrives at the meeting with them in hand. He has self-determination because he has reviewed the program, or agenda, and has come to conclusions on the matter in question. Most likely he is chairing the gathering, but not necessarily so.

Someone else may have been designated as the leader for a variety of reasons, and his personality may fall into one of the other three categories. Should it happen that a leader does not exist in the mix, then the success of the group may be impaired, or made difficult, but not necessarily impossible.

The nascent team will have a "combatant" amongst the group. This does not mean that his personality automatically questions everything that is presented, but he will not be silent. He will force the leader to prove his points, and back up his suggestions with solid background and reasoning. He will not meekly accept that which is set forth, and will fight the leader for intellectual territory. It is not beyond the realm of possibility that this member may possess both the personality of a leader as well as that of a combatant.

A "compromiser" will be present who will hopefully smooth the friction between the strong personalities of the leader and the combatant. He will step in and explain points in a different way than presented in order to negotiate a better understanding between the leader and the combatant. He very well may negotiate a compromise between the other two, taking the best of both arguments. However, it is to be understood that the combatant is not basically a presenter of ideas, but one who has doubts about the correctness of what has been presented. He tends to relate what won't work, but very seldom has a suggestion as to what will work. Hence, the work of the negotiator is of vital importance.

The last personality is the "follower." He either executes orders, or does nothing. He adds little to the solution, but can play an important role in implementation.

The first condition of a self-directed work team is ownership. Until everyone buys into the concept, the notion of self-directed teamwork is fantasy. There can be no consensus that is productive if all, or part, of the group is not convinced of the correctness of their effort, and not convinced that the result of the effort will be implemented, unless the conclusion is congruent with a determination previously made by someone who is not a part of, but has authority over the team.

Without interest in the project, and without a determination that there is a solution, the members will not perform to their best effort. In athletics, a team takes the field convinced that it will lose, most likely will not be disappointed. The team, or individual brimming with self-confidence is difficult to overcome . In some cases, the two are mixed. We have an athletic team made up of individuals convinced of their superiority, and also members who are sure that they don't have a chance. Just like the team, the results will be mixed. If the opposition is not too difficult, then the team will win, but on other occasions may lose to those who are equal, or near their own potential. The mixed group will realize better success if the confident members can provide the leadership and inspiration necessary to exhilarate the doubters into a new reassured feeling of "can do!"

Whether we are examining athletics, industrial groups, or organizational committees, the basic principle remains the same. It is impossible to obtain a maximum effort unless all the members buy into the effort. Only then will each perform with confidence and not be discouraged by any setbacks that might be encountered during the process.

A principle must be applied to the mission that is consistent with the talents being devoted by the members. Some problems are too small for the talent assembled, and some problems are too large. Someone must make a determination of the ability levels to be assigned to the problem solving team. That person, or persons, must also be aware of the mix necessary if productive solutions are to be the result of the effort.

So the first hurdle of team existence is ownership by all members, which may be difficult. Until the concept is accepted, we have two problems. First is ownership, which can be thrust upon the members, but must be bought into, and the second is that the seeds of conflict have been sown through the imposed familiarity of membership on the team. Conflict between the members arises quickly. The leader arrives with all the solutions. The combatant questions the solutions and says they won't work. The compromiser tries to bring the two together, and the followers are quietly sitting back to await the end of the meeting, or receive orders as what they are to do.

What will solve the dilemma, and bring the team together where they can all make a meaningful contribution? Some catalyst must strike the entire group and bring them to a sense of trust in one another. The old saying is that two heads are better than one, but it is not very often followed. No doubt one member of the group, usually the leader will have a good agenda toward appropriate solutions, and perhaps the group will adopt most of his ideas with some correction and alteration. Those alterations and corrections will make the difference between moderate success, moderate failure, and exemplary productivity.

On the other hand, the question of qualification arises. All too often there does not exist on the team anyone with the proper background and experience to intelligently address the subject. And most often that deficiency is not realized by the proper authority. Each team member must acknowledge that as an individual he does not have all the answers, and trust the knowledge and ability to contribute by his teammates.

It is vitally important that it be recognized whether the team is composed of a proper mix of those within and without the expertise related to the question.

Let us take a simple problem and submit it to a team: "How much are two and two? The leader arrives with a determination that the answer is three,. He knows that there is a quantity of two, and since something has been added, obviously the answer will be somewhat higher, and therefore the answer is three. The followers say, "okay". However the combatant questions the leader.

"What makes you think the answer is three. You can't just add things together and come up with answers. I know what I'm talking about because just yesterday morning, my wife added two eggs to two cups of flour and she didn't get three waffles, she got five!"

The leader replies that we aren't talking about waffles. He continues with the argument that if you have two of something and then add some more, you will get a higher number which is three. The combatant is now becoming belligerent. "Well. isn't two eggs something, and isn't two cups of flour adding more, and I'm telling you my wife got five, not three."

Now is the time for the negotiator. He steps in and points out to the leader that no doubt he is on the right track, but we need to resolve the question raised by the combatant. He now points out to the combatant that his analogy is a good one, but is slightly flawed by the fact that he is adding two different things...eggs and flour. His analogy would be better if he added two more eggs to the first two. The question now appropriately becomes, "How many eggs do we have?" He continues by pointing out that the results of his example were waffles, which did not exist when we began, and therefore the addition resulted in the creation of something not existent when we started. The result as indicated by the combatant is not responsive to a mathematical problem, but more related to the field of science, or invention. It is pointed out to the combatant that his thought process is excellent in questioning the result given by the leader, but needs to go further. The negotiator goes back to the leader and points out that while there is a flaw in the example of the combatant, he has nevertheless made the point that the team has not yet delved out enough information to come to a conclusion to the problem. While the leader might very well be right in his answer, there has not been enough information provided for everyone to buy into the leader's decision. More research needs to be done, and more information provided for the team members. How is the appropriate answer achieved? It may take research by the committee, or it may be necessary to add more expertise to the group. They must come in contact with the information that one and one is two. Then they must discover that one and one and one and one is four. From this information, they can arrive at the correct conclusion to their problem.

There is no danger here in not having a math expert, but rather of being devoid of the proper expertise to research the problem and arrive at a productive and correct conclusion. At the same time, a math expert amongst the mix whose credentials are impeccable could have saved the committee research time.

Individual competency is that which makes a

member an asset to the team. Each must have something to contribute in the way of background and knowledge, and trust must be established among the team members. Trust is absolutely essential to accomplishing the team's mission, and the unqualified arrival at a common goal opened to all members generates an atmosphere conducive to positive and enjoyable participation by all.

The grand total of accomplishment is the sum of the resolved differences amongst the team members, and that grand total is greater than the sum. Laziness, and/or indifference, is the enemy of the effort that will sabotage the results. It is manifested in an unwillingness to hear conflicting views; unwillingness to evaluate assumptions; unwillingness to accept initial principles; and failure to pursue non-responses.

Today's society demands teamwork, but at the same time buys into the true concept with reluctance. It cannot be created by mottoes, buzzwords, or catchy slogans. It is established, like so many things…after recognition of the individual parts necessary to create the machinery of conversant productivity. The task is not easy, but is absolutely necessary.

For the moment, let us presume that you are the head of an organization, and as such, responsible for the appointment of committees to carry out various tasks for the general group. Some of these committees will be operative in nature, and therefore necessitate the investigation of what expertise is necessary to complete the tasks of the committee. The answers here are simple. It is simply necessary to establish the particular needs of the committee in terms of manpower and expertise. However, it must be noted that it is essential that a chairman be appointed that can be relied upon to see that the committee's assignment is completed. It is also essential that the chairman be given members who will actively assist and support the chairman's efforts. Therefore, an operative committee can be made up of a respected leader, knowledgeable in the necessary expertise, and the necessary manpower consisting of entirely followers. Not to be overlooked is the necessity of appointing people who can get along together, and work together.

More difficult is the selection of those committees that are investigative in nature. Suppose we appoint only members we consider to be leaders to our first committee deemed investigative in nature. Have we not provided a scenario that dooms our group to unproductive wrangling without solution? Further, if we continue this attempt to load each committee with all leaders, we will run out of leaders for subsequent committees. Unproductive or slow moving committee work will result if we load committees with any one of our categories. All leaders, all combatants, all negotiators, or all followers doom our organization to poor investigative committee work.

Assembling groups of people to take charge of an assignment is not easy. Much consideration is necessary to arrive at the proper balance of personalities in order to insure success.

Let us take a phrase heard somewhere long ago, the origin of which is not remembered, nor of much importance. However, the thrust of the words fits our discussion appropriately, "An ox can pull a cart up a hill, but a bird can nest in a tree."

A determination of the original problem can be developed from the few words contained in the phrase. We will presume that the purpose of the cart is to move goods, or an object of some weight, from one place to another. To accomplish this task takes more than just the strength of the ox. Certainly the ox has qualities that are vital to our project, but he is also greatly lacking in other important aspects.

Preparing for the accomplishment of this task necessitates someone with the proper expertise to harness the ox and hitch him to the cart. Certainly the ox is incapable of accomplishing this part of the task. Next, whatever is to be moved on the cart has to be loaded. It well may be that those parties have not the strength necessary, and either others, or additional help is needed.

Once the ox is harnessed and hitched, and the cart loaded, it might seem that the ox can complete the task alone, but he cannot. The ox is incapable of receiving instructions as to the destination of the cart, and so a driver must be added to the project. Also, we must not overlook the possibility of other obstacles to success.

While the ox and his driver are capable of viewing the road ahead to anticipate dangers, or problems, they cannot see over the hill. There is no way for them to anticipate any difficulties that might lurk just over the brow of the hill, nor can they be certain the strenuous effort of the ox will end in fruition since there may be important information unknown to them. Will they stop on the hill to contemplate this dilemma? Will they hesitate, and perhaps return to the starting point fearful of continuing? Will a project this far nobly begun, end in failure because all contingencies were not accounted for?

Our bird that can nest in a tree is in a position to be of help in our example. He can see over the hill, determine the safety and prospects for success. He indeed becomes a vital part of our project. In our phrase, or example, we had several different needs, and neither the ox, nor the bird could supply all of them. In fact, there were some that neither the ox nor the bird could supply, but needed the assistance of others. And so it is for any endeavor assigned to a group, or a committee. If it were not so, the person appointing the committee, or assembling the group, would have either performed the task necessary himself, or would have given it to just one person.

How many times have you seen someone stand up in a meeting and state that such and such should be done, or some particular matter should be looked into, and the presiding officer agreed, and appointed the person on his feet as the chairman of the committee to accomplish that which had been suggested. The presiding officer then looks around the room and assigns others to assist as members of this new committee. The additional members of the committee are selected in one of two ways, depending on the particular motivation of the presiding officer. There are some presiding officers who select people because they have nothing to do. This may be suitable, but it might also be that they have nothing to do for a reason. The second method is to pick those who are already very busy, knowing that they can be relied upon to complete tasks. This is not any more reliable than the first way.

Our presiding officer needed to take the matter under consideration until he had time to put together a committee with the necessary expertise, personalities, and tools. He may, or may not, feel it appropriate to include the person who prompted the creation of this new committee. This action must be done with careful thought, and perhaps with some advice from others. If it is not worth the time and effort necessary to insure success, then it is not worth bothering with at all.

There is one more consideration in this area and

one further category of committee that has been left out. It is prudent and necessary to prepare for the future of your organization. This can only be done if a number of the younger members are trained to assume the various positions of responsibility in the future. It is, therefore, the duty of every presiding officer of an organization to be alert to assigning younger members to be active in the committee work. They are not a part of our mix of four categories in assignment consideration. They are added for the purpose of exposure and assimilation of committee problems and operations. What they learn will not only assist them in performing tasks in the future, but we also thereby build a bridge by which valuable information from previous endeavors is not lost.

A person in charge, or presiding over a large group is disadvantaged if he does not know the expertise and background of each member. The size of the group may very well make it impossible to be fully aware of the capabilities of everyone. However, the more time spent in researching and discovering the abilities of as many members as possible will stand him in good stead. This is one of the several tasks necessary in preparation to preside over an organization. It also points out the extreme importance of becoming personally acquainted, and delving into the background of every new member of the group.

Many who are aware of the necessity of this endeavor to the success of their tenure, establish a questionnaire of some kind in an effort to familiarize themselves with the abilities of the members. There is nothing wrong with this approach, provided it is not the only attempt at investigation. Nothing substitutes for personal knowledge and contact. There are many among us who do not care, for personal reasons, to quasi volunteer for duties by filling out questionnaires. Oh, we may put something on paper to show a spirit of cooperation, but the full scope of one's ability very well may not be visible by the answers given. At the same time, these individuals respond very positively to personal contact and inquiry. The search for talent amongst the members is of vital importance, and each presiding officer must develop ways to accomplish the same by various means.

All too often those who are non-attendees are written off as not being interested in the proceedings and efforts of the group. While such might be true in some individuals, it is not correct in every case. There are many who do not attend simply because they have nothing to do, and have not been given an assignment. It is not within their personality to simply attend and sit on the sidelines, and yet they have a great capacity for productive contributions. It does not serve the whole to discount out of hand, any of the parts.

Be aware, be careful, be smart, and do your homework before appointing committees in your organization. They, not you, will decide your success!

To the reader: What follows does not suggest solutions. It addresses an attitude that perhaps should be addressed.

Chapter XI
Change

> *"No one is so good they cannot fall,*
> *nor so bad they cannot climb."*
> *- O. Henry*

An examination of the above quotation brings a question to mind. Suggesting an answer leads to another question, and so it goes. If one does not climb, then apparently no matter how adept one is at hanging on, there is no risk of falling. Indeed, would it not be a consideration that time, or environment, or untoward influences will eventually assure that one will fall? Most likely!

One may be uncoordinated, undisciplined, uneducated, and untalented, but one can still climb. Each will have a different innate ability, and each will have a different acquired ability; but nothing prohibits the attempt, nor precludes success.

Application of the above quotation can be made to any endeavor whether it be physical, or mental. It applies to all circumstance whatever the setting, but suggests a confrontation of theory. Is O. Henry saying that no matter how well planned our position, no matter how careful our safeguards, and no matter how securely established, there remains a danger? What position can we establish that is absolutely so well safeguarded that a fall is totally impossible? The only safeguard that demands consideration is time.

Let us examine those things protected by time. No...not those things, but those people.

Remember, the quote refers to a person. It is not true that all people revered George Washington. He sent an army of five thousand to burn the capital city of the Iroquois Nation during the Revolution. The Iroquois Nation consisted of five tribes bound together by democratic agreement. Two members of that nation had joined the British at the insistence of Joseph Brant, and two had recognized the colonists as a new nation, but one member had remained neutral. The neutral were the ones whose town was the capital, and were the ones slaughtered. The descendents of that Indian Tribe call the "Father of Our Country", the Burner of Towns."

Albert Einstein was reported as having flunked math in school. It is doubtful that he was greatly admired by his math instructor. Time leads to revelations unflattering to revered heroes. On the other hand, time can also bring to light those who were overlooked, or discounted in their lifetime. In some cases, the sands of time wash over the names of many who should have been remembered, but were not. Time provides no safeguard against failure, nor barrier to success.

Perhaps numbers would provide a safeguard. If we expand our pursuit to groups of people rather than an individual, it may be that we can discover a safe haven.

A quick check of history, and we review the Romans, the Greeks, the Incas, the Persians, the Egyptians, etc. All were great civilizations in their day; but all, for one reason or another, fell into disrepute, and were cast on the pile of the once great.

Well, it does not appear that there is safety in numbers that precludes a fall. Apparently, when num-

130

bers are involved, the only difference is that the crash is greater. How do we assure ourselves that we will not fall? O. Henry said that none are so bad they cannot climb. He provided the answer in his quotation. If you are to attempt to avoid a fall then you must climb... and continue to climb. There is no respite provided. Once you quit climbing, the fall becomes an eventual certainty. There is a concentration of the task at hand while climbing, and the mental processes are focused on the objective, which is progress. One may find the present path blocked, but in retreating to seek out another path, there is no sensation of having lost the battle. Even a slip is not categorized as falling, or failing. Again, it is only a minor setback, and a warning to be more selective in the choice of footholds. As long as the mind is comfortable that progress is being made, and does not mentally capitulate in response to minor setbacks, the body will perform far beyond what might be deemed its reasonable limits. It is only when the mind succumbs that the body suddenly collapses before it is entirely spent. Even when the body cries out, and demands rest, the mind considers this only one of those minor delays in progress.

A prime example of the mind and body relationship is exhibited in track and field. It is seldom that a runner collapses in the middle of a race; however, we often see the runner completely collapse just past the finish line. Only when the mind has been satisfied with the completion of its objective, has it permitted the body to succumb to exhaustion.

Climbing is progress, commonly thought of as in an upward direction. However, the direction depends on your goal. It may consist of climbing down, or across, as well as up. It very well might be a combination of several directions in order to strive toward your objective.

For our discussion, it would be proper to use progress as a synonym for climbing, and if we think in terms of recognition and success, it would be appropriate to substitute falter for fall in the quotation. Our new consideration of O. Henry's quotation becomes, "No one is so good they cannot falter, nor so bad they cannot progress."

Ah! You want to use the word, "succeed", instead of progress in our substitute quote. We cannot do that. To do so would establish a given of success. To succeed is to reach a pinnacle not to be surpassed, or it is to attain a preset goal which you have determined is satisfactory for your purposes or desires. The quotation, both O. Henry's and ours, is one of action, and not one of conclusion. To fall, or to falter, is not conclusive; nor is to climb, or to progress, conclusive. All of these terms indicate a direction of action, but do not establish the ultimate consequence.

Have we now established two goals? One, not to fall or fail: and two, to climb, or progress? Not really...the thrust of our premise is that if we climb or progress, then we are eliminating the risk of a fall or failure; so we have really considered the one by attacking the other. A determination of progress has reduced the danger. Progress has now become a lifelong vocation in everything we do. Whatever our everyday job, we now must strive to learn more and more about it. We no longer accept that we are an expert to the end that there is no other avenue of advancement in knowledge possible in our field.

Whatever our hobbies, or extracurricular activities we no longer accept that what we know, or are able to do, is acceptable. Our family can look forward to continually improving relationships, and our church will be pleased with our increased activity and understanding. All of the preceding invokes a consideration that is contrary to the basic nature of man. It involves change. To assure progress, and minimize the risk of faltering, we must change, and be receptive to change in the future.

Let me develop an example. We have a businessman who began as a very bright young man. He set up his store in a downtown area where everyone worked and shopped. His store exhibited a very attractive sign that hung over the sidewalk, and the windows were attractively decorated with the goods he offered. Inside, his displays were neatly arranged on tables, or on shelves behind the counters. The incandescent lighting was adequate for customers to examine his goods. He had several clerks who met the customers and saw to their needs, rang up the purchase on the cash register, wrapped their goods, and gave them their change and receipt. In the office was a telephone, file cabinets, and a double entry set of books. These are typical of the small businessman before and after World War II.

Where is that small businessman today? If he didn't get a fax machine, a computer, cut down his sales force, let the customers fend for themselves, and move to a mall…he's out of business! But is this progress? Our example is not progress, it is survival. If one does not survive, then progress is not obtainable. In our example, the businessman may have engaged in survival only. It he was the last to change, he only survived and made no progress. However, if he was the first to change, then he engaged in progress, and is progressing even further in business growth while others are engaged in catching up.

Pick out several corporations engaged in the same line of business. Somewhere there is a ranking of those corporations relating to their gross sales and profits. Chances are the rankings change little from year to year. All of them are trying to pass the fellow ahead of him on the list, except the one at the top who is trying to keep anyone from catching him. The scenario is simple, basic, and prevalent in the world today. People, corporations, or organizations that are on top are there because they took our quote to heart. They began to climb and progress and it was only when others realized they were falling farther behind that they jumped on the bandwagon. In most cases those behind copied, and did not innovate; hence, they remain in the same relative position. As has been said, "If you are not the lead dog, your view never changes!"

What of those who were once on top and did not climb? What of those who were confident that their position was safe, and that chances were slim and none that they would fall, or fail? In every case you can find, they, sooner or later, found themselves insignificant and substantially forgotten. O Henry was right! Either climb or fall, either progress or fail! There are no other options.

Change is the magic word, but it is also a potential trap. First, we have the resistance to change. None of us are receptive to change. We are quick to accuse the other fellow of not being adaptable, but we are just as guilty. We must constantly be searching, studying, and quantifying. We must be looking forward to potential difficulties and dangers so that our path can be altered. A relaxed acceptance of the status quo invites eventual calamity. We must climb, we must progress, we most move forward. So there we are! All have been investigated; we have a consensus, and are now determined to change. No!...we have a another problem.

We have decided to change, but what is to be

changed? Let's make it easy. We are dressed to go out, and meet the wife by the front door all shined up and with a big smile. She gives us a sideways glance and remarks, "Do you expect me to go out with you looking like that!"

"What's wrong with the way I look?" you inquire.

"Well, you have on a pink shirt, an orange tie, a green jacket, and purple slacks. We're going out to dinner, not to the circus!"

Obviously we thought we looked okay, but a very important part of our enterprise disagrees. And so the discussion begins. No need to relate who wins the debate; the question is what is to be changed. There is nothing wrong with any of the clothes we have on, individually. We have been informed they do not go together, and are not to be worn at the same time. Now, what do we change? We have several options.

If we consider the matter, it is obvious that changing the tie and the jacket might get us by the inspector, and would not consume a lot of trouble or time. It's certainly worth a try. Whether our course of action works or not, we have attempted to manage our change in an intelligent manner…we managed change! In our example, we might have changed everything and not progressed. We might have changed the slacks and the shirt which would have been more difficult and consumed more time and energy. To constantly monitor one's position and look for ways to improve, is to live a life to its fullest and make a positive contribution to society. The same goes for organizations.

Management of change is not a reactionary involvement on a part time basis. Letting a situation, or events, become complex before being addressed constitutes operation by default. We have then permitted events to manage us which becomes a vicious vortex that will draw us into perhaps an unmanageable predicament, and at best, the solution will be ineffective.

By habit, we are prone to continue like we always have. Only when a minor crisis appears do we squirm for a while and hold our breath while the minor crisis goes away. Imperceptibly, change is beginning to affect our institution, but we are unwilling to recognize the danger. We trust time to cure the minor ills, and when it is too late, we will be shocked by the incursion of a major problem. Even then, we will wring our hands and talk the matter to death. Surely time and patience will correct our problem with very little effort on our part!

Down the road we will discover that we have waited too long and have permitted the swirl of change to destroy our organization. Go to your history books and look for these events. You will find it crowded with them.

Dr. Curt Chezem, editor of "The Oregon Scottish Rite Freemason," reported the following numbers in the January 1996 issue: "The last year for an increases in Masonic membership growth in the United States was 1958. This might be justified if the population of the U. S. was declining, but the reverse is true; hence, the statistic becomes even more alarming. The average age of Masons in the United States is approximately 68 years. Again, if the population were declining, we could understand and accept this statistic. We might find some solace in the fact that people's life expectancy has increased, and that families are also smaller; however, this does not account for such an advanced average age among the Craft." Accountability lies in the lack of interest by those who have never served in the military, served during the Viet Nam War, or somehow avoided service during the Viet Nam War. Oh yes! You know members of the Craft who fall into one of the above three categories, and so does this writer.

What you cannot do is equate the membership of those three categories with the numbers who petitioned after every major conflict in the history of this country. A careful examination of the records quickly indicates that Masonry was flooded with petitioners on each such occasion.

Why was the last increase in membership 1958? What is the significance of that particular year? Is there something to be learned from that particular statistic? In 1958, the depression kids had all reached maturity. They were brought up in times when it was necessary to bond to friends and relatives, if there was to be any hope of survival. Those same kids were here to welcome their brothers, fathers, uncles, cousins, and neighbor's, home. They learned a lesson in how vital it was in times of war to rely, and depend on one another… not only the military man next to you, but the Generals in the rear, the government in Washington, and especially those back home doing without certain foods, vehicles, shoes, and other items needed for the war effort. Survival depended on the workers doing their job in the war plants, putting in long hours, doing without raises in pay, and making sure their work was of exemplary quality.

Further, those depression kids were encouraged to seek out Masonry. A great many of them were brought a petition for the Order of DeMolay, and instructed to fill it out. DeMolay assisted in forging the principles and attitudes being exemplified by the returning servicemen. Masonry flourished after World War I, by the influx of returning servicemen, and then realized some losses because of the economics of the depression. It did not lose the interest of the populace, but some of the populace found it necessary not to be members for economic reasons. It flourished again after World War II with great numbers of petitions by returning servicemen, which was followed by the influx of depression kids.

It would now seem that we have a problem. The problem was foreseen, and predicted by several, but was not addressed. It was not addressed because it was thought there was nothing to do, "We are what we are, and we have always survived, and therefore we always will!" We all fervently pray that the statement is true, and that it will always survive. "This is not the first time in Masonic history that the Craft has been faced with declining membership, and the Craft did not change. Why should we be concerned? These losses in membership do not mean we have failed. They are simply minor delays in the continuing progress of Masonry. O. Henry's quote is safe with us. We can climb, and in doing so we will not fall!"

The previous quote is what many might say in response to the statistics quoted. The error is in not considering all the circumstances germane to the issue. What is the likelihood of another major conflict in the world that will draw the United States into a commitment on the scale of any of the engagements previous to 1950? What are the chances of this country suffering through another depression on the same scale as the one during the thirties? The chances are remote on either consideration. What is more important, is that to rely on prosperity as the result of extreme strife is not admirable. Calamity and strife can forge great qualities in individuals, or in organizations, and can be the inspiration to great progress once overcome. They can be the great stepping stones to higher heights, but not as the result of their imposition on others. An individual does not acquire strength of character, and determination of purpose by witnessing the difficulties of others. He only learns the great lessons from his own experience. The same is to be said for organizations.

As individuals, and as an organization, it is imperative that we constantly monitor our position, and our progress. Do we see the secure footholds ahead that will permit our continued progress? Do we need to back up and pursue another path in order to continue? Have we taken into consideration all the present factors, and made an intelligent examination of what appears to lie ahead? Having done these things, are we ready to look toward and change with eagerness, or do we contemplate these things with anxiety?

There is only one event that will doom our effort to failure…only one exercise that will destine us to fall. Only one consideration that will weaken us as individuals, detract from us as an organization, and deprive society of what has always been an important integral part of its fabric…and that is if we do not take the initiative to talk about it in a cooperative and concerted effort from the lowest levels to the most exalted.

What is to be done? How are we to address these types of problems? We are human, so we don't want to change. We want things to stay as they are! Everything has always been great, why must we change" The answer is simple. Whether we like it or not, everything changes, each in its own way, and in its own time. We can choose to ride the tide and see where it takes us, or we can fashion a set of oars, and do our best to manage the direction in which we travel.

To the reader: A personal experience of the wife and myself prompted this paper. As you examine this paper, contemplate the need to assist others without inadvertently reducing their ability to function.

Chapter XII
Squirrels and People

What a lovely setting. A very comfortable cottage with a view of the tree studded hillside behind the luxurious lawn and small gentle stream. Three large trees, one a Magnolia, grace the scene. Truly, it is a comfortable and relaxed experience to sit amidst and ponder. To animate the panorama are songbirds, and occasional visits from a pair of squirrels. Our furry friends would sit in the low crotch of the biggest tree where they had a glorious view of the surroundings. They didn't come every day, but seemed to enjoy working their way from the hillside, branch to branch, until arriving in our backyard where they paused in their daily chores for a half hour or so, and then moved off.

It seemed a good idea to put some peanuts in the crotch of the tree so that our friends night have a little repast while enjoying our yard. In this way we could show our appreciation of the many hours of entertainment they provided, and the pleasant animation they added to the panoply of nature. They would run, jump, and do acrobatics in the air, and seemed to enjoy entertaining in appreciation for the free meal. As time passed, we moved the peanuts to the back deck, and our little friends quickly discovered the change.

During the summer, it took only a few evenings

to encourage the lively and inquisitive pair to take peanuts from our hands. Our little granddaughters were amazed and thrilled during a visit to Grandma and Grandpa's house to witness Grandpa feeding the wild squirrels "right out of his hand," and had a great story to tell their playmates when they returned home.

However, we soon found ourselves faced with eight in our backyard! Obviously the word spread that there was an easy meal available twice a day, as my wife had begun to put peanuts out every morning in addition to the evening fare. While there was no variety to the menu, simply peanuts; nonetheless, it was both regular and effortless...just show up and enjoy the repast.

Summer, fall, and winter passed with peanuts making up an increasing part of our bill at the local Kroger. As nature restored her beauty in the spring, we soon discovered that we were having little visitors that we hadn't seen before. Yes, our morning and evening ritual was now serving a second generation. The numbers continued to grow and the bill at Kroger's reflected the increase in our number of little dependents. Noticeably missing from the exercise was the Olympian quality acrobatics, and gymnastic type maneuvers. What had seemed a sense of appreciation by our little visitors had deteriorated into an almost panic driven effort to compete for the ample supply of peanuts. Indeed, observation indicated that some who were late arriving found others with bulging midsections, and little scuffed places in the green grass where that which could not possibly be consumed, was buried for future reference. No thought had been given by first arrivals to consider those who might be tardy!

Very often those who were late, and whose appetites had not been satisfied, arrived to discover their peers scurrying around the yard deciding on a place to bury the last of the repast. The late arrivals would follow to see the location of the buried treasure, and quickly obtain what they adjudged was their right. Their intentions did not go unnoticed. The hoarders soon learned to stop, scratch at the ground with their paws, duck their head into the ruffled grass, and move on without dropping the peanut from their mouth. Observing the ritual, it was readily apparent that the late-comers were not fooled by the procedure. They relentlessly continued to follow the little gray hoarder with the flashing bushy tail, checking each stopping point until the desired cache was discovered.

What at one time had been enjoyed as an act of concern and generosity had now become a labor of attempting to satisfy the demands of an ever growing community of greedy and contentious little gray streaks of anger. Occasionally my wife would be tardy in getting the peanuts out in the morning, due to some household chore that required immediate attention. Or upon my arrival from work in the evening, we might have some project that distracted us from getting the peanuts out on the back deck, and our little furry friends were forgotten. On those occasions we were quickly faced with an irate entourage. They would bark and flash their tails, They would jump up and bang against the back door. Some would climb the porch railing so they could look in the back window and raise Holy Ned! And no more acrobatics and entertainment. No, all that stuff had become history. Just get it out here, and be on time about it!

Indeed, we found out that what had started out as a gesture of kindness, and an effort to be of some small assistance during the bitter weather, as well as helping out during those times when the food supply

142

was short, soon was looked on by the squirrels as an entitlement. Apparently, we must weigh carefully the assistance and aid we mete out with the best of intentions. Perhaps we should teach and show others, rather than do it for them.

Organizationally, we do for others, and they decide they can't, and that we must do for them. Then one day we say, "You haven't, you can't, and you didn't; therefore, you aren't!" Maybe it's better to provide food for thought, rather than food for the tummy. Perhaps it is more productive and kinder to show and assist, rather than to do for!

Germane to the issue of population growth, and industrial change, is the movement of population centers. Many small, but busy, communities have lost the industry that was responsible for their activity and success. Perhaps our example might have been the center of a railroad repair shop, a timber cutting enterprise, a lumber mill, or perhaps a grain mill, or coal tipple. All of the preceding are dependent on natural resources available, and when they play out, the community shrinks, or perhaps disappear altogether.

Being the active center of not only a working class of people, but also management, Masonry came to town very soon. Very often Masonic Bodies remained long after the ability of the community to preserve the activity necessary to survival for such an enterprise. Lacking the ability to perform all the requisite functions, these, now small, bodies depend on folks from over the mountain to visit and assist in the performance of work, or the accomplishment of inspections. Many times the Craft is unwilling to move charters when it is necessary. Moving charters is not an event to be avoided, but is extremely vital that they be moved only after due consideration, investigation, and a proper program of communication with those that will be impacted by the decision.

It may be that there is a possibility of future influx into the community that would greatly alter the status quo. In those cases it is necessary to supply the aide needed to assure the continuance of Masonry in the immediate area. If so, we are faced with the difficulty of balancing our assistance so that those being aided do not become like the squirrels in our tale. In some cases it is merely a matter of moving the charter a few miles down the road, or across the mountain in order to create the spark that will renew Masonic activity in the general area. Moving a short distance from a dead area into an active one seems discordant. Why would Masonry flourish only a few miles away? Why would interested people drive in only one direction, but not the other? The answer is not readily visible, nor is it accompanied by an awareness of those that participate in what might seem like unwarranted behavior; yet the answer is basic human nature. To drive twenty miles to a community that has become devoid of industrious activity is to the subconscious a regressive activity. To drive twenty miles in the other direction to an area growing in population, one spurred with an influx of industry and business, is to the subconscious, a progressive activity. The philosophy of human nature is vital to our consideration before making decisions regarding the movement of charters. We again must be aware that relocating does not remove the need for assistance in reactivating our group in question, nor does it remove the danger of creating a problem like we did with the squirrels.

It is significant that all problems existent in any organization were, and are, easily predictable. They sprout from the seeds of complacency, and prosper from the fertilization of inattention. We cannot claim to be proper stewards if our only interest and time are dedicated to our own ratification and advancement. We only serve in an admirable fashion when we are constantly aware of what is, or may be, ahead.

Again, the danger in all, and of all, is that we step in when to do so is not only counter-productive, but makes the very objective we seek unattainable. Is there a proper formula of when to assist, and how much? Is there an established procedure outlining how to determine what type, and the amount of aid needed to an apparent floundering organization? Are there certain parameters setting forth the judgment that now is the time to consider moving a charter? Is there a guideline on how to determine that ability of a group to pull itself back into an active and responsive organization? No, there isn't!

So how are we to decide when, how, and to what extent to pursue our concerns? Well, now the question becomes somewhat easier. It is proper and vital to be well acquainted with the comings and goings of all. It is essential to study and examine the history of our organization on the local level. From this study, we can learn much of what to do, when to do it, and what not to do. By being interested and concerned each with the other, we establish an intelligent and sensible relationship where we not only enjoy the satisfaction of extending the proper assistance when appropriate, but we can also expect the same in return.

This endeavor was inspired by two events.

The second was the relationship with the squirrels in my backyard. Pondering on the attitude development of my little gray dependents, I recalled reading sometime ago the words of President Theodore Roosevelt in his First Annual Message to Congress n

1901, which constitutes the other premise for what has been here said. Our good Brother said it eloquently as follows:

"When all is said and done, the rule of Brotherhood remains as the indispensable prerequisite to success in the kind of national life for which we strive. Each man must work for himself, and unless he so works, no outside help can avail him; but each man must remember also that he is indeed his brother's keeper, and that while no man who refuses to walk can be carried with advantage to himself or anyone else, yet that man at times stumbles or halts, that each at times needs to have the helping hand outstretched to him. To be permanently effective, aid must always take the form of a helping a man to help himself; and we can best help ourselves by joining together in the work that is of common interest to all."

In all we do regarding human relationships, we must never forget the lesson of the squirrels, for after all, perhaps squirrels are people too…or maybe it's the other way around!

To the Reader: Speculative Masonry uses physical structures as an allegory to teach great moral truths. All structures must have a solid foundation if they are to survive. The following thoughts occurred to the author while watching the young men of a DeMolay Chapter perform their degree work on a class of candidates.

Chapter XIII
Building the Structure

Masonry in contractor's parlance consists of brick, or block, or stone, and mortar. If the mortar is properly mixed and tempered, the brick, or stone, of good quality, the design structurally sound, and the workmen skilled, the completed edifice most likely will stand for centuries.

Masonry, in a philosophical context, consists of solid citizens with a belief in one God, cemented into a Brotherhood of Man under the Fatherhood of God. Time has established the design structurally sound, and the building blocks of the highest quality. At issue is the mortar.

Masonic Brethren are the cement that holds the structure of Freemasonry together. As the workmen at an edifice use up the mortar in the mixing box, more must be properly prepared for their use. So Freemasonry uses up the expertise and talent of its membership as that membership moves on to that Celestial Lodge above.

A skillfully erected edifice is an accomplished endeavor that requires only periodic maintenance to preserve its beauty, service, and viability. It is only necessary to leave a very few workmen behind to provide such service. The main body of workmen move on to another site to repeat their skills.

Freemasonry requires a full complement of skilled craftsmen to maintain its philosophical structure. There is no luxury of a completion of the objectives, for the Master Architect's drawings provide for continual strengthening of the edifice and added adornment. Such never ending labor creates problems for the philosophical worker not experienced by the construction laborer. Freemasonry rightly depends on volunteer apprentices who seek to learn the craft of their own volition, and without solicitation or encouragement. For this unique form of maintaining a skilled working crew, it is essential that the general citizenry be impressed with the accomplishments of Freemasonry, and inspired by the skill and assiduity of its membership. It cannot remain viable in any other way.

Historical research of membership numbers furnishes interesting statistics. Following the American Revolution, the Craft experienced an increase in membership as well as an increase in the number of lodges. After the War of 1812, there was a spurt of membership, and growth continued in spite of the Morgan affair of the late 1820's and 1830's, although not of major proportions until after the Civil War.

After the Civil War, there was a great increase in membership and activity which continued into the Twentieth Century. Another surge of activity occurred following World War I, but there was a dampening of enthusiasm during the Great Depression. The last great influx of petitions followed World War II. Since then, there has been a general decline which has gained momentum in recent years. It is to be noted that the Supreme Architect has been placing his call to those veterans in ever increasing numbers to the point that their numbers are nearing depletion.

It is curious to note that the terrible experiences of war somehow touches men's hearts and souls that they seek the comfort of the Masonic Fraternity. But Freemasonry is much more than a refuge for those who have stared the Grim Reaper in the face and survived. For the Craft to stand idly by and permit the dissolution of that symbolic mortar so necessary to its edifice is not an option; nor is passive conjecture that perhaps world events will somehow solve all our problems.

Answers to our consideration are complex, but to quote Winston Churchill, "Out of intense complexities, intense simplicities emerge." To quote a carpenter from Nazareth, "Teach the children in the way you would have them go, and when they grow old, they will not depart from it."

Therein lies one of our simple solutions. Frank S. Land of Kansas City, Missouri, formed an organization for young men in 1919 that surpassed any concept ever conceived for that age group. One of the requirements is that local DeMolay Chapters be sponsored by a Masonic Organization.

The Order of DeMolay began in 1919, and its alumni now include outstanding leaders in all fields of endeavor, and has supplied Freemasonry with many skilled Craftsmen. However, as we discuss these matters today, DeMolay suffers the same problems as the Craft, and therefore it is important that we investigate collateral issues.

Raising children is a frustrating adventure experienced by parents from time immemorial. Each generation is faced with the dilemma that the young people simply do not have a firm grip on life's purposes, have no understanding of values, and with all their education, remain, to some extent, naive of the actual world and its workings.

I was not in attendance; I had the privilege of reading the text of a talk given by a prominent West Virginia Mason titled, "What is happening to the youth of Today?" the young men in question suffered through the Great Depression, won World War II, petitioned Masonry in tremendous numbers, and led the Order Of DeMolay to its zenith. His talk was delivered in 1931!

At issue is how we are to capture the spirit, zeal, and enthusiasm of the young men he was concerned about, and instill it in today's emerging citizenry. Indeed, the matter is not really an issue, for an issue is a debatable consideration. It is more correctly identified as a problem which is an accepted given to which there must be found a solution.

In 1980, it fell my good fortune to be both the Grand Commander of Knights Templar in West Virginia, as well as the Executive Officer of DeMolay. In those capacities, an investigation was made into the membership roles in both Templary and DeMolay in the various states for the previous ten years. A direct correlation was discovered. Membership in Templary and DeMolay went up and down together, and in the same percentages in all states with one exception... West Virginia. The West Virginia phenomenon is understood, but will not be explored here. It is reasonable to suggest that down cycles in competent leadership for DeMolay had a dampening effect on the interest of young men in the Masonic Fraternity, and a resultant down cycle in Craft membership. Loss of Craft membership results in difficulty locating suitable leadership for DeMolay. Acceptance of the correlation here exhibited must not be shrugged off as an unchangeable fact. To do so is to shrink from challenge, and surrender the battlefield. As numbers shrink, more responsibility falls on the few, and they must step forward and shoulder the weight of preparation for success.

The Supreme Council of DeMolay, like most human endeavors, has made occasional errors in judgment, but that is not to denigrate the overall outstanding benefit to our youth, the family, society, and the Craft. Working with these young men is educational, uplifting, highly rewarding, and satisfying.

One of the great enigmas of present day society is the lack of financial stability in so many of our organizations, and the loss of membership in an ever expanding population. DeMolay is no exception,

A number of years ago, the Supreme Council, in an attempt to address this problem, lowered the minimum age for membership. The point was argued strenuously from this quarter that you cannot put Junior High boys, High School youths, and College young men in the same tent. The youngest group will take over, and then leave in droves as they reach the next category. This problem had been solved years before with the establishment of The Priory of Knighthood for the college men. Time has proven the argument sound, but the matter should not detract from the opportunity presented to the Craft by this organization.

There are ways to handle the age issue on a local basis without any changes in International Law. Poignant to this discussion is the ideal mechanism presented, to put Craft Masonry, and all its adjunct groups in direct contact with the young men right up until their twenty-first birthday…what more could one seek? An immediate, and common reply is, "Yeah, we oughta do that," which is a totally unsatisfactory statement. Other replies heard much too often are: "I served my time working with DeMolay, it's someone else's turn," "I'm busy with Boy Scouts (or some other organization)" "I'm too old to work with young people," "I don't know anything about it (to which some add - and I'm too old to learn)" "I'm sure you could use some money, and I'll be glad to help financially, but I just don't have any spare time," "I couldn't get along with my boys, I sure as hell couldn't get along with someone else's."...there are more but you get the idea.

Let's review. To say, "We oughta do that," puts the matter on hold until such time someone steps forward and blazes a trail. Even then, the trailblazer usually ends up alone as the others hang back feeling they are not needed. If you have worked with DeMolay previously, then you are a valuable resource, and should make yourself available for consultation and advice, and as such you must keep in contact on a regular basis.

Busy with some other group requires an assessment of priorities, and no one can do that for you. Perhaps a careful examination will bring to light some opportunity to support DeMolay, if even in a small way, and perhaps bring some valuable insight from your experience in the other group.

Growing too old to work with young people is a self-imposed malady much like the man with a cramp in his foot on the leg that was amputated years ago. No matter how strong the brain's opinion, it just ain't so! Each individual is a storehouse of life experiences and knowledge, and there is an obligation to make that knowledge available to those who are following. Not knowing anything about DeMolay is not a deterrent, nor a shortcoming. The Laws, Rules, and procedures are easily absorbed. The most important requirement is that you have some relevant connection with young men, and indeed, you have the highest recommendation possible…You once were one! All you need is to remember those years in an honest manner.

A willingness to help financially is commendable, but conjures up memories of giving our own kids a couple of bucks and sending them off to the malt shop, the movies, or some other gathering place for young people that will get them out of our hair. We did it because we felt pressed for time on some occasions. Everyone's children are important, and we must make time for them.

Because you felt an inability to communicate with your own boys, is absolutely no criteria precluding the ability to have a good exchange with someone else's. Further, there is the consideration of those who never had any children and feel unqualified. Good gracious! It is without contention that all parents begin the task of working with their children totally unknowledgeable about the institution. The very first agreement reached between grandparents and grandchildren is that the youngster's parents don't know the first thing about raising kids!

An excellent example of a substantial contribution to DeMolay by one who thought he had nothing to offer follows:

While serving as Chapter Advisor of the local chapter, a program was instituted of inviting a local Mason every other month to speak at a chapter meeting. He was to talk about his vocation, and answer questions following his presentation. The program met with good response from the young men of the chapter. We had attorneys, doctors, business men, politicians, and even a retired member of the Baltimore Colts professional football team(Yes, the Indianapolis Colts were once in Baltimore).

One such invitee, who was Past Grand Commander of Knights Templar of West Virginia, was reluctant to accept, reasoning that his job at Wheeling Steel of shipment routing would be of no interest to the young men. It was suggested that he touch briefly on his vocation, answer any questions, and then go into an explanation of the structure of Masonry, vis a vis the two Rites, and the several appendant organizations. With a lot of trepidation, he finally agreed. On the specified evening, the Sir Knight was astonished at the interest and questions regarding his job. Those programs usually lasting twenty to thirty minutes, he tried to close, but the young men had been told he would explain the structure of Masonry, and they insisted the Sir Knight do so. He was there for another full hour before the questions subsided. The Sir Knight was pleased and excited at the reception he had received, and had a warm feeling of having made a solid contribution. Everyone has a valuable contribution to make to our young people. We simply have to investigate the Craft, discover the talent available, and put it to good use...there's a job right there!

An argument heard all too often is that the youth of today are different. It is pointed out that there is just too much competition for their time and energies. A myriad of school activities, cars, jobs, computers, television, and a wider range of athletic activities, are all cited as reasons for the decline of DeMolay, and the impossibility of it being brought to the forefront. These are not reasons for failure; they are excuses for a lack of willingness to meet a challenge.

Sales of American automobiles began to decline at one point in history because of the competition from foreign manufacturers. American companies decided what the consumer ought to have, geared their procedures to a product of modest quality, and until faced with the advent of the foreign imports, relaxed and enjoyed a very profitable enterprise. For some time the competition was ignored, but falling sales figures finally jarred them into the realization that they had a choice of meeting the competition, or quietly folding their tents. Catching up took a while, but today their product is competitive. Importantly, the U. S. companies exhaust every effort to continuously improve their product. No longer do they simply make a minor change in cosmetics from year to year.

There are two choices in the everyday world... vigorously battle the competition, and blaze exciting new chapters in history, or fade into obscurity as a footnote. "Youth of today are different, they do not respond like they used to," is another excuse for failure. Oh, the buttons may change in arrangement or location, but the basic human instincts and responses are still there. Find the buttons, and proper manipulation will create the sought after response that can then be channeled into devotion and respect for God, Country, and Family values. The thought that basic human responses have changed is contradicted in the following factual event.

"The trip has been a perfect nightmare to me, and I hate to even think about it. What good it has done I do not know. I am going to let it mellow, and then some day, I will tell you what I think about it. The President feels that it has strengthened him a great deal. I am not so certain, but it is so new, and so many of the horrors of it all are still so fresh in the mind that none of us who took part in it is capable of giving an unbiased view of it. I only know that we were on the go for ninety days, and in a whirl of noise and confusion and indigestible food from the beginning to the end, with the national air being drummed into one, day and night, and badly mannered fellow citizens screeching and screaming out, 'Hello Bill," from one town to the other. I am thinking about writing a lecture on the bad manners of our children - no reverence, no politeness, and no courtesy to anyone. There should be a department of manners in every public school. Of all the cities visited, there was only one where the children along the line of march took off their hats and spoke respectfully, and that was Boise, Idaho. When I asked Colin Cobb the reason for it, he confessed with some shame that an English woman was at the head of the school system. It was better when we reached the south, but even there we sometimes heard saucy little brats yell out, "Hello Bill," and sometimes, "Hello Fatty!"

Who is the President referred to? When did this event occur? What is the prognosis for the "saucy little brats" mentioned? One might easily surmise that the event happened in recent years, the President is Clinton, and as for the "saucy little brats." if something, or someone, doesn't straighten them out, this country is in for serious trouble. If so, one would be in error! The quoted excerpt was taken from a letter written by Major Archie Butts to his Aunt Clara, November 13, 1911. Archie Butts was personal aide to President William Howard Taft. The "saucy little brats" did straighten out. They fought World War I, raised their children during the roaring twenties and the Great Depression. They were the stalwarts who toiled in the quarries, worked in the vineyards, and brought the Craft, and our Country to the forefront of civilization. They fostered the Order of DeMolay, and raised it to an outstanding organization for young men. Indeed, those "saucy little brats" turned out quite well. The point here is that the little brats were not abandoned. Parents and society took an interest, worked with them, and they developed into good citizens.

Prospects for apprenticeship to learn the Craft of practicing Freemasonry must come from somewhere. They cannot be manufactured, cloned, or purchased in kit form; nor will wishful thinking create a substantial atmosphere of interest in assisting with the continued work on the Masonic Edifice.

The simple solution is recognition that volunteers to learn the Craft of Speculative Masonry comes from the adult male population, which comes from the teenage male population, which comes from families. The Craft survives only as long as it creates a favorable impression on families, teenagers, and adult males. Each comes from the other, and is a product of that which came before. When the Craft no longer works as a team in dedication to a viable and favorable image, it begins to deteriorate, slowly, but surely. The average age of members increases, officers become difficult to find, ritual work degrades, activities decline, and brethren start making presentations such as this one.

Operative Masons were learned and skilled in their crafts, and labored hard and long for their wages, and the right to continue as members. As Speculative Masons, we have no right to do less.

To the reader: The impetus to the following thoughts were prompted by the question being propounded to this writer regarding the compatibility of Masonry and Religion. The question is an important one. What follows is intended only to stir the reader to make his own investigation of the question in order to be comfortable with his own determination.

Chapter XIV
Masonry & Religion

Scholars have expended substantial amounts of time examining the history of Masonry to determine its lineage, its origins, and its connections in history. There are many areas of agreement, and some disagreement. Those interested in the history of the Craft, having read the work of each of these scholars, will decide on which theory is personally the most intriguing, and tends to bolster their perception of the matter. One might even amalgamate certain pieces from several into a personal belief regarding these matters that are historically in question. The one statement that none of these scholars has found, nor has suggested is that Masonry and Religion are mutually exclusive.

Can a person be both a Democrat and a Conservative? Can a person be both Republican and a Liberal? The answer is yes on both counts. They are not mutually exclusive. Democrats and Republicans are each members of an organization, and being so, have thereby enlisted under a specific banner for whatever reason. Liberal and conservative are merely philosophical tags hung on particular points of view on an issue in question. While a person consistently remains a member of his organization, he most likely will adopt

158

different tags depending on the matter at hand.

While there are certainly a multitude of religious organizations, there does not exist an entity formally organized simply under the banner, "religion." The word identifies a concept only in the broadest terms, unless accompanied by an identifier, or tag, which then only partially reduces the question, such as Christian religion, Jewish religion, Shinto religion, etc. When the matter is again divided in order to be specific, the word religion disappears.

What then are the specifics regarding religion? Is the Catholic Church a religion? Are Presbyterian, Methodist, Greek Orthodox, or Baptist, religions? Apparently not, as that word is not used in their identification. It would seem that all the myriad denominations and sects are organizations that have established certain rules, regulations, practices, and interpretations which they believe, for one reason or another, to be the correct approach to religion. How are we to view and define religion?

Perhaps we can agree when it is here suggested that religion is the expression of man's belief in a superhuman power as the creator and ruler of the Universe. It might be questioned whether the power thus described is a force, an ethereal spirit, or the manifestation of a divine being. The answer depends upon to whom the question is posed. Indeed, there have been those who believed that this superhuman power was divided between several entities rather than one.

Hence, we have arrived at a conclusion to which it is hoped we can all agree. Religion is an expression of belief, and in itself is not an organization. That expression of belief is in a superhuman power as the Creator and Ruler of the universe, represented by some as one God, and through history, by some as more than one God.

The myriad of denominations, sects, and religious cultures are paths, or roads, to the ultimate goal which is religion. Each has established its own litany of practices and forms assuring its followers that these constitute the proper landmarks to guide them along the correct path to their goal. These landmarks are set forth in the "Holy Book" of each, including historical background, teachings, and instructions in proper conduct. Perhaps it is appropriate to say that there are many roads to religion, all of which are acceptable to someone. If so, it seems curious that so many of the several approaches are derived from the same set of instructions.

An individual that believes in more than one God is not eligible for Masonic consideration. It is requisite that the applicant believes in a Supreme Being, and one Supreme Being only. Beyond that there are no other requirements that fall in the general category of religion. there are no further professions to make, no ceremonies or rites that are religious in nature, and no other religious questions, except in the one Masonic Body that is Christian in nature, and requires the applicant to profess a belief in Christ.

Followers of the Christian Religion are eligible for consideration in any, and all, Masonic affiliated bodies. Non-Christians, but believers in one Supreme Being are eligible for consideration in any, and all, Masonic affiliated bodies except the Commandery. These statements are not new, nor enlightening. They have been recognized and known by all Masons throughout the history of the Craft. What apparently is not understood by all too many is the extreme limitation of any religious concept to Masonry. The question has been posed to this person three times in the last year whether the questioner can remain a Mason and still be loyal to his church. Brethren, it is here suggested that someone has placed a doubt in the minds of these three Brothers. Surely research and study on their part did not confuse their position...someone planted the doubt.

There is no valid reason for anyone to even remotely suggest that it is not possible to be a Mason, and a staunch member and supporter of a Church. However, if some Church has established some sort of edict against Masonry, or perhaps some rule that suggests it is improper to withhold any information for which the Church might ask, then a conflict does exist, and the issue is promulgated by that specific Church group, and not by Masonry. Any church that exercises any of the preceding engages in convoluted thinking, and does itself more harm than good. It is only paranoia that leads some clergy to rail against Freemasonry, and attempt to undermine the rational thinking of really good people.

How self destructive is the attempt to monopolize the minds, time, and resources of humans, thereby smothering any inclination toward study, investigation, and the resultant self determination? History confirms such efforts result in short term success, but long term failure in those instances where the objective is political power related. Time soon erodes the ability of those in power to maintain the suffocation of truth and reason, and control is lost, sometimes in a violent upheaval.

More difficult is the unwilling effort at control and exclusion resulting from either fear of the unknown, or lack of understanding and rapport with other agencies. The human species is territorial by nature, and tends to react negatively to any activity that gives

161

the appearance of intrusion, or is not understood.

Mistakenly, the Masonic tradition has been eyed with suspicion in some religious circles. Misinformation, mistrust, and jealousy have habitually created great chasms of contentious conduct between people who otherwise preach, or subscribe to, the qualities of patience, charity, and good will toward others. Those deeply dedicated to a denomination, or any religious culture that has a full understanding of the Craft are comfortable with the aims and purposes of the Masonic Fraternity.

There are two diverse mental approaches to life. One is that which has an aimed approach to the future. The other is that which approaches the future aimlessly. Some individuals make a determination of goals and formulate a plan they believe will be successful. Time and consideration are devoted to their approach, and once their journey has begun, it is difficult to dissuade them from it. Only unexpected obstacles will cause them to hesitate in order to adjust, and then renew their journey.

Those who approach life aimlessly are not necessarily doomed to failure. Good fortune, or dumb luck, very well may shine upon them at an opportune time, and events project them into great success. To put the matter into a short phrase...some people make it happen, others let if happen to them. These two categories, however, have subdivisions which are important. Some of those who have goals and plans are honest and diligent in their deliberations. For example, a youngster might be fascinated with the game of basketball, and decide at an early age that his goal in life is to play the game professionally. The obsession blocks out any appeal to at least have a contingency plan. He is not interested in an education other than as it presents an opportunity to learn and play basketball. As he reaches late teens, he becomes aware that not only is he devoid of any coordination, but also that he is slow of foot, and destined to never be any taller than five feet four inches. The decision to abandon his dream is easy for him to accept at that time. It might have been difficult to deter him from his goal at an earlier age, yet the obvious was probably apparent to those around him.

Conversely, perhaps our young man was prone to listen and digest information pointed out to him, and change his aim in life much sooner, as well as concentrating on a contingency plan along the way. Much more difficult if we change the physical characteristics of our example and make him six foot three, give him some modest speed and coordination a little above average. The decision still might be obvious to others, but becomes more difficult for our young man. He now becomes more resistant to logic and advice. He rejects anyone, and anything, that gives the appearance of intrusion into his determination. There is admiration to be heaped upon our example provided his mind is open to those things that do not infringe upon his goal. To be a good basketball player, and to be well educated are not mutually exclusive.

Those who approach life aimlessly are easy to steer, at least for a while. They are always ready to change course at a mere suggestion. If all goes well, they remain easily led; however, if they suffer through bad experiences, their readiness to follow suggestions disappears, and as they have no self determination, failure in life becomes a companion.

All of the paths to the human mind, whatever their nature, are strewn with thorns of resistance, and gates locked against intrusion. The one possession of each person capable of being totally and completely hidden from society is the mind. Being so, it is jealously guarded. The thorns can be avoided, and the gates unlocked, but the process must be considered carefully.

What is thought out and decided in the mind is not easily surrendered. These decisions can be changed, but in a limited number of ways. They can be bought, but purchasing means just what is inferred. The resolution of the targeted individual was not changed, but merely traded for monetary considerations; and therefore, subject to being reversed by those with larger purses. They can be altered through intimidation and/ or threats, but again the process is a question of who has the biggest stick.

Success comes only through a slow and careful presentation that hopefully will stimulate a revisit to thought processes by our targeted individual. The change must be his idea, and carried to fruition by his determination. The mind strenuously resists being bullied by another's influence. It resists moderately, reasoned, but aggressive presentation. It only temporarily, and modestly resists any new information on a subject not previously considered. The great negative reaction comes when new information directly contradicts that which had been accepted, and upon which firm decisions, or attitudes, had been formulated.

Since Masonry makes no effort in the area of solicitation for membership, its candidates come only from a pool of individuals who have developed a favorable impression of the Craft. Hence, the candidate seeking admittance is tacitly saying, "I think your organization a good one; therefore, I seek the opportunity to become a member and have you prove to me my judgment is correct."

The Craft, upon accepting the petitioner, is faced

with a mind seeking to be reassured, and eager to learn and participate. The petitioner arrives with convictions already established regarding the denominational approach to religion. Imagine the conflict stirred in the candidate if he were to encounter attempts to alter, in any way, those deep seated convictions.

Research your memory of ministers who have been members of the Craft, both nationally known figures, and those in your locality. It is beyond question that they were, or are, outstanding examples of their faith, or denomination; and it has been my experience that they were, or are, very active members of the Craft…do you not agree?

Within the strict definition of the word, one cannot argue with anyone claiming Masonry is religion, for the term only designates those who believe in something spiritual. However, modern society tends to incorrectly expand the word religion to encompass form and ceremony which cannot then include Masonry.

Forms and ceremonies of a religious nature instruct the congregation on the proper manner to reach their goal of acceptance into the world beyond. Each denomination, or sect, has differences with the others in method details, but none have a different ultimate goal. Some are tolerant of others, but think they are mistaken on some minor points. Some think others are mistaken on major points, and some have no tolerance for others at all, because they believe the others to have everything wrong. Some are not tolerant of others, and are militant in their attitude and conduct.

Perhaps those who take Masonic ritual and apply interpretations to conjure up some special significant hidden reference, or meaning, do the Craft a disservice. The lessons are not more, and no less than what is communicated. There is much to learn in Masonry, but an interpreter is not needed. What is needed is an acceptance of what Masonry is, and what it is not. Masonry is, or should be, a collection of the male population recognized as morally and ethically above reproach and professing a belief in one Supreme Being. The impetus for such an endeavor should not be exclusivity, but for mutual support,. assistance, and strength, both within the Craft, and the community. While each member is accepted because of his good reputation, thereby providing a good example for those with whom he comes in contact, the gathering of an area's most respected men into one organization, whose sole purpose is the promulgation of respect, good will, and stability among, and throughout society, is a gestalt of positive influence not attainable in any other forum.

Churches aspire to such ends, but are hampered by the contentions regarding interpretation and practices, thereby prohibiting the unification under one banner such as occurs in Freemasonry. All sects, denominations, churches, or coterie that society labels as religious, use a book such as the Holy Bible, the Koran, the Talmud, or some other that they consider as the rule and guide of their faith. Passages are pointed out as documented evidence of what one must do, what one must believe, and what one must follow if there is to be any chance of recognition in "the world to come," or citizenship in an afterlife.

Practically none of the religious groups recognize any "Holy Book" but their own as being anything more than literature. Only their own designated Holy Book is ascribed as being Holy and worthy of being placed on the altars of their religious edifices. Only their own contains the proper instructions, rules, and

166

guidelines appropriate to their followers.

Masonry recognizes and respects the right of each citizen to follow his chosen religious beliefs, and to select his own "Holy Book" as a guide. Masonry considers binding the obligations taken by an adherent on whatever his "Holy Book" might be. The Craft has no opinion, and advances no theories on who is right, who is partly right, or who is wrong in the matter of religious beliefs and ceremonies. It's only position in the area of religion, is that only in the strict definition of the word…a belief in one Supreme Being.

While churches use their "Holy Book" as a set of instructions, Masonry uses the history delved from the Old Testament of the Holy Bible pursuant to the construction of King Solomon's Temple to stir self examination of the precepts of faith, hope, and charity, and foster a spirit of mutual support in society.

Religious groups support the inspired, make great effort to draw the wayward into the circle of their teachings, and strive to assist in correcting the direction of their lives. The success of these religious institutions is vital to peace and tranquility in the world at large, and Masonry believes each citizen should take an active part in the church of his choice.

Masonry is not an institution for the rehabilitation of a loss of proper moral and ethical conduct; not is it a vehicle for teaching these precepts to those who are without. Masonry is not a religious philosophy, nor a religious practice. It takes no stand, nor promotes any opinions in regard to methods, practices, or ceremonies of worship; and is therefore not in conflict with any Church whose basic tenet is a belief in one Supreme Being. As Masons, we believe and put our faith in a Supreme Being…beyond that, each Brother's religious opinions are his own. It is imperative that every member of the Craft understand this, as well as society.

There is not now, never has been, and never will be any conflict, competition, cross purpose, or contention between Masonry and organized Religion. If somehow, some way, such should occur, Masonry would immediately disappear, for the membership would never stand for that kind of misdirection of purpose.

To the reader: Events and/or circumstances sometimes cause one to reflect on the past. Perhaps change is inevitable in one direction or another; and that change can stir memories that evolve into either questions, or determinations. Reflection on the night this writer was permitted to begin his Masonic journey prompted the following paper.

Chapter XV
Where Did It Go?

The year was 1954, a very busy time for this young chap of 23 years, but there are some things that one simply must take time to do. My grandfather, a copper miner in East Tennessee, and also an ordained Methodist Minister had been Chaplain of his lodge. My father was now Master of his Lodge, and it seemed the right time for me, if the Craft was agreeable. The membership favored my application, and my journey began.

Of course the text of the work was impressive, but the presentation was impeccable. Astonishment and amazement best describe my feelings as my father did his work as Master. While he always had my respect, obviously his abilities had been vastly underrated in this quarter.

My Grandpa was killed in a mine accident in 1908, leaving my Grandmother with seven children, five of them girls. My Dad was in the third grade, and was taken out of school to pull a little wagon delivering groceries for his Grandfather's store. When he was fifteen, Grandmother secured a position as housemother in one of the dormitories at Athens Preparatory School, in Athens, Tennessee. One of her stipulations before she accepted the job was that the school agree to edu-

169

cating her son. The school agreed provided my Dad would work on the farm, evenings, and Saturdays. The school's farm provided milk, meat, and vegetables for the student's meals.

At that time, Athens Preparatory School consisted of two years of education. The first year was devoted to the grade school level and the second year was high school work. Upon graduation, the student was considered ready for college. My Father completed the two years, and along with the previous three years before Grandpa was killed, comprised the sum total of his education. It hardly seemed possible that he could perform in the manner being witnessed. Information he passed on to me several years later presented some explanation.

As my Father was passing through the Craft lodge officer's line, his work was not considered proficient, and it appeared that he would be dropped. A Past Master from another lodge stopped one day at my Father's store and accosted him in no uncertain terms.

My Father did not describe the conversation as a friendly one, but rather more on the order of a father laying down the law to a wayward son. The Past Master "ordered" my Father to be at his home at 7:00 p.m. that evening.

Dad was glad when he was told at eleven o'clock that night that he could go home, but was dismayed when he was instructed that from now on he would appear at 7:00 every evening except Sundays, and lodge meeting nights, for a four hour session until further notice. This continued for several months, and Dad described it as one tough ordeal. He hated going every night! He wanted to quit! He wanted to drop out of line! He would do anything rather than face this big gruff man every night who taught like a Marine Drill

Instructor. Dad's reply to my query as to why he didn't just quit was, "Well, he wouldn't let me!"

That scenario occurred over fifty years ago. What a mindset! Here was a man who made a decision that he would not let a Brother fail. He did not ask if he could help; he decided on a course of action and implemented it. On the receiving end was my Father, certainly no shrinking violet, to whom it never occurred to tell this good Brother he didn't want his help, and to mind his own business. This big man confronting him was a Past Master, someone to respect and do your best to accede to his wishes.

To be Master of one's lodge was considered a highlight in life. This was something to be cherished, and it commanded the admiration and respect of everyone, both in and out of the Craft. Given the opportunity, it was not something one passed over lightly; and no doubt the stature of the accomplishment at that time influenced my Father's grit in facing this tough teacher every night.

Today it is difficult to get officers, much less those that will dedicate themselves to the tasks as they should. Perhaps there are two reason for this. First consideration is numbers.

It is a given that from numbers comes a better opportunity for quality. It does not necessarily follow, but the odds are in your favor that the bigger the pool, the more likely to find what you seek. Let's use athletics for an example. A Division 1A school is permitted 88 athletes on scholarship, while a Division 2A school is permitted just 65. Of course there are occasions when a 2A school can, and does, defeat a 1A school on the gridiron, but they are rare, and you sure wouldn't bet that way. And so it goes through every endeavor. You very well might find outstanding quality in a small group, and you should not overlook the possibility, but essentially, whatever quality you are searching for, is more easily found in a larger group. Hence, if our numbers dwindle, our officer problem increases dramatically.

In the previous paragraph, two verbs were used that perhaps the Craft has forgotten. They are search and find. There were days when the sidelines were full and membership rolls were large, and only regular attendees were considered for appointment to Masonic office. Also there were many more young members than today. It was proper to afford the honor of office to those who expressed their interest by regular attendance; however, now the sidelines are sparse, and officers must be searched for, and found. The unconscionable is to stand in the East, or pen in a bulletin, "Anyone interested in being an officer, please contact me." This is self defeating! You have just advertised to the world that no one wants these jobs, and human nature is such that if you don't want it, then I don't want it!

Many years ago a rather recently raised Master Mason sat next to me in our Craft Lodge on election night. He had performed admirably with his catechism, seemed self assured, and had a good voice. He was nominated for a Steward position, and I could feel him straighten up in the next seat. He was elated to have been nominated. Then there were four others nominated, all of whom refused. The Brother in the adjacent seat elbowed me, and quietly asked with much concern, "What's wrong with this job, and how do I get out of it?" I encouraged him not to withdraw his name, and he was elected. However, he did not appear for installation, and to my knowledge has never attended a Craft Lodge meeting since.

What went wrong here? Very simply the lodge

shot itself in the foot. They should have done their homework before election night. All those considered officer material should have been contacted to make sure they would accept nomination with the understanding that their election was not assured. Some might scream politics here, but such is not the case! Politics is when the elections are controlled by not permitting certain names to come on the floor, or lobbying for the election of a certain preferred individual.

In this story lies the second reason that it is hard to obtain officers. The perception is that the job is not a desirable one and that nobody wants it. "Where did it go?" That aura surrounding being a presiding officer. That mystique infiltrating the psyche of members as they contemplate the stature among the Craft of those who are, or have, presided. The dream that perhaps someday the mantle of authority would be falling on their shoulders.

A few years ago I sat in a seminar on relations between management and hourly people. One of the questions propounded was, "What was the most exciting thing that ever happened to you?" There were many answers. Some said when they found Christ. Some said it was when their first child was born. Others related that it was when they were married, but one gentleman of about sixty years of age stood up, and with dignity and pride stated that the most exciting event in his life occurred many years ago when he was elected Master of his Masonic Lodge! The younger folks, both men and women, Craft and non Craft, looked at the gentleman with admiration.

My thoughts turned to the evening those same responsibilities had evolved upon my shoulders. The good Brother was right! Very few experiences elevate the spirits, or mellow the demeanor as much as being installed Worshipful Master of a Craft Lodge. Circumstances and time may lead to the responsibilities of other Masonic Bodies, perhaps even on a state level, but there is something special about being Master of one's lodge. Many make the statement that there is nothing superior to being a Master Mason, and they are, of course, correct. It is much like saying one is a student. The graduate student studying for a Doctorate is still just a student, and the foundation established previous to the current study will make the task either more difficult, or easier.

The Master of his Lodge has the awesome responsibility of introducing the neophyte to the mysteries of Masonry, and upon his shoulders rests the enthusiasm, or the indifference, the candidate develops from his first encounter with the Craft. Is the responsibility of the college professor heavier than that of the first grade teacher? No, in my considered opinion, if one were to weigh the two tasks, the duties of the grade school teacher are much more difficult and important then those of the professor. Upon the grade school teacher lies the responsibility of infusing the student with a thirst for knowledge, and it is their approach that will leave either a good, or bad, taste for education in the psyche of the student. The importance of education is only exceeded by the requisite ability of the primary teacher to infuse the excitement of a great experience upon their charges.

Instructors in higher education hold the position of glamour, notoriety, and additional monetary rewards, but their status is secondary to the fundamentals in properly reaching the minds of students incumbent upon the primary teacher. Such is the position of the Worshipful Master. To be elected Worship Master is an unmatched event in the Masonic life of a Brother.

Such is done by those who have sat in lodge with him, witnessed his dedication and proficiency, worked with him in the community, and known him well for some time. They have trusted him with a big responsibility, and it is vital that as the new Worshipful Master stands in the East, he sense that, nay, he knows that he is respected, and holds a position admired by every member of the lodge.

How different if the new Master feels that no one wants this job, and that he has been somehow maneuvered into it.

There is no question that any position that is power related usually draws plenty of aspirants, and any position that commands a place in history is doubly attractive. All of the Presidents of the United States are recorded in history, and their tenures in office reviewed ad infinitum. Some other very prominent positions are not remembered as their influence over affairs is tempered by the limits of power and recognition. Who was President of the United States in 1902... Theodore Roosevelt! Who was Speaker of the House...I haven't any idea. Who was Secretary of State...I haven't a clue. Even in their day, there were all too many that had no idea who the Speaker was, or the Secretary of State. Today, millions of dollars are spent seeking the position of President. Even would be Governors spend several million dollars seeking the position. But how much is spent to be a City Councilman?

Would one rather be President of the U. S., or King of England? The President has considerable power, while the King has relatively little. Perhaps there would be differing views on the question, but once one recognizes that the President can not serve more than eight years, cannot pass the mantle to a relative, suffers the slings and arrows of the opposition, and is held responsible for much over which he has little control, the downside of his place in history comes to the fore. The King, however, is not burdened with any limit on his tenure other than mortality and reasonable conformity to established actions and behavior. He is not blamed for any perceived shortcomings of the government, and is not subjected to the rigors and cost of seeking the position. Further, he knows that one of his children will one day take his place when he has left this earthly vale. Monetarily, the compensation far exceeds that of the President. Seems like being Monarch far outdistances that of being an elected official!

However, there is more to be considered. A President can make a difference in his country. He can provide great assistance in protecting his citizens, move the economy forward, and improve the lives of his constituents. These are things the King cannot match. If the desire is to establish an identity in history, provide very little service, but to be honored by constituents for no other reason than the position held, then King is the answer. If one desires to attempt to make a difference, to move society forward, to provide a prosperous and safe environment, and to plan for the future, the choice would be President.

Being Master of a Craft Lodge places the individual in the historic annals of that particular city. It is not a position of ceremony and reception of accolades, but a task of great responsibility and importance. On the dedicated assiduity of the Master lies the future of Masonry in that particular locale. He supervises the base of all Masonic structure, and if he fails, all of Masonry fails in his jurisdiction.

While the venue is much smaller than being President of the country, there was a time that the Master of the local Craft Lodge was admired and respected as much, and in some cases, more. His election depended on votes from people who knew him personally, and he could not obtain the office by sound bytes, speeches, promises, or enormous expenditures of money. Indeed, such activity in an attempt to be elected Master of his Lodge would absolutely doom the Brother to utter failure. He had been selected to progress through the line, and having done so successfully, earned the support of his brethren. In many respects, his election was more distinguished than that of a President.

It is no doubt true that this feeling continues in some local jurisdictions, but with the decline in membership, and the attendant difficulty in capturing the imagination of good officer material, there is no doubt that in all too many cases the newly elected Master wonders how he got stuck with this job that nobody wants!

What are the solutions in those areas where the problem exists? How do we make the job appear what it really is, an extremely noteworthy and desirable opportunity? The answers lie in that often misused word, "perception." Minds are trained by what the eye sees, the ear hears, and the body experiences. If the eye sees what appears to be interesting, pleasurable, or exciting, and the ear is told that what the eye has seen is true, then the mind encourages the body to conjoin and experience the event. Once the experience is complete, the mind will then judge whether it agrees with what the ear has been told, and the eye has seen, However, if the eye witnesses an apparent bland event, the ear hears nothing to encourage an interest, then the mind rejects any consideration of permitting the body to engage in the activity.

Perception comes from what the eye sees, and

the ear hears; hence, the mind makes its decisions based on perceptions that may be either true, or false. In our discussion, those who might provide great service are lost because of an incorrect perception. Therefore, the answer is to correct the perception so that it correctly demonstrates the stature of serving in the chairs, and especially to be elected Worship Master. Such corrections cannot be made in an instant, but can be accomplished in a relatively short period of time.

Mark Twain demonstrated the matter of perception eloquently in his book, Tom Sawyer, when Tom created a perception of white washing a fence that had his friends demanding an opportunity to enjoy the enterprise. We are not trying to hornswoggle someone into a mundane labor.

We are attempting to create a true and accurate perception, The task can be accomplished with ease. First, it is necessary that the installation attract a large crowd. Surely no one would attend an exercise of unimportance; hence, a large crowd emanates a correct perception that what is happening is consequential.

Second, if it is noteworthy, then it will be mentioned in the media. The installation must be mentioned in the newspaper with a nice article, and a photo of the new Master, and not some little two sentence notice at the bottom of the page. Perhaps you feel that your local paper is resistive to such cooperation, but if you find someone in the lodge with enough expertise to write a nice article, and locate a member of the lodge that has some horsepower with the paper (Like an advertiser), you can most certainly convince the paper that they should print the story.

Third, invite members and officers of other nearby Craft Lodges to be in attendance. This will indicate that the event has wider significance than just a regular lodge meeting event.

Fourth, invite officers of the closest Royal Arch Chapter, the closest Commandery, and any other near-by Masonic affiliated bodies to be in attendance. The success of their organizations depends on the activity of the Craft Lodge, and they need to be constantly re-minded of the need for their interest in lodge events. Their presence will lend to the occasion.

Fifth, make sure you provide for a nice dinner before the installation, Decorate the tables, have place cards, and a competent emcee. This gives the event even more importance, and raises the perception that this is an evening to be remembered.

Sixth, this is an opportunity to recognize the Past Masters of the Lodge, and to make some positive comment about each one, It must be perceived that those who have given of their time and talent are never forgotten, but retain a place of respect and admiration in the hearts and minds of the Brethren, and an hon-ored place in the history of the lodge.

There is no corner on the marketplace of ideas in this quarter, and once the Brethren dedicate their concentration to the matter, they will conceive an on-going program of raising the perception to a high and accurate standard.

"Where did it go?" It is imperative that we find it, no matter how difficult it is, or how long it takes. There is no other viable option!

To the reader: There are several opinions on the question of, "What is the Highest Degree in Masonry. The Scottish Rite devotee will say the 33rd. One must admit it has gotten a lot of mileage over the years. Some might say the Order of the Temple, and more recently, there is case to be made for the Order of the Purple Cross. Following is a summation of a debate held a few years ago. The summation is biased in that it reports the high points of only one side.

Chapter XVI

Is the Royal Arch the Highest Degree in Masonry

In addressing this subject, it is necessary to first address the semantics of the question.

Reference to the Royal Arch leaves nothing to conjecture. The phrase refers to those ceremonies which constitute the conclusion of the work presented in Royal Arch Chapters all over the world. Admittedly, the ceremonies vary from jurisdiction to jurisdiction, but the basic background and fundamentals therein contained are consistent, even though presented with some variation.

The next part of the question as stated, needs examination, and reference is made to the words, "the highest degree." The term has been used in society for many years to connote perfection in areas of reference other than Masonry. The words have been descriptively used in a fashion not necessarily complimentary; such as, "He is a scoundrel of the highest degree." And to confuse the issue, some bards have used the reverse, perhaps inappropriately by reporting that he is, "A scoundrel of the lowest degree." Hence, we must

establish the grounds upon which we relate the term,

"the highest degree."

In general terms, it is submitted that these words are correctly used when an area of expertise is established, and when that knowledge, or skill, is further developed and refined. Time and diligent effort may well bring us to the point that we can say, "It has reached the highest degree."

Let us further clarify by example by considering a common substance such as water. If we take water to the highest degree, we reach 212 degrees Fahrenheit at sea level. If we try to reach a higher degree, we no longer have water, as it will turn into steam. Some might argue that we still have water, but in a different form. That type of argument prompts this preliminary discussion in order to establish the parameters along which we will keep our discussion. If steam is to be considered water, then there is no answer to our question other than, the highest degree in Masonry has not yet been discovered, or established. Indeed, the highest degree in Masonry very well might be judged not to be of this life. However, if we can agree to confine our research to a constant, and to agree that we will limit our considerations to one form, and discard all that is not an elevation of the matter in its basic form, then we establish a frame of reference which will permit further discussion.

There is also another consideration concerning the term, "the highest degree." If man had not the equipment to bring water to 212 degrees, but was only able to raise the temperature at sea level to 175 degrees, then would not the lower degree be the highest degree? It is possible that what we consider the highest degree in Masonry stems only from the limitation of our knowledge, or an ignorance of that which is beyond.

Therefore we submit the following ground rule for this discussion; the highest degree represents the limit to which a specific discipline, art, or skill, has been developed, or discovered by man to date.

Let us now examine the final words in our question, "in Masonry." Perhaps some feel that this prepositional phrase is self-descriptive, conclusive, and leaves nothing to question. While it is obvious that the phrase refers to that fraternal organization so prominent throughout history, and to which so many of us belong; it certainly does not include all organizations to which Masons belong. Example: Masons belong to the Elks, but Elks are not included in Masonry. The same can be said for the VFW, the American Legion, and the list goes on. Then it becomes consistent to say that the mere fact that Masons are members of an organization does not make that organization necessarily a part of Masonry, even if the membership is limited to Masons.

There are a myriad of fraternal organizations in the world, but Masonry should not be included in this general category. While a fraternity is a group of men, or boys, joined together for fellowship, or some other purpose, Masonry is much deeper and more complex. Historically, Masonry has been a discipline and an art, containing within the confines of its guilds, the carefully guarded knowledge necessary to the construction of magnificent edifices. With the loss of the operative nature of the Craft, it has used those disciplines and arts through allegories to search for the path of truth between God and man. It is not necessary for this treatise to pursue this point any further. It is only essential to establish that Masonry cannot be truly labeled in that fashion. It is necessary to agree that germane to our issue is only that which can be categorized as Masonic

182

as it relates to the discipline and arts of Masonry, and that which is merely an assembly of Masons is not part of this discussion.

Let us further examine our prepositional phrase. There have been more than 1400 degrees in Masonry. They are nearly impossible to count, If we accept all of these as part of our question, then perhaps we are in for many years of study. But if we examine some general categories, rather than to examine each degree, perhaps we can reduce the size of our task. In addition, should we consider that which has gone? Is that which falls by the wayside of any importance unless resurrected for a specific purpose at some later time? I think not, but certain conditions and considerations might change that view. At any rate, at this juncture in human events that which has gone before has had an effect and guided us to where we are now, not only in Masonry, but in all things. They need to be studied and understood, else our decisions are flawed and our perspective skewed. Having said that, our focus is not blurred by a lack of knowledge of the myriad of Masonic Degrees that have fallen into obscurity. The fact that they have done so, eliminates them from consideration in our present question.

Let us first examine the origins of Masonry in order to establish some further guidelines.

When did Masonry begin? Some say in 1813 with the formation of the United Grand Lodge of England. Some say in 1717 with the formation of the Grand Lodge of London. In each case, the very name belies the assumption. If the Grand Lodge of London was uniting Lodges of Masons in 1717, then it is without argument that Lodges of Masons existed previous to that date.. The next time frame that is often mentioned is when lodges changed from operative to speculative.

There is no definitive date for either occurrence, and indeed in recent years it has become more and more apparent that non-operative Masons have been members of the Craft since before recorded Masonic history. So we find ourselves digging into ancient history to find the origins of Masonry. Maybe we should consider King Solomon's Temple. There remains on record the expertise and skills with which that structure was erected, but we certainly cannot say that operative Masonry originated with King Solomon's Temple as it is obvious that the artisans arrived on the construction site with the knowledge and organization of Masonry already in hand. Perhaps it is necessary to go to the oldest recorded structure of any consequence to see if Masonry was extant at that time, or if it realized a natural development between the construction of the oldest know edifice and King Solomon's Temple.

The oldest structure known to man still stands in Egypt - the Great Pyramid of Gizeh - which according to some authorities was completed on the date of the beginning of the age of Taurus in 4699 B. C. That date is not subscribed to in this quarter, as research leads to an agreement with those who place the date at 2623 B. C. Either date is long before the Exodus occurred, but after known cataclysms. Is it possible that operative Masons had anything to do with the construction of the Great Pyramid, or were the arts and sciences of Masonry unknown at that time?

The prophecies of the Great Pyramid that have come to pass are of no interest in our present study as we are only concerned with the arts, skill, and disciplines involved in its construction, and whether they can be related to the techniques of Masonry as taught by the Craft.

The design and construction of the pyramid is

184

based on what is commonly called the pyramid inch. In reality it is supposed to be the same as the British and American inch, but the centuries have eroded our inch so that it differs from that of the Pyramid inch by one half the width of a human hair. The Pyramid inch is one five hundred millionth of the diameter of the earth from North to South Pole. How was that known in 2623 B. C.?

If the land mass of the earth is laid flat and a line drawn through the center of the widest land mass from North to South, and another line drawn through the broadest land mass East to West, they would cross exactly on the site of the Great Pyramid. Where did that information come from?

The Pyramid indicates the North Star of that astronomical time, and does so more accurately than any technology of man's, until men went into space. In fact, the very slight deviation that exists is due to movement of the earth in that area resultant from an ancient earthquake. The Solar year, the Solstice year, and the Astronomical year are all correctly indicated in the Pyramid. The exact circumference of the Earth and its exact weight were more correctly indicated by the Pyramid than was done by science until we put men in space when we found out that the Pyramid was more nearly correct than man had been with his calculations. The stones were cut more accurately than we are able to do today, and the mortar used was superior to any in existence today.

In the construction, Geometry, the Fifth Science, was used extensively as well as a thorough knowledge of the stars, the Earth, the Sun, the Moon, and their relationships to one another. The workmen obviously had a thorough knowledge of Pi, as well as the 47th Problem of Euclid. The list goes on and on including

185

cross references between the Pyramid and the Holy Scriptures. From whence did all this knowledge of the arts and sciences stem?

Several theories have been put forth concerning the construction of the Great Pyramid, but most of them have been put to rest. One that has neither been proved, or disproved to date, proposes a land mass in the Pacific Ocean before a big cataclysm. Called the Land of Mu, the people of that land are alleged to have been, in some respects, more advanced in astronomy, mathematics, arts, and sciences than modern man. Also, they are alleged to have been very far advanced in human relationships. It is theorized that some of those residing in the western part of the land survived by traveling west into what is now China. Hence, it is set forth that all knowledge traveled from the East. It is alleged that the survivors from the Land of Mu, sometimes called Hyksos, became know as the Shepherd Kings, and that they appeared in Egypt, instigated and supervised the building of the Great Pyramid, and then departed. It is said that their knowledge of the Universe matched their ability to spread harmony and good will wherever they traveled.

Another theory is that Enoch, who according to the Bible, was taught by Shem, had a vast knowledge of what we would agree are the arts and sciences of the Craft, and that he was the architect of the Great Pyramid, and a Grand Master of Masons.

The point is here made that history and archaeology repeatedly make the case of Masonry, or some form thereof, originating long before recorded Masonic history. If one disclaims all except that which can be documented, and cross checked concerning the origins of Masonry, one must still admit to its existence in at least a combined speculative and operative mixture a

186

few hundred years before the foundation of the Grand Lodge of London in 1717.

Having examined the question of origin briefly, it is time to turn our attention to a determination of what is to be included within the parameters of Masonry, as relates to our question.

While there are a myriad of degrees that fall within the general category of Masonry, many of them can be excluded from our question quickly. Many degrees have been set forth to honor, or set aside, those, who from their dedication and devotion have made more than a passing contribution to the Craft. It is altogether fitting and proper that such designations are made in order to exalt those whom we admire and appreciate. The question is whether these degrees and organizations are to be considered a part of our subject? Our original question infers a reference to the basic Masonic system of education in the arts and sciences, and their analogy toward construction of proper relationships, both between men, and between God and man. We previously stated that we would consider only that which pertained to the elevation and development of a particular art, discipline, or skill; and as these honorary degrees represent a reward for dedication to those who receive them, rather than an elevation of the art; it is fitting that we here strike all honorary degrees from consideration in the question.

Next is consideration of those organizations whose prerequisites include that the petitioner must be a Master Mason in good standing, of a properly chartered Lodge of Freemasons. These groups of Masons do an outstanding job of charitable contributions to society. Their work in several fields of medical research is exemplary, and they are to be admired by the world in general, both Craft, and non-craft. But they do not

187

meet our determination to eliminate all that does not elevate the Craftsman in his knowledge of the arts and sciences, and therefore must be eliminated from our consideration.

The preceding determination leaves us with the two basic systems - that of the Scottish
Rite, and that of the York Rite.

Let us first examine the Scottish Rite. By their own statement, the Scottish Rite abandoned their own first three degrees in England, Scotland, Ireland, and the United States. Their statement reads, "In deference to the age and authority of the York Rite System." The Scottish Rite then attached themselves to the first three degrees of the York Rite System in the above named countries. No doubt the Scottish Lodges practiced the art of Masonry entirely compatible with those in England, but unlike the early English and Irish Lodges, they used a two degree system: whereas, the English and Irish Lodges had just one degree. They sprang from the same origins and therefore constitute no confusion to the question as relates to the first three degrees. However, there is the matter of the rest of the Scottish Rite, vis a vis, the fourth through the thirty second degrees.

Chevalier Ramsey, a Scottish Mason, who moved to the continent, invented many degrees, one of which was similar to the Royal Arch. He tried to interest the English Lodges in his invention, but was turned away. Over the years he invented many degrees, and indeed the Scottish Rite system has had approximately 1200 degrees in total. Over the years the Rite of Perfection sorted, sifted, and changed until the name was changed to the Scottish Rite, and the present system evolved.

It hardly seems fitting that we consider that

which is invention along with that which comes from antiquity, and which offers no expansion, or edification, on the original arts and sciences of Masonry. Scottish Masonry began with the construction of the Abbey at Kilwinning by Masons who traveled to Scotland for that purpose at the end of the Fifteenth Century

In view of the recognition of the invention of degrees, rather than they having some basis in history, and in view of the Scottish Rite's own view of the age and authority of the York Rite System, it seems plausible to eliminate the Scottish Rite from consideration in our question.

By process of elimination, we are left with the Degrees and Orders of the York Rite. Let us first consider the Orders of the Commandery which presently represent the culmination of the York Rite System.

The Knights of the Red Cross were established in 312 A. D. by Constantine, and were the forerunners of the Knight Templars. From before recorded Masonic history, one of the qualifications to being accepted a Knight Templar was to be a Mason. This is not to infer that such has been the case since 312 A. D., not that it was a requirement for membership before the martyrdom of James DeMolay. This prerequisite of being a Mason was extant with the emergence of the Templar Order following the inquisition.

Some historians contend that Masonry was brought to Western Europe by the Templars returning from the Crusades. Perhaps they brought back certain mysteries and ceremonies indigenous to the Middle East, but there is little to support the thought that Masonry itself was thus originated in the Western World. To prove, or disprove, this theory is of little consequence to our question. It is suffice to say that with the emergence of the Templars after their dismemberment by Phillip the Fair of France, and Pope Clement the Fifth, there was a prerequisite to membership on being a Mason.

The fact that the Templars were connected with the Priuere DeSion, previous to the "cutting of the Elm" has no consequence in our question either. The evidence that the Priuere is Hermetic Masonry, and at one time constituted highly selective degrees of the Scottish Rite in France, obviously has no bearing on the question, whether true or not.

We have already made the case for discounting the Scottish Rite from our question, and therefore any roundabout connection with the Templars has no bearing.

We previously determined that the question pertained to the arts and sciences of Masonry. The Templars being strictly military in their background would seem to eliminate them from the question, unless it could be established that they were an integral part of the system from the beginning. Even so, the divergent backgrounds preclude consideration of Templary as a part of the basic disciplines of Masonry. It would appear that the two merged together through common members for mutual benefit. As we have circumstantially submitted that Masonry predates the time of Christ, and that the earliest lineage that can be given to the Templars is 312 A. D., again it seems appropriate to eliminate them from the question.

The preceding has led many to the opinion that the Commandery has no place in the York Rite System, but there is little argument to the appropriateness of the Order of the Temple being a part of the York Rite System. It is just as suitable as having both the Old and New Testaments in our Holy Bible. Truly, the suggestion that Masonry alludes to Christianity in its content is just as correct as the suggestion that the Old Testament alludes to Christianity. At the same time, we cannot say that the Old Testament, in fact, contains the Christian Religion, but only alludes to it and prophecies its coming. In the same manner, Masonry does not contain the Christian Religion, but only alludes and prophecies in the same manner as the Old Testament in the context of being a search for Truth.

It must be noted that much of this preface raises many interesting questions that would provide for interesting future debate. This preface is set forth here on the basis of research to outline the parameters along which we set forth our determination.

Hence, we turn our examination upon that which is left, the Master Mason Degree, and the Holy Royal Arch.

The Masonic system of symbolism as now constituted presents us with a triple set of antagonisms - that of ignorance and knowledge, darkness and light, loss and recovery. It is without dispute that the present Master Mason's Degree leaves the candidate with a task unfulfilled. His journey through the revelations of the three degrees brings him from ignorance to knowledge, from darkness to light; but he is left with a loss. The recovery is effected in the Royal Arch Degree...but is it the highest degree?

In the beginning we said that the highest degree meant the extent, or limit, to which a discipline would be taken. Obviously in Ancient Craft Masonry, this would mean the Royal Arch Degree. But we cannot yet accept this statement as fact in regard to our question without further establishing the Royal Arch Degree as indeed an integral part of Ancient Craft Masonry.

Lawrence Dermott calls the Royal Arch, "the root, heart, and marrow of Masonry." Dr. Oliver stat-

191

ed in reference to the Royal Arch, "It is indescribably more august, sublime, and important than any which precede it, and is, in fact, the summit and perfection of Ancient Craft Masonry."

Quoting from "A History of Freemasonry and Concordant Bodies," published in 1907 by a Board of Editors, "It has been well settled by our recent writers on Masonry, such as W. J. Hughan, A.F.A. Woodford, R. F. Gould in England, D. Murry Lyon in Scotland, that as early as 1723 a ritual was in use; but no reliable evidence that prior to A. D. 1717, there was more than one ceremony with a word, words, and signs. The Master was so called after he became the presiding officer of his lodge; and when an Apprentice was to be 'drafted,' two Apprentices should be present to witness the ceremony. Apprentices, then as now, in all countries but the United States, constituted the membership of the Lodges, and in that degree all business was, and is yet, transacted. About the middle of the century, upon the introduction of the Royal Arch Degree into England from France by Chevalier Ramsey, the ritual of the Third Degree was changed, and the most important secrets were placed in the Royal Arch; and hence, since then, a Mason who has only received the Third Degree is not a Master until he has been elected to preside, and not even then is he a Master Mason proper, until he shall have received the secrets of the Royal Arch, which can only be given to a Past Master."

It is noted that research indicates that the proposal by Ramsey was rejected by the English Lodges, and that they made their own separation of the Third Degree, rather than use the degree that Ramsey proposed.

Quoting Dr. Oliver again, "I have now before me an old Master Mason's tracing board or floor cloth,

192

which was published on the continent almost immediately after symbolic Masonry had been received in France as a branch for the Grand Lodge of England in 1725, which furnished the French Masons with a written copy of the lectures then in use; and it contains the true Master's word in a very prominent position."

Again, another quote from Dr. Oliver, "The Royal Arch Word was anciently the true word of the Third Degree," and he refers to a French writer of 1745 as stating that "the Master's Word was originally…but that it was changed after the death of Adoniram." It is believed that the writer referred to by Dr. Oliver is Guillemain de St. Victor.

Previous to 1717, there was only one degree in Masonry in England. That degree consisted of all the teachings that were a part of the three degrees into which the Craft was separated in 1717 at the formation of the Grand Lodge of London. Previously, Entered Apprentice, Fellowcraft, and Master Mason simply denoted Masonic, relative, or official positions. In 1717, three degrees were established. Desaugliers, Anderson, Payne, and possibly others were the architects that designed the Fellowcraft Degree which was accepted in 1719. They introduced the Master Mason's Degree no sooner than 1720, and no later than 1723. While this action might seem to be an innovation, it was not, in that it was a mere separation of that which had been one, to that which is now contained in three.

However, a rift occurred when in order to prevent those who were Masons, but outside the jurisdiction of the Grand Lodge of London, from visiting what they considered regular lodges, they transposed certain significant words in the lower degrees, and invented a new one for the Third. Those who deserted in protest to what they called innovations labeled

193

themselves as Antients, and called the original Grand Lodge, the Moderns.

The Antients under the leadership of Lawrence Dermoitt, engaged in a mutilation of the Third Degree by separating it into two degrees. The second of these two degrees was termed the Holy Royal Arch, and contained the ceremonies that had previously constituted the conclusion of the Third Degree. Hence, we can see that in fact, the Craft has never been without the recovery of that which was lost.

Quoting Hughan, "The chief feature in the new ritual consists in a division of the Third Degree into two sections, the second of which was restricted to a few Master Masons who were approved as candidates, and to whom the peculiar secrets were alone communicated."

The Antients realized much success, as prospective candidates found the Grand Lodge of Four Degrees of more interest than the Grand Lodge of Three Degrees. The Moderns, late in the century, also divided the Third Degree into two sections, but it was too late to stem the popularity of the Antients.

Modern researchers such as Harry Carr, Roy Wells, and Vatcher, make the case that they doubt the origins of the Royal Arch Degree. They state that a study of the records gives no indication that the Third Degree was incomplete, or that there is any indication of a discovery of that which was lost. At the same time, these Brethren insist upon the value of the Hiramic Legend, and the Vault Legend. To quote Roy Wells, "It cannot be emphasized too strongly, however, that the direct link between the Craft and the Royal Arch is the 'Word' that was lost, then found."

These modern researchers speak of a two degree system in England, but such is not the case according to earlier Masonic authors. It is my view that there is some confusion created by the ceremony of ascending to the chair. It would be very easy to pick up this ceremony, and detect a two degree system, when indeed, there was only one ceremony in communicating the secrets of Masonry to a candidate.

For those who cannot locate any indication of early Masonry being incomplete, and therefore presume that the Royal Arch was not taken from the early ceremonies, I submit that proves the point. If early Masonry was complete, then it necessarily must have contained the true word of a Master Mason!

Amman Marcellin, a Pagan Historian who lived from 330 to 390 A. D., describes the Vault Legend, and that the book that was found contained the Gospel of St. John.

Orbis Miraculum, dated 1659, recites the Vault Legend, and again that the book contained the Gospel of St. John, which begins, "In the beginning was the Word, and the Word was with God, and the Word was God." The Vault Legend in reality concerns Julian, the Apostate, who abandoned the Christian Religion and endeavored to rebuild the Temple of Solomon to disprove the prophecy of Daniel. Workmen accidentally discovered the vault, and lowering a workman down by means of a rope, he found himself in water up to his waist. Feeling about he discovered a book resting on a column,. He brought the book up with him, and they found it wrapped in a covering. The book was in excellent condition, and when opened, it contained the words from the Gospel of St.. John. Following that discovery, fire prevented the workmen from rebuilding the Temple, and thus the prophecy of Daniel was preserved.

Any attempt to divorce the true Master Mason's Word from Masonic ceremonies previous to1717 proves fruitless. At the same time, it must be admitted that rituals were not extant, and there is really no way to document the ceremony of that day. However, rituals adopted after 1717, such as the Claret Ritual states, "The Supreme Degree to which you have been admitted is the real Master Mason's Degree."

Much has been made of the compromise between the Antients and the Moderns upon formation of the United Grand Lodge of England in 1838. There is a view that the Moderns gave in to the Antients by permitting the Royal Arch to be included in Article II of the compact which stated, "That pure Antient Masonry consists of three degrees and no more; viz., those of the Entered Apprentice, the Fellow Craft, and the Master Mason, including the Supreme Order of the Holy Royal Arch." Perhaps the opposite is the true interpretation of the story.

When the two Grand Lodges merged, it was the Antients who surrendered their views on the subject as they cited four degrees in their Laws and Regulations, "Antient Masonry consists of four Degrees - the first three of which are, that of the Entered Apprentice, the Fellow Craft, and the Sublime Degree of Master, and a Brother being well versed in these degrees, and otherwise being qualified, as hereafter will be expressed, is eligible to be admitted to the Fourth Degree, the Holy Royal Arch.

This degree is certainly more august, sublime, and important than those which precede it, and is the summit and perfection of Masonry"

Your attention is directed to an excerpt from the minute book of the Grand Chapter of England, recording the proceedings of a Special Convocation on 30 November, 1813. "The Grand Lodge of England under

196

H. R. H., the Duke of Sussex, had entered into preliminary Articles with the Grand Lodge under H. R. H., the Duke of Kent for a Union of the two Grand Lodges under one Grand Master. That by those Articles, the Royal Arch was acknowledged as the perfection of the Masters Degree."

The Oxford Dictionary equates perfection with completion, the words are synonymous.

The Templar Encampments of the times met in January 1760, and changed their prerequisite from Master Mason, and thereafter required that the applicant be a Royal Arch Mason, and a believer in the Christian Religion, with no mention of Master Mason.

The evidence is preponderant that the Royal Arch Degree was originally a part of the Third Degree, and previous to that, a part of one degree conferred in English Lodges. This argument is finalized by the Second Article of the Compact of 1813, where it is stated that the Master Mason Degree in order to be complete, included the Holy Royal Arch. This clause of the Article represents views of the Moderns, who won the day over the Antients, who had introduced a four degree system. The Moderns had clung to the three degree system established in 1717, but the phrase, "including the Supreme Order of the Holy Royal Arch," again reflects the concurrence by both Grand Lodges that the Royal Arch is indeed a part of Ancient Craft Masonry.

If we consider the question in relation to Ancient Craft Masonry, we must discard all the offshoot and honorary degrees, the Scottish Rite, and the Commandery. Further, if we consider the extent, or limit, to which the instruction and education of Ancient Craft Masonry can be taken, and finally, recognize that the Royal Arch is in fact, the conclusion of the Master Mason Degree, and furnished with the recovery of that which was lost, thereby concluding our three antagonisms, then the answer to the question becomes affirmative.

The Holy Royal Arch is the highest degree in Masonry!

Nonetheless, it is really a matter of acceptance. There is no one with the authority to say one way or the other. No one will, or should, disagree that once an individual is raised a Master Mason, he is just as much a Mason as anyone walking the face of the earth, but his knowledge is limited. There are gatherings which he cannot attend, and subjects upon which he cannot speak. If any Brother chooses not to accept the premise that the Royal Arch is the highest degree, who is to contradict him? If any Brother chooses not to subscribe to circumstantial evidence, who is to argue?

What is so, is what is believed until conclusively proven different: and then only if the proof is accepted. In the meantime, what is so, is that which is universally accepted; and upon this question there is certainly no agreement.

To the reader: The question of the Ineffable Name is one that has been addressed many times before.

The following is an effort to spur the reader toward examining the question in depth that he might draw his own conclusion.

Chapter XVII
The Ineffable Name

The most important single point that we can study in Masonry is the "Ineffable Name." Quoting from the Royal Arch Mason textbook, "It can never be too often repeated that the WORD is in Masonry, the symbol of TRUTH. This truth is the great object of pursuit in Masonry - the scope and tendency of all its investigation - the promised reward of all Masonic labor. Sought for diligently in every degree, and constantly approached, but never thoroughly and intimately embraced; at length, in the Royal Arch, the veils which concealed the object of search from our view are withdrawn, and the inestimable prize is revealed.

This, which Masonry makes the great object of its investigation, is not the mere truth of science, or the truth of history, but is the more important truth which is synonymous with the knowledge of the nature of God, that truth which is embraced in the sacred Tetragrammaton, or Omnific name, including in its significance, His eternal, present, past, and future existence, and to which He himself alluded when He declared to Moses, "I appeared unto Abraham, unto Isaac, and unto Jacob by the name of God Almighty; but by my name JEHOVAH was I not known to them."

Ineffable means not to be spoken. Tetragrammaton means the four lettered name of the Deity. We are familiar with the Biblical passages referring to the inability of anyone except the High Priest to correctly pronounce the name, as the Hebrew language was written without vowels, and the High Priest was the only one in possession of the knowledge of the correct pronunciation.

Traditionally, the Patriarchs from Methuselah to David, pronounced the WORD in the several following ways: Jeva, Juha, Jeveh, Johe, and Jehovah. The question we will here address is...what is the correct pronunciation?

First, let us establish some background for the theory we will put forth.

This reverence for the name of God is to be found in all the ancient rites. The Ineffable Name itself is said to have been preserved in its true pronunciation by the Essenes, who communicated it in a whisper during their rites, and only in syllables separated so as to make the word a mystery.

The Egyptians used the sacred name as a password for gaining admission to their Mysteries.

In the Brahminic Mysteries of Hindustan, the name given to candidates in their rites was AUM, and it was forbidden to be pronounced. It was to be the subject of silent meditation by the Hindoo.

In the rites of Persia, an Ineffable Name was communicated to the candidate which was Mithras, their principal Deity. It is interesting to note as a sidebar that the principal day of celebration of the followers of Mithras was December 25th.

In the Mysteries introduced by Pythagoras into Greece, we again find the Ineffable Name, but expressed in an entirely different way. It was expressed by symbol, consisting of ten dots placed in a triangle, just like bowling pins. The apex having one dot, denoted the monad, or active principle of nature; the second row having two dots represented the duad, or passive principle. The third row having three dots represented the triad, or world emanating from their union; and the fourth row having four dots represented the quaterniad, or intellectual science. The whole number of dots , totaling ten, the symbol of perfection and consummation. This figure was called by Pythagoras, the tetracts, a word equivalent to tetragrammaton. This symbol was deemed so sacred that on it the oaths of the Pythagorean Rites were administered.

Among the Scandinavians and the Jewish Cabalists, the Supreme God in their Mysteries had twelve names, but the most sacred one was Alfader, the Universal Father. Among the Druids, the sacred name of God was Hu.

The list goes on, but the important note on all these various names of Deity is that they were considered both male and female, or bisexual. This statement is to be viewed in the spiritual sense as indicating that the Deity had the manifestation of power, both generative and prolific. This infers a power of creation from a single source.

Now let us turn to Genesis 1, 26 & 27, "And God said, let us make man in our image, after our likeness; and let them have dominion over the cattle, and over all the earth. So God created man in his own image, in the image of God created he him; male and female created he them." Do not be misled by the final clause, "male and female created he them."

Let us now turn to Genesis, Chapter 2, Verses 20, 21. and 22. "And Adam gave names to all cattle, and to the fowl of the air, and to every beast of the field; but for Adam there was not found a help meet for him. And the Lord God caused a deep sleep to fall upon Adam, and he slept; and He took one of his ribs, and closed up the flesh instead thereof; and the rib, which the Lord God had taken from man, made He a woman, and brought her unto the man.

It is apparent that originally man had both the generative and the prolific, for the Bible states that God withdrew the female part, symbolized by the rib, and thereby separated one into two. Where before, the one was both generative and prolific, now the continuation would depend on reuniting the two. If so, then it follows since man was originally made in God's image that God is both male and female, both generative and prolific.

Let us examine the theory put forth by Dr. Lanci concerning the Ineffable name.

The Tetragrammaton consists of four letters: yod, heh, vau, heh. These letters appear right to left; hence, the letter on the extreme right is yod, and we then continue right to left.

Of these letters, the first, yod, is equivalent to the English "i" pronounced as the "e" in the word machine. The second and fourth letter, "heh" is an aspirate, and has here the sound of the English "h." The third letter, "vau," has the sound of an open "o."

Reading the letters from right to left, and the writing them down from left to right as we read English, we have IHOH. In the Hebrew language there is no such word, nor can you make anything out of the letters by separating them in any combination. Now, Lanci proceeds to the discovery of this true pronunciation as follows; "In the Cabala, a hidden meaning is often deduced from word by transposing, or reversing, the letters, and it was in this way the Cabalists concealed many of their mysteries.

Now to reverse a word in English is to read its letters from right to left; but in Hebrew, the contrary takes place. Since the normal mode of reading Hebrew is right to left; therefore, to reverse the reading of a word, is to read it from left to right."

Lance applied this cabalistic mode to the tetragrammaton when he found that IH - OH being read in reverse, makes the word HO-HI.

In Hebrew, Ho is the masculine pronoun, equivalent to the English He; and HI is the feminine pronoun, equivalent to the English "she;" and therefore, the word Ho-HI: literally translated is equivalent to the English compound HE-SHE. That is to say that the Ineffable name of God, in Hebrew, being read Cabalistically, includes both male and female, the generative and prolific energy of creation. This theory, as set forth by Dr. Lanci, joins with all the ancient mysteries in deducing that God is both male and female, represented by the point within a circle, and another proof of the connection between Freemasonry and the ancient Mysteries.

What are we to make of this presentation by Dr. Lanci? Frankly, it is impossible to refute the premise in any other way than to simply discount it out of hand, and state, "Nobody really knows."

It is agreed in this quarter that the evidence is circumstantial, but it is also agreed that it is compelling. On two occasions, the opportunity presented itself to question individuals knowledgeable in Ancient Hebrew. No background, or reason for the question was stated, merely the inquiry as to the meaning of Ho and HI, in ancient Hebrew. The answer received on both occasions agreed with Dr. Lanci's statement, that they are equivalent to the English pronouns, he and she.

Masonry is indeed a search for Truth, and part of that Truth is the Ineffable Name. Has Dr. Lanci concluded that part of our search? Perhaps, but we will not be absolutely certain in this life. More importantly, if we accept the good Doctor's theory, is our search for Truth over? Certainly not!

The correct pronunciation of the name of Deity is a fascinating enigma in the pursuits of Masonry. While the attention of certain degrees is the mystery of this pronunciation, at the same time, Freemasonry is not concerned with what the petitioner calls the Deity. The only interest is that he believes in one God.

These facts bear out the Universality of Freemasonry, the tolerance for diverse views on religion, and the aptitude for a persevering search for Truth.

Truth does not begin and end with the Ineffable Name and its correct pronunciation. Truth begins and ends with the desires, intent, and instructions of the Creator. All that He manifests is Truth, and part of our search is for the ability to irrevocably establish ourselves within the parameters of emulating that example.

To the reader: Here we take a few moments and discuss one of the principal characters in the York Rite Order of Red Cross. Suggested reading pursuant to this discussion: Ezra, Chapter 1.

Chapter XVIII
Cyrus, the Great

M asonic tradition follows closely the construction of Solomon's Temple, its destruction, its rebuilding, and the events pertaining thereto. In the Royal Arch, we are attendant to the circumstances surrounding preparations to rebuild the Temple. We are informed that it was Nebuchadnezzar who destroyed the Temple, and carried the people away captive into Babylon; and not only the Royal Arch, but also the Order of Red Cross follow history in relating that it was Cyrus, the Great, who permitted the Jewish people to return to their country to rebuild the Temple.

The circumstances that prompted the invasion of the Jewish lands by Nebuchadnezzar was the intense rivalry between Egypt and Babylon, and the desire of both to control the ports along the Mediterranean Sea. The Jewish people did not relish subjugation by either, but if it was inevitable, they much preferred domination by Egypt from which Moses had extricated them. Three times the Jews revolted against Nebuchadnezzar, but were put down each time.

When Nebuchadnezzar had conquered the Middle East, he turned to the construction of the city of Babylon. It covered four hundred square miles, and was five times the size of the city of London. It was constructed on both sides of the Euphrates, and was surrounded by walls three hundred feet high, and 85 feet wide at the top, wide enough for four chariots abreast to drive. It contained one hundred gates, and the river within the city was spanned by bridges at convenient locations. Two hundred and fifty towers placed upon the walls afforded additional strength and protection. Within were palaces and beautiful edifices of all types which caused the wealth and splendor of Babylon to be the favorite theme of ancient historians. The prophet, Isaiah, even while denouncing Babylon ,spoke of it as "the glory of kingdoms, the beauty of the Chaldees excellency." Babylon, the Great, as the prophet Daniel called it, was situated four hundred and seventh five miles east of Jerusalem.

Let us now turn our attention to Cyrus, who was born seventy years after the death of Nebuchadnezzar.

According to Herodotus, Astages, the King of Media, was warned in a dream that his kingdom was threatened by the son of his daughter Mandane, who was not yet married.

In an effort to protect himself from this danger, he married his daughter to a Persian named Cambyses, who took her with him to his own country. Later, Astyages had another dream which was interpreted that his daughter's son would reign in his stead. Alarmed, Astyages sent for his Lieutenant, Harpagus, to carry the infant to his own house and kill it. Harpagus took the baby as instructed, but due to the pleading of his wife, he determined to submit the deed to another. He called one of his herdsmen, and ordered him to leave the child on the bleakest part of the mountain to perish, and threatened him with the vilest penalties in case of his disobedience. However, the herdsman and his wife had no more stomach for the deed than did Harpagus and his wife. While they were torturing themselves with pity for the child, but fear of retribution from Harpagus, fate intervened, and provided the herdsman and his wife with a child that was already dead. They presented this dead child to Harpagus as proof of their compliance with his orders. They then raised the grandson of Astyages as their own.

When the child of Mandane was ten years old, an ancient brought him to the attention of King Astyages, and he became the ward of one of the king's slaves.

One day, when Cyrus was playing with the children of his neighbors, a certain game where it was necessary to make one of the players, king, Cyrus was chosen, and all the others, as subjects, promised to obey his commands. But one of the boys, the son of a rich Noble of the Court of Astyages, refused to do as he was bid by Cyrus, and according to the rules of the game, he had to submit to a beating at the hand of the boy chosen as king. Angry at this treatment, the boy complained to his father, who, indignant, went to Astyages, and reproached him with the story of his son's treatment at the hands of the son of one of the king's slaves. Cyrus was brought before the king; but when he was asked how he dared to treat the son of a nobleman in such a manner, the boy answered that he had done only what was right. The rules of the game were known to all who had joined it. The other boys had submitted to and obeyed his commands. The son of the nobleman alone had refused, and he had been punished as he deserved.

"If any wrong has been done by me,:" the boy said, "I am ready to suffer for it." Something in the boldness of the lad as well as something in his looks prompted the king to send for the herdsman, Mitridates, and wrung from him a confession. The king did not turn his vengeance on Mitridates, but dismissed him. The king now summoned his Lieutenant, Harpagus, and evoked the most terrible punishments upon him. Harpagus made light of the severe treatment, but deep down harbored a determination to get even with the king when a suitable opportunity presented itself.

When Cyrus reached manhood, the kingdom of Lydia, Media, and Babylonia were flourishing. Lydia was ruled by Croesus, Media by Astyages, brother-in-law of Croesus, and Belshazzar ruled Babylonia. Croesus was not only the brother-in-law of Asyages, but was also in close alliance with the Babylonians, the Egyptians, and the Greeks; and being at the height of his power was looking toward still greater increase in his dominance.

At this time, Harpagus, still vexed over his treatment by the King, Astyages, had been stirring up the great Median chiefs behind the king's back. When he felt there was enough support, he prevailed upon Cyrus to overthrow the king and assume the rule of Media. The same was accomplished in time for Cyrus to subjugate the lesser tribes that owed allegiance to the Median King, and to strengthen his position.

Croesus, hearing of the events chose this time to attack; but Cyrus, with a powerful army, bottled up Croesus in Sardis, and discovering the secret entry to Sardis up the cliffs, a few of his soldiers surprised the guards, and opened the gates of victory over Croesus, and the assumption of rule of Lydia.

Cyrus sent Harpagus to subjugate the Greek cities of Asia Minor, while he himself turned eastward to pursue his conquests in Upper Asia and Assyria. His greatest achievement in this was the taking of Babylon. He laid siege to the city for two years, but it became apparent that the city was self sufficient, and that the siege would have no effect. He conquered the city by turning the waters of the Euphrates, which ran through the middle of the city, and when its bed was dry, he entered the city by this road, and captured it with little resistance.

One of his first acts was the issuance of the decree which permitted the Children of Israel, under the guidance of Jesua, Zerrubbabel, and Haggai, to return to their country and rebuild their city and their Temple, concluding their seventy two year captivity.

Cyrus was now the sole master of the vast Assyrian Kingdom which was now brought back to something like the unity it had before the great Median revolt, But he was not content, nor was it, perhaps, possible for him to rest in the enjoyment of power and possessions extorted by force, and dependent upon force to hold. The new empire, like the old one, was destined to break into pieces by its own weight. Cyrus was kept in constant activity by the necessity of resisting the inroads on his empire by the tribes in the north and far east. While endeavoring to repel invasions, and maintain order, he met his death.

After a reign of thirty years, he was slain in 529 B. C., in battle with Massagetae, a tribe of Central Asia. He left his kingdom to his son, Cambyses, who had been named after Cyrus's father.

Thus it was that through this man, Cyrus, whose entire life consisted of intrigue, greed, conquering and subjugating peoples, the Jews found a sensitive ear to their pleadings to be permitted to return to Jerusalem to rebuild their city and their Temple.

Tradition informs us that the work on the city and Temple were caused to cease by Cyrus's son, Cambyses. After several years, an embassy consisting of Zerrubbabel, and four other Jewish chiefs, repaired to the Court of Darius, to obtain the protection of that Monarch from the encroachments of the Samaritans, who had interrupted the labors of reconstruction of the Temple. The history of this embassy is found in the eleventh book of the Antiquities of Josephus, whence the Masonic ritualists have undoubtedly taken it.

The Degree of the Order of Red Cross has no analogy with the chivalric Orders of Knighthood. It is purely Masonic and intimately connected with the Royal Arch Degree, of which, in fact, it ought rightly to be considered as an appendage. It is, however, now always conferred in a Commandery of Knights Templar in this country, and is given as a preliminary to reception in that Order. Formerly, the degree was sometimes conferred in an independent Council, which Webb defines to be "A Council that derives its authority immediately from the Grand Encampment, unconnected with an Encampment of Knights Templar.

Since the martyrdom of Jacques DeMolay, the last Grand Master of the Order of the Temple, there have been one hundred and twenty five Masonic Knightly Orders. Of all these, only the Order of Red Cross, or Knight of the Red Cross, said to originally have been Knight of the East as instituted by Darius; Knight of the Mediterranean Pass: Knight of Malta; and Knight Templar, are the only ones to have flourished in the United States, and become a part of the York Rite System.

To the reader: West Virginia has had its share of outstanding Masons. Three that have presided over either National, or International Masonic Bodies. One that was Lieutenant Commander of the Scottish Rite, and several that have been International, or International officers. Following is one from my home town whose name is not as readily recognized as some of the others, but whose stature in the history of the Craft in West Virginia is second to none.

Chapter XIX
Morgan Nelson

History is a multi-faceted marvel. It is a great teacher from which one can receive an outstanding education. It sets examples, both good and bad, illuminating them from every angle of time to spotlight and interpret their impact on society. It furnishes heroes to be admired and emulated, as well as villains to be despised and abhorred. But perhaps best of all, is that while history is providing all of the preceding, it is also marvelously entertaining.

Each of us has at least one hero, but most likely we have several, one for each field of personal interest. These personal heroes might be contemporary, but they are probably historic figures, or they were contemporary only to the extent their lives overlapped ours. In addition to our personal icons, history is replete with famous people in every field of endeavor, and it behooves the good citizen to study their lives. However, there are a multitude of people whose lives were exemplary and worthy of emulation, and yet remain obscure.

Often times fame eludes heroes because of who they are not. They are not the General, not a Captain of industry, not a national politician, nor a publicized athlete; or for a variety of reasons, their story was never told. Contributions to progress and to present day enjoyment and opportunity often go unrewarded, particularly when that dedication is in a field not of universal interest.

Masonry is not without its heroes, but we must define the context in which we use the term. There are those who have the talent and resources to serve the Craft in various capacities on local, state, and national levels. The unselfish giving of their time and assets is deeply appreciated by the Craft. Such contributions make it possible for Masonry to enjoy constancy, as well as worldwide fraternal relations. These good Brethren are to be admired and appreciated, but they are not exactly heroes.

How exciting it is when we discover that some famous, or well known person, is a member of the Craft. Whether we feel that their membership somehow gives the Craft validity, or that we have some sort of personal connection, is hard to determine. Needless to say, neither is true. It is interesting that we have a fraternal connection with famous, or well known people; but their membership adds no more to the validity of the Craft than your membership, or mine. We are grateful and enthused that these notable figures loved, and respected, and served the Craft, but they are not heroes in that context.

In the early days of the colonies there were those who spent a lot of time studying and learning various degrees from the ritual authorities of the day. They then traveled from town to town communicating their knowledge for a fee. Proliferation of Masonry throughout the colonies by degree peddlers provided a much needed service, but we could hardly call these good Brothers, heroes.

Your shelves and mine are full of wondrous Masonic literature which took thousands of hours of research, study, and assembly to prepare and publish. These Masonic journalists have provided valuable information as well as food for thought in regard to the history of the Craft. Their work has been invaluable, but they are not heroes.

Among Masonic heroes are those who blazed trails by establishing Masonic Bodies where they had not been before, under difficult circumstances. They are those who took a stand publicly supporting the Craft, when it was not popular to do so. They are those who gave unstintingly of their time, resources, and talent to further the cause of Masonry under difficult circumstances. Meanwhile. they supported and raised a family, performed admirably in their chosen profession, and were outstanding leaders in their community.

In my view, just such a man was Morgan Nelson, a name no doubt unfamiliar to you, but hearing his story may bring to mind a similar Masonic hero from your local history.

Morgan Nelson was born in Massachusetts in 1792, during the administration of Worshipful Brother George Washington. Details of the next twenty eight years of his life are not available, so much is left to speculation regarding this period. We do know that he was a member of Lodge No. 60 in Baltimore, Maryland. What we don't know is when he moved to Baltimore, or where he was educated. Sometime later he moved to some location in Kentucky which is not difficult to understand. It may be that he moved west in an effort to establish himself in his chosen profession of law, or it may be that the War of 1812 encouraged him to aban-

213

don the Eastern Seaboard. We just don't know. In any event, he came to the City of Wheeling, Virginia, in the year of 1820, from Kentucky, and immediately affiliated with Ohio Lodge #101, A. F. & A. M. which had been chartered by the Grand Lodge of Virginia in 1815.

Brother Nelson must have had readily visible signs of leadership, as he was elected Worshipful Master of Ohio Lodge in 1820, the same year he arrived in the city. He was elected again the following year, and the minutes of Ohio Lodge speak eloquently of his proficiency and leadership.

In 1822, a Brother by the name of John Truax affiliated with Ohio Lodge from Morton Lodge No. 87 in New York. His date of affiliation was August 5, of that year, and it is of particular interest to note that a petition was presented to Ohio Lodge on November 21, 1822, asking a recommendation to the Grand Master for a Dispensation of Charter for a new Lodge in Wheeling, under the name of Wheeling Lodge No. 128, naming Morgan Nelson for Worshipful Master; Oliver Wilson for Senior Warden; and John Truax for Junior Warden.

There is no record in Ohio Lodge regarding Oliver Wilson. The petition was granted, but a protest was filed with the Grand Lodge against forming a new Lodge. The Grand Lodge of Virginia issued a Charter for Wheeling Lodge on December 12, 1822.

This brings up a lot of questions. Where did Oliver Wilson cone from, and how did he fit into this picture? Why was a new Lodge desired so soon after the arrival of John Truax, and isn't it curious that the sitting Master of a Lodge would be one of the petitioners for a new Lodge to be established. Certainly one of the thoughts that comes to mind is that Ohio Lodge had gotten so big that it was deemed expedient to establish another.

When Morgan Nelson arrived in 1820, the population of Wheeling, Virginia, was 1567, and the membership of Ohio Lodge was 53. While the city was growing by leaps and bounds, Ohio Lodge had raised just eight to the Degree of Master Mason during the two years Nelson was Master. There would not seem to be a bulging membership problem.

Another consideration would be the meeting place. In those days attendance was excellent at Lodge meetings, and perhaps it was felt that quarters were too cramped for the membership, thus necessitating some of the Brethren to meet on another night which would entail establishment of another Lodge…perhaps!

At the same time that the petition for Dispensation for forming of Wheeling Lodge No. 128, was filed with the Grand Lodge of Virginia, a petition was filed with the Grand Chapter of Virginia requesting formation of a Royal Arch Chapter in Wheeling under the title of Wheeling Union Chapter No. 19. A Charter was issued by the Grand Chapter of Virginia on December 5, 1822, naming Morgan Nelson, Most Reverence High Priest; Peleg Mason, King; and William B. Hubbard, Scribe; together with all such other Companions as were then, or should at any time thereafter become members. They were authorized to confer the Mark Master, Past Master, Most Excellent Master, and Royal Arch Degrees. Another consideration is that the formation of a Royal Arch Chapter in Wheeling did not meet with the approval of everyone, and a rift occurred which prompted the formation of the new Lodge. This thought seems unlikely, but certainly not beyond the realm of possibility.

A curious fact is that Peleg Mason, and Wm. Hubbard were not residents of Wheeling, but lived in

215

St. Clairsville, Ohio. Both were attorneys as was Morgan Nelson.

Worshipful Brother Nelson made the arduous trip to Richmond to attend the Grand Chapter Session on December 5, and stayed until the Grand Lodge session on December 12. Such a trip in those days required difficult travel through the mountains, and was not accomplished without considerable expenditure of time. Nelson brought both Charters back to Wheeling on his return. On February 23, 1823, both Nelson and John Truax demitted from Ohio Lodge.

A fire in Wheeling in 1875 destroyed some of the early Masonic records, but we do know that Wheeling Union Chapter met in the Lodge rooms of Wheeling Lodge No. 128.

Ohio Lodge did not work a candidate in any degree during 1823 and 1824. They also issued ten demits during those two years, most of whom affiliated with Wheeling Lodge, and petitioned Wheeling Union Chapter. Could it be that our thought that there was a difference of opinion regarding the establishment of a Royal Arch Chapter in Wheeling is valid, and that Brother Nelson persisted in moving the Craft forward...perhaps!

In any event, both Ohio Lodge and Wheeling Lodge flourish to this day under the auspices of the Grand Lodge of West Virginia. Nelson served as High Priest of Wheeling Union Chapter Royal Arch Masons from 1823 through 1846, except for the year 1836. His driving influence kept the Chapter alive and it flourishes to this day.

Peleg Mason, and Wm. Hubbard served as King and Scribe for just the one year, and then left Wheeling Union Chapter. At the first meeting of the Chapter in 1823, several petitions were received, and cleared the

216

ballot, and then were worked in the several degrees.

In 1822, Morgan Nelson was appointed District Deputy Grand Master of the Grand Lodge of Virginia, and was still serving in that capacity, as well as being the official representative of the City of Wheeling on May 23, 1825, when he received General Marquis La-Fayette at the Wheeling wharf on behalf of the City of Wheeling, and on behalf of the Craft. The General was accompanied by his son, George Washington LaFayette, M. Lavasseur, and Collin King. That evening all three entered Ohio Lodge No. 101 as visitors, and the General was escorted to a seat in the East, where he was welcomed by Worshipful Brother Nelson, District Deputy Grand Master, as follows:

"Illustrious Sir, on behalf of the Brethren here assembled, permit me the pleasure of bidding you welcome within these walls dedicated to friendship and brotherly love. In common with our fellow creatures, we cherish the warmest sentiments of admiration for the principles and actions which have marked every period of your life.

Accept the homage of our gratitude for your arduous exertions in the great cause of American Liberty. It is no small addition to our joy that you suffer us to address you by the endearing appellation of Brother. That while many of the monarchs of the old world exhibit towards Freemasonry the like spirit of hostility as towards the cause of human liberty, you deem it not derogatory to your dignity to level yourself with the fraternity and signify your approbation of those philanthropic principles which are the basis of our institution.

Be pleased, sir, to accept of my right hand that ancient token of Brotherly love, and allow me to express my fervent wish that the evening of your days

217

may prove as serene and happy as your past life has been eventful and glorious."

In reply, the General expressed his thanks for the kind sentiments expressed toward him, and stated that it was gratifying to him to meet in western Virginia, the same cordial reception with which his Masonic Brethren had often honored him in other places. He further said that he has always entertained a high esteem for the Masonic Institution, but more especially since it had experienced the bitter persecutions of the European despots who had vainly attempted its destruction.

Following the pleasantries, Worshipful Brother Nelson escorted the General to Shepherd's Hall for an evening of dining and dancing. Shepherd's Hall was built in 1792 by Moses Shepherd and his wife Lydia Boggs Shepherd. These two were close friends of Heny Clay, and through that friendship were able to get the National Road brought to Wheeling instead of Wellsburg which was the much more sensible route. Not only did the National Road come to Wheeling, but it was brought right to the front door of Shepherd's Hall, and then made a ninety degree turn to head into the city, six or seven miles away. This necessitated building two additional bridges, which contract was awarded to Moses Shepherd. Present Route 40 still travels the bridge built over Wheeling Creek by Shepherd, near the front door of his home. Shepherd's widow was the center of entertainment in Washington, D. C. until her death. No one in the Nation's capitol would dare attempt any sort of social gathering without the advice and influence of Lydia. Shepherd's Hall remains standing today, and is the present home of Osiris Shrine. A.A.O.N.M.S.

To stir your imagination, take note, and put together what we have thus far. Moses Shepherd was a Mason; Henry Clay was a Mason, and the Senator from Kentucky; Morgan Nelson was a Mason, who moved to Wheeling from Kentucky. Any connection here, or are these facts just coincidence!

Worshipful Brother Nelson was instrumental in the construction of the first Masonic Hall in 1826, located at 1130-32 Market Street., in Wheeling, It was occupied by the Masonic Bodies from 1827 to 1844, when it was sold at a sheriff's sale for debts. Imagine, when Nelson came to Wheeling in 1820, there were just 53 members of the Craft in town. Just six years later, there was another Lodge, a Royal Arch Chapter and a Masonic Hall had been constructed in a prominent section of downtown Wheeling. Records indicate that Nelson worked very hard to save the building for the Craft, employing every legal avenue open to him, but the Morgan Excitement during this period had put such a damper on the activities of the Craft, that he finally had to succumb to the inevitable. It was purchased by the city and used for a city hall for some years.

In 1828, Morgan Nelson was married to Mary A. Graham in the First Presbyterian Church, located on Fourth St., (Now Chapline St. Moses Chapline was a member of Ohio Lodge) by the Reverend William Wylie. This marriage was blessed with five daughters. The Church remains standing and regular Sunday Services continue.

He was instrumental in the founding of the first savings Bank in Wheeling, known as the Wheeling Savings Institution, and served as a Director. He was a member of the Board for the construction of the Suspension Bridge over the Ohio River which was the longest span of its kind in the world when it was completed. It remains in use today, although Route 40 (National Road) has been replaced by I-70, so only local traffic going to Wheeling Island uses the old Suspension Bridge today.

Nelson did not abandon the desire for the Craft to have its own home. He was instrumental in organizing the activities which resulted in the construction of Washington Hall, just one half block south of the previous Masonic Temple, and on the corner of what is today 12th and Market Sts.

This structure was much larger and more beautiful than the one lost. It not only contained shops on the street level, but also a concert room on the second floor where the leading entertainers of the day performed including Jenny Lind and Edwin Booth. The third floor contained meeting rooms which were used by the Masonic Bodies. The Brethren moved into this beautiful structure in 1854, but sadly, it burned down in 1875 during sessions of the State Legislature being held there. It is believed that the fire started from a heating stove, it being very cold weather.

Worshipful Brother Nelson was a member of the first class of candidates in 1838 when Wheeling Commandery #1, Knights Templar was instituted as a subordinate Commandery of the Grand Encampment. At the first election of officers he was elected Prelate, and served as Eminent Commander in 1848-49-50. A fellow member of that first class of candidates was Richard Harding, grandfather of the noted author, Richard Harding Davis.

Chartering of Wheeling Commandery caused problems amongst the Craft. The Grand Commandery of Virginia was incensed at the actions taken by the Grand Encampment, and indicated they would withdraw from that body. The position of the Grand Encampment was that the Grand Commandery of

220

Virginia, like so may other Masonic Bodies during the Morgan Excitement period, had been dormant; hence, their actions were reasonable, and in the best interest of the Craft. The Grand Master of the Grand Encampment, Wm. Hubbard, a close friend of Morgan Nelson, and one of the petitioners for the Charter for Wheeling Union Chapter, Royal Arch Masons, handled the matter diplomatically and with gentleness. The matter was resolved, in 1853, when Wheeling Commandery voluntarily withdrew from the Grand Encampment, and joined the Grand Commandery of Virginia.

Between the formation of Wheeling Commandery in 1838, and joining the Grand Commandery of Virginia in 1853, John R. Hall, Richard W. Harding, Wm. P. Wilson, and Morgan Nelson had served as Eminent Commanders of the Wheeling Encampment. Wheeling being a subordinate of the Grand Encampment during those years, these Sir Knights held the recognition of being Past Grand Commanders, and members of the Grand Encampment. Nelson served as Senior Warden of the Grand Encampment, and in 1856, Wm. Hubbard, who had served as Grand Master for nine years, declined to be further considered for that office, whereupon Sir Knight Morgan Nelson was elected Grand Master. Nelson declined to be installed, and the Deputy Grand Master refusing to be considered, Sir Knight Hubbard was unanimously elected and prevailed upon to serve another term. Reluctantly Hubbard acquiesced.

While Nelson was actively involved in the formation of Wheeling Commandery, he was not the prime mover. That distinction belongs to Sir Knight Philo Stocking, who was a member of Genessee Commandery of Batavia, New York. Stocking had been the Junior Warden of the Masonic Lodge involved in the

Morgan Excitement. Fearing for the safety of his family, he left New York and settled in Wheeling, Virginia, becoming an active Mason and leading citizen.

In 1836, Nelson and eight others petitioned the Grand Council of Ohio, requesting a Charter for the establishment of a Council in Wheeling. The petition had the recommendation of Steubenville Council #2, located in Steubenville, Ohio, of which body the petitioners were members. The Grand Council of Ohio stating that they being the closest Grand Council to Wheeling granted the Charter for Washington Council No. 6, Morgan Nelson being named Thrice Illustrious Brand Master.

In 1842, Washington Council was notified by the Grand Chapter of Virginia that they had taken over the Council Degrees from the Grand Council of Virginia, who had surrendered them voluntarily. It had been deemed, upon investigation, that the Grand Council of Virginia had been improperly formed, and was thus illegal. Washington Council was ordered to cease their operations and close. Morgan Nelson took up the challenge, and communicated with both Virginia and Ohio on the matter. His position was that the Grand Chapter of Virginia had no jurisdiction over Washington Council, it being chartered by Ohio. The Grand Council of Ohio sided with the Grand Chapter of Virginia, and three long meetings were held by the members of the Council in regard to the request from the Grand Council of Ohio that the Charter be surrendered and returned to Ohio.

The minutes do not give any particulars regarding the discussion, or what decision was agreed. However, the results are as follows as of this writing:

1 - Washington Council #6 was closed in 1843, and the Council Degrees assumed by Wheeling Union

Chapter No. 19, whose High Priest was Morgan Nelson.

2 - When West Virginia Masonic Bodies established their own Grand Bodies after the dissolution of political ties with the citizens east of the mountains in 1863, the Grand Chapter of West Virginia continued the practice established in Virginia of being in control of the Council Degrees.

3 - In approximately 1970, one of the Wheeling Banks contacted a prominent York Rite Mason in Wheeling (George Gorrell) and asked him to examine a document they had found in one of their old vaults. The document was the original Charter of Washington Council No. 6, from the Grand Council of Ohio. The Charter has been preserved, framed, and hangs in the Masonic Building in Wheeling to this date.

4 - As of this writing, there is no fraternal recognition between the Grand Council of Ohio, and the Grand Chapter of West Virginia.

Most Excellent Companion Morgan Nelson was elected Grand High Priest of the Grand Chapter of Virginia in 1852 and again in 1853. As such, he was the only Mason from west of the mountains to preside over any Grand Body in Virginia.

Meanwhile this outstanding Mason continued to be one of the leading attorneys in the Wheeling area, and a leader in the rapid growth of the city.

Most Excellent Companion Nelson's health began to fail, and on December 21, 1858, he filed his will, leaving his estate to his wife, Mary A. Graham Nelson, and to his four surviving daughters, as well as to the widower of his other daughter. He passed away on Christmas Day, 1858. The Grand Chapter of Virginia adopted suitable resolutions upon his death and the altars of the Royal Arch Chapters of Virginia were draped in mourning for one year.

Now let us review the record, looking for the items that would lead to the selection of this man as a Masonic hero.

Arriving in a new town, he affiliates with the local Masonic Lodge, and is quickly elected the Worshipful Master. Two years later, over the objection of the Lodge, he obtains a Charter for a new Masonic Lodge in Wheeling. Time proved the intelligence of his determination.

At the same time, he obtains a Charter for a Royal Arch Chapter in Wheeling. He serves as High Priest for many years, including during the Morgan Excitement.

At a time when Masonic Bodies are closing, and members are demitting because of the Morgan affair in New York, he not only maintains the validity of Wheeling Union Chapter, but starts a new Masonic Body in Washington Council #6, Also during this difficult time, he assists in the formation, and serves as an officer in Wheeling Commandery, Knights Templar.

He is instrumental in the construction of a Masonic Building in Wheeling, and when that property is lost, he is the prime mover in the construction of a new, bigger, and more beautiful Masonic Building within ten years of the loss of the first one.

He is elected Grand Master of the Grand Encampment, but refuses to be installed

This good Brother is a leading light in the establishment of suitable banking facilities in Wheeling, works on getting a bridge over the Ohio River which is the longest suspension bridge of its day.

He is a confidant of one of the most outstanding Grand Masters the Grand Encampment has ever had. He is selected to represent the city, and Masonry in receiving and entertaining General Lafayette.

He is twice elected Grand High Priest of Virginia, the only Mason west of the mountains
to serve as presiding officer over a Virginia Grand Body.

A lot of this good Brother's accomplishments were achieved in times without a receptive atmosphere for Masonry. His record indicates that he made good sound decisions, and was not dissuaded from them regardless of opposition from others, no matter their standing, and time has proven the soundness of all his actions.

He represented the Masonic Bodies of Wheeling in Richmond for many years. An accomplishment when it took more than a week to travel from Wheeling to Richmond. For example, when he went to Richmond in 1822 to obtain the Charters of both Wheeling Lodge, and Wheeling Union Chapter, the event would have entailed nearly a month of his time. Just going to Steubenville to receive the Council Degrees, and be active in their activities entailed more than three hours travel each way.

On January 24, 1867, Nelson Lodge #30 A. F. & A. M. was chartered in Wheeling by the Grand Lodge of West Virginia. It was the first such action by that Grand Body, and how fitting that the first Lodge chartered by West Virginia would be named after this dedicated and outstanding Mason.

When Morgan Nelson came to Wheeling, the population was 1567, and the Craft numbered just 53. When he passed away, Wheeling had grown to almost 18,000, and the Craft had grown and prospered as well as the town, with the Masonic Temple being the heart of activity, both for the Craft, and for town affairs.

Worshipful Brother Morgan Nelson was buried

in Mt. Wood Cemetery, atop Wheeling Hill, overlooking the Great City and Valley that he had adopted, and done so much to develop, both in the workaday world, and in Masonry. During the long history of our country, it seems to me that the Supreme Architect of the Universe has seen fit to supply us with outstanding leadership from the Masonic Community. Whether Masonry brings out these qualities in men, or whether men of this quality are attracted to Masonry, is a moot question. It is more important that it is here resolved that the world is a better place for Morgan Nelson having been here, and as Masons, it is the earnest intent of each of us that when we pass on, history will say the same of us.

The career of Morgan Nelson, in all its facets, was a brilliant and illustrious one. Nelson Lodge can well be proud of the origin of its name.

To the reader: Given the proper setting, such as a warm, quiet evening under the stars, one's mind may drift into areas previously not considered. One might reflect on the past, contemplate the future; or explore questions relative to life and its meaning. Just such an evening stirred this scribe into the area of how Masonry might be evaluated in the cold light of logic. What is the rationale that over the centuries has continued to keep Masonry a viable institution? Is there something about the Craft which touches the members that is not readily recognized? The thoughts developed randomly, and after a month the following paper was written. However, the intent is here stated that the purpose is to stimulate the reader into making the same examination.

Chapter XX
The Logic

L ogic is the science of proof, or the science of reasoning; and there is no better locus upon which to lace the wreath of masonry than on the armor of knowledge known as Logic. Logic, derived from the Greek word "logike" (reasoning) has two sides. The doctrine in Hellenic thought is essentially reason. The other side from the Hebrew is a doctrine of word. Bringing the two sides together we arrive at "reasoned word." Many scholars, in the annals of history, have undertaken to define logic as it relates to philosophy, psychology, or science, but in this quarter, the simple definition, "reasoned word," speaks volumes.

If one knows many of the great truths of life, he has wisdom and knowledge, and is so recognized. If one is full of wisdom and knowledge, he then must know many of the great truths of life. It would seem to this writer that the individual couldn't have one without the other. In seeking either, he arrives at a comfortable grasp of both.

Arrival at this respected station is occasioned by the search for the reasoned word, but the road to it is obfuscated with side roads that are dead end at the least, and misleading at best.

A study of the small game hunting dog, and his quarry, provides an excellent example of searching by logic, and the evasive turns truth can take. Logic enters the picture before the hunt begins, as the hunter must choose the proper equipment to assist in bagging the quarry. This selection process is not difficult, for previous generations, and their findings, have accomplished much, and having passed the test of time, are accepted without controversy. The quarry in this first example will be the rabbit which dictates not only the selection of equipment, but also the decisions on where, when, and how to seek the rabbit. But first a license must be obtained from those in authority whose responsibility it is to decide the proper qualifications necessary to be issued permission to pursue wild game.

To enter the fields and woods alone in pursuit of the rabbit decreases the odds of success dramatically. One would have to be lucky enough to stumble onto a rabbit, and then would have very little time to get off a shot as the rabbit scampered away. Further, if the rabbit becomes aware of the hunter, he will endeavor to hide, or sneak away undetected. Seeking a rabbit in this manner is certainly not impossible, but difficult. The equipment will be hunting boots or shoes, hunting coat, hunting pants, cap, shotgun, and such other clothing under the hunting coat and pants as the weather dictates.

An explanation of these items have all been decided by logic, and are as follows: A beagle hunting dog will be of great assistance to our hunter, and greatly increase the chances of success. A beagle dog has a good nose for locating and tracking, not enough speed so that the rabbit is pushed so hard it will hole up right away, small stature to more readily maneuver through the briars and thickets, and yet durable enough to withstand a full day in the field.

Hunting boots, or shoes, as there will be lots of walking over rough ground, and therefore proper footwear is essential. Hunting coat, as it is made to ward off briars, has a suitable lined pocket to carry game, has individual shell pockets, and lots of other pocket space. Hunting pants to ward off briars, and hunting cap to keep sun off the eyes, and woodland bugs and debris out of the hair. The shot to be executed will be at a small animal on the move, and over a short distance. The long range of a rifle is not needed, and to hit a rapidly moving small target would be difficult; hence the appropriate selection is a shotgun.

Hunting for rabbit after dark is not an option, for even though rabbits may be active at night, to shoot them in the dark is impossible. So daylight hours are the choice. The dog will locate the quarry, who will run when discovered. He will not run far, but will wait to see if he is being tracked. As the dog working the track gets close, the rabbit will move off again. While not being overly intelligent, the rabbit, nonetheless, reasons that running in a straight line will not be effective in losing the dog, and he really does not want to go into unfamiliar territory; so, the rabbit begins to corner each time he sits down and awaits the dog. The dog has to search to the sides to discover the new direction the rabbit has taken; but if the dog is good at his trade, he will not be confused, and will continue to keep the rabbit slowly on the move.

The quarry has one more trick up his sleeve, and that is to circle and cross his own track. Having done so, the dog must determine which track is the most recent, and continue to move his quarry. The rabbit will continue to corner, and circle until either he loses the dog, or tires of the game. The rabbit will then attempt to retire to his burrow in the ground. Indeed, the dog will never be successful in bagging the rabbit on his own. In circling, the rabbit exposes himself to the hunter who has positioned himself anticipating the rabbit's actions. If the dog is good at tracking, and the hunter gets a clear shot, most likely the rabbit is doomed.

Let us change the quarry from the rabbit to the raccoon, and see if logic determines that changes are necessary.

Mister Raccoon is active at night and tend not to move all a great deal in the daylight unless disturbed. However, the raccoon nests in, and readily makes use of trees while the rabbit remains on the ground. Obviously, there is no way to locate and chase a raccoon in the daylight if he is up a tree somewhere; hence, our hunt will have to be at night when the raccoon is on the ground feeding. Once it has been decided that our hunter and his dog will have to work at night, how is the raccoon to be bagged?

Certainly, moving the raccoon and tracking him, as was done with the rabbit augers no chance for success. You can't shoot a moving target in the dark. Some changes will have to be made, and logic will determine these alterations. If it was known which tree the raccoon was situated, then he could be located with a good flashlight, and in that light, shot with a 22 caliber rifle, or pistol. A shotgun would not be effective shooting into the top of a tall tree for two reasons. One, the branches and leaves would reduce the effectiveness, and two, the shotgun would put several holes in the animal's pelt which is what the hunter is after.

230

If the raccoon can be pushed hard enough by the dog, he will tree; and if the dog remains at the tree, barking up, the hunter will recognize the change in the dog's voice, and hike to the location and bag the quarry.

To push the raccoon into "treeing," a bigger, faster, hunting dog will be needed. So, in addition to the previous listed changes, the hunting dog will have to be changed to a Black & Tan, Blue tick, Red Bone, or Walker; and a good flashlight has been added.

The quarries tactics are different only in that the raccoon will tree instead of going into a burrow in the ground, and he will move over a considerably larger area. The raccoon tactics include going up a tree, circle the trunk to the other side, and come back down; an event the hunter calls tapping the tree. He will also go to water, hoping the dog will not find where he came out of the stream. However, the experienced dog will not lose his quarry, and eventually close in to where the only option for the raccoon is to tree so the dog can't get him. In so doing, however, he is now vulnerable to the hunter.

Logic determined that the hunter's chances of success in working were rather poor when pursuing the rabbit, and near impossible in regard to the raccoon. The dog's chances working alone were non-existent in either case. But when logic put the two together, with proper knowledge, training, and equipment, the odds were heavily against both the rabbit and the raccoon.

The hunter and his dog found that logic dictated they work together to land their quarry, but the cat needs no co-conspirator. He locates the paths along which the rabbit travels, and then lies patiently waiting to ambush his quarry. His logic is that sooner or

231

later, the rabbit will travel this path again, and when he does, the outcome heavily favors the cat. In this case, we have two different ways to arrive at the same result, both logical.

Let us move on to a completely different situation regarding logic. where time changes the result and the approach. As little babies, we are born with a lack of ability to communicate, a determination to get what we want, and a great shortage of patience. When things are not to our liking, we react violently by screaming, crying, and shaking our hands and feet. This behavior works very well as we soon get attention, and therefore the logic is that this behavior pattern will work very well in making the world conform to our agenda. Even after we learn to communicate, we resort to this behavior when things do not go our way, but after a few years the world will not accede to our desires; and in fact, may become highly resistive to this infantile attitude. It is difficult to accept that decisions made on the basis of previously workable logic later turn out to be unworkable when circumstances change

Examples set forth here are basic and simple, but for a specific purpose. There are two human attributes that operate the world's machinery, to wit: knowledge and beliefs. We are not born with either, and the path to both must be selected carefully for the danger exists that one may develop an egocentric sphere of wisdom and beliefs that are inherently flawed.

Knowledge, truth, and wisdom, are to some degree interchangeable, but logic cannot be added to that list. Logic is the path to knowledge, truth, and wisdom; and further, it is also the path to beliefs. Besides being the only correct path to knowledge and beliefs, logic is also the metaphorical armor; and thus, protector of both knowledge and beliefs. When knowledge, truth, wisdom, or beliefs are attacked, the defender is logic, and yet logic is not finite. It is subject to addition and correction. Time, circumstances, or new developments may necessitate revisiting the logic that previously shaped particular knowledge or beliefs. There is never a danger in revisiting logic, but disaster lurks for those who refuse to review it.

Masonry as an institution is engaged in a never ending search for Truth. As such it should follow the path of logic in a continuous pursuit of knowledge, wisdom, and Truth. Such an effort is not a collective, but an individual one, for the Craft enjoins upon each member to strive toward the self professed goal of "More Light in Masonry." Masonry does not have an exclusive on logic, nor a monopoly on the search for Truth. All persons should be engaged in these pursuits, but all too few are. The Craft, if properly understood, should attract those men of good moral character, who believe in a Supreme Being, to travel the paths of logic, seeking truth and knowledge.

The Craft issues a license, as was the hunter, by favorably accepting the petitioner for membership. Through degree work, the proper equipment is issued by communicating lectures and symbols of the Craft. The Craftsman, armed with the good will and promise of assistance when requested, embarks on the lifelong pursuit of truth and knowledge. Membership in Masonry is a privilege and an opportunity. The Craft is historically rooted in order and symmetry, both operative and speculative; and has been a positive influence on men and society for hundreds of years without interference in the operation of other lawful institutions.

Wisdom comes with the accumulation of knowledge and truths. It is the wise citizen who understands the interpersonal and tolerant relationships necessary

233

to a peaceful and productive society. Wisdom is attained by logic.

Knowledge comes from formal schooling, formal training, and the experiences of life. It is accumulative and its storehouse receives additional deposits of knowledge from each generation. Knowledge is also attained by logic. Truth is said to be the foundation of every virtue. It is admired and set aside as the ultimate attribute, and yet truth is evaded and suborned on a daily basis. The search for the great truths in life should not be sullied by the studied, or unconscious avoidance of small ones.

Truth is also pursued and found by logic. There is so much more to Masonry than the important decision at the ballot box, or the learning of ritual, the teaching of candidates. the holding of meetings, and the payment of the bills of the lodge. Opportunities to pursue research touching upon the great truths of life by the Brethren can be inspired by Masonic programs, both within and without the lodge. With all such activities, these, and other deliberations must be approached with logic. Personal agendas, personal desires, competitive attitudes, piques, and jealous withdrawal from open minded discussion will not properly serve the Craft.

A word that pervades society today is "consensus." A meeting of the minds upon which all can agree is an admirable goal in virtually all organizations. However, it is imperative that compromise not be substituted for consensus. To compromise is to meet in the middle with everyone giving up approximately the same amount of ground. Such an event only serves to quiet the discussion; however, to reach a consensus upon which all may agree, is properly reached by the assiduous application of logic, Logic is the battleground of adulthood!

To the reader: If one contemplates, there is much to stir the thought processes. In the following, a line from a movie was the impetus to the paper. There is much to learn in life, and perhaps we inadvertently overlook many of its lessons.

Chapter XXI
It Takes a Lot of Lights

A lazy summer night's breeze wafted softly through the foliage, gently stirring the leaves in a symphonic harmony of movement. At the top of the hill a break in the trees provided a lookout alongside a country road, and there, framed in the valley between the hills and the horizon, were a myriad of twinkling city lights shining passionately in the night.

A pair of headlights pierced the dark with their mournful stare as they wound their way through the trees along the narrow macadam road, and up the hill. Reaching the top, they seemed to glance at the overlook, and flashing approval, eased their charge off the road, coming to rest in a self effacing manner high above the display of Edison's genius below.

A handsome young man with dashing blue eyes and a shock of blond hair switched off the source of power to the two purveyors of illumination, and turning the key, quieted the purr of the engine in the 1941 Plymouth convertible.

A glamorous young lady with long blond hair cascading down over one eye as though to hide the impact of both those deep blue eyes from the world, graced the front seat. Her soft inviting lips parted, and from that delicate throat a soft, but slightly husky voice spoke,

"What a beautiful sight!" The young man turned his attention to the panoramic view below and replied, "Yeah, it takes a lot of lights to make a city."

The scene just recounted is from the 1946 film, "The Blue Dahlia." The two actors in the convertible were Alan Ladd and Veronica Lake. The script line, "Yeah, it takes a lot of lights to make a city," is an intriguing thought that merits consideration and study. It will be the focus of this treatise.

For every existence, there must be a beginning. Towns and cities are no exception. Some are born from adventure and singleness of purpose. In may cases, a family moving west seeking new opportunity found a location of personal appeal and settled. If other families were alike motivated, the opportunity for establishment of a community became a possibility, but not a given.

One, two, or just a few families do not make a town. There are commercial considerations, and if they cannot be satisfied, there is no one to supply the products and services necessary to sustain the families needs. Without that support, valuable productive time must be spent traveling to the nearest town to trade for those items beyond the ability of the family to produce. Of course a family, or perhaps even several, can sustain themselves off the land through their own ingenuity and labor, but a town will not develop unless there is some motivation to attract additional growth.

Good farmland may gender additional interest; however, farms, by their very nature, demand that the population be spread over a wide area, and therefore, in and of themselves, the development will not generate a town, much less a city. The farmers must get the results of their labor to market which means transportation. Hence, roads, waterways, or railroads now become a requisite.

Minerals such as coal, iron, salt, or some other natural resource will generate the establishment of a community, but again those natural resources must find their way into the hands of those artisans capable of manufacturing them into useful products. Obviously, transportation is a necessity if growth is to occur. Most often, time will draw the manufacturers to the source of the raw materials in order to reduce the cost of transporting raw material. Locating the manufacturers at the source now produces all the ingredients necessary to develop an area in a prosperous community, provided they have a ready ability to transport the finished product to remote markets.

So what is represented by that panorama of twinkling lights seen in the valley? What do they represent? From our brief review, we know that they are not merely faceless entities that can be neither faced nor understood such as the stars we see at night. They are much more than mere trappings of beauty presented for our enjoyment by the Great Creator. There is a great story behind each and very one of those lights, and each light represents an integral part of the whole as it contributes to the brilliance of the glow.

See those lights stacked up near the junction of the smaller river with the large one? That's an office building with the lights on for the janitors to perform their tasks. During the day it is filled with office workers, each making a contribution to the prosperity of the town. And out there on the right in the suburbs, near the base of that hill, those several lights are descendants of the original family whose first cabin was on the site of the office building.

Down river from the office building the lights are rather orange in appearance. Those are lights from the manufacturing plant that employs almost four thousand people. Those orange lights are responsible for four thousand of the small lights you see near the base of the hill on the left, all lined up like soldiers on parade up and down the streets of the residential area. Each light in the business, and/or, manufacturing section joins with a light in the residential area to make up a fascinating tale of family history, perhaps unimportant in a larger sense, but of vital concern to those whom each light represents. All those lights lined up in rows near the office building represent the grocers, dry goods stores, shoe shops, and all the other providers of necessities for the many people of the city, and for each other.

But there is much that is not readily seen. One of those lights down there is the Mayor of the City. Several others are Councilmen's homes. Still more are the firemen, the policemen, the sanitation workers, and all the many service providers for the community. Indeed in this case, lights are people, each with a job, each with a responsibility, and each with his, or her, own talents and abilities.

From high on the hill in the distance, one light would be of no importance, and perhaps overlooked as merely the moon reflecting off some object, but altogether, united in concert in a proper setting, the display of cooperation, hope, unity of purpose, an illustration of man's responsibility to man, unparalleled.

Is there something missing? Yes, unfortunately there is. Those who have no responsibility, and make no contribution to the community, have no light, and make no light. In the daylight, they can be seen wandering the streets, or loafing in an alley, but the community, for the most part, ignores them. Certainly there are those who try to assist these non-contributors, and that

239

is a proper thing for individuals to do. The question regards the glow in the sky at night, darting among the clouds as they roll over the valley. These non-contributors are not part of the escape. The city as a whole is no better off for their presence, nor are the individual citizens somehow elevated by their cluttering up the scene. This does not infer that these non-contributors should be completely ignored. Every effort should be made to gather then into the arena, and exhibit to them the rewards of sharing the responsibility of progress and prosperity. Until that happens, if ever, they wallow in the darkness and make no contribution to the beacon of community life we see from the hill at night.

How does the multitude of lights affect others who are not a part of the town we see? They are beacons in the night as they light up the sky from afar. They present a promise of safety, prosperity, and opportunity. They promise a chance for security for self and family to those who are willing to join and be a part of contributing to that beacon. They uplift the spirit with the knowledge that one will never have to meander in darkness without purpose or goals again.

As so often happens, the phrase uttered by Alan Ladd in that movie, "It takes a lot of lights to make a city," may not have made much impression on theatergoers at the time, particularly with Veronica Lake in the scene, but pensive examination of the phrase brings out a deep and philosophical consideration. This consideration translates directly into many facets of life, and particularly into Masonry.

As men and women with certain skills see the opportunity to make a valuable and rewarding contribution to our selected settlement, so Masonry seizes on the prospect of becoming an integral part of establishing an aura of friendship and brotherly love amongst a

240

gathering of right thinking people, who believe in the Brotherhood of Man under the Fatherhood of God.

Light, to Masons, is not an unfamiliar term, and refers to that interest and investigation which brings a better understanding of those issues whose resolution brings true Brotherhood into proper focus.

Anciently, the builders jealously guarded their knowledge to prevent others from overcrowding their trace. That mentality persisted as late as the latter part of the nineteenth century amongst the puddlers of the iron mills, and nailers of the nail factories. Modern technology has stripped these trades of their ability to control relevant knowledge, and modern Masons have no desire to withhold their teachings from any who meet the criteria of a belief in a Supreme Being, and can pass the test of the ballot box. However, much like the future of our selected settlement, Masonry's philosophy and impact depend on an accumulation of small glimmers that work together to form a mighty beacon in the night.

Traveling across the sands of time, we are struck with those gatherings of people who prospered for a time in a location, and then the community turned into a ghost town. No longer did their light shine in the sky at night to lead a prospective contributor to them. No longer a hub of activity generating a prosperity and security. Nothing but ruins of what once was. Did those people so situated disappear? No, for what they deemed good reason, they moved on to establish something even better and more secure in another location. Perhaps the raw resources played out. Maybe better transportation was established at another location. Or perhaps some calamity of nature wiped out their effort. In any event, what was did not disappear, but relocated, establishing continued progress in a new venue.

Masonry cannot survive in a location with only one small twinkle, much as no town existed until there were enough twinkles to make a light. Masonry in its establishment depends on the contribution of many, much as the town does. Members are needed to handle the financial considerations of the Craft. Members are needed to perform the work of ritual instruction. The variety of talent needed for the prosperity of a Masonic Lodge is just as extant as that of a town. With it, Masonry grows and prospers. Without that variety of talent it withers and must move on, or die.

Suppose we have no one capable, or willing to learn the information necessary to perform the ritual work? Then we cannot accept new members, and when the present ones are taken by time, the lodge is gone. Assume that no one has the ability, or willingness, to properly advise the lodge regarding financial matters. Without some minimal resources, the lodge will have to close. We find that we are unable to hold meetings because the members have other things to do, and will not attend. Again the lodge closes.

Festive occasions are always welcome, the festive board attracts activity and discussion, but we can't find anyone able, or willing, to perform the tasks necessary for such a gathering. No one wants to provide adequate instruction in the observance of the various Laws and Regulations of the Craft, so we soon fall into confusing and unmanageable problems. A Brother, or his family, is in need of assistance or guidance, but there is no one with the expertise, or willingness, to handle the matter properly.

Masonry, like a town, is not something that just happens. The proper execution of a Masonic Body necessitates common purpose, willingness to participate, and dedication to the principles of cooperation and work. Like the town, Masonry has all too many of those who simply wander the streets as citizens, making no contribution to the whole. They are not to be ignored, but rather to be brought into the main stream and taught the lessons of common effort for the common good. While their lights may be out, they must be rekindled that they can add to the Great Light.

At the same time, the talent and expertise of each and every one, both in the town, and in Masonry must be examined and slotted into that part of the light that will make the best contribution. It is folly to burden a citizen, or a Brother, with a task for which he has no ability. His interest will falter and disappear. His contribution will be without value. His light will flicker and go out. For the town, the resources were raw materials and transportation. The goal was prosperity and security for all who chose to stake their future on what they saw. Working together, and each making his contribution, the goals were achieved for all who worked diligently, not only for themselves, but for the common good.

For Masonry, the resources are men of good character, who believe in one Supreme Being. The goal is bringing to a community the stability of men who can best work and agree, no matter the problem, and enjoy the spirit of pleasant associations with all whom they come in contact. Working together, and each making his contribution, no matter how big, or how small, but each in his own capacity; the goals are achieved which greatly benefit the participant, his family, and his community.

"It takes a lot of lights to make a Masonic Fraternity.:" Is your light on, and if not, what are your intentions? If your light is on, are you holding back on the candlepower?

You are reminded of a phrase uttered by one of the greatest Teachers in history…"Let your light so shine before men that they may see your good works, and glorify your Father, who is in heaven." Indeed, it is altogether fitting and proper that all should contribute to society, and no doubt each in his own mind feels that in his own way, he has done so. Each justifies his present position with success, limited only by opportunity. Each justifies any lack of participation with self-determined priorities. Indeed, man is the great justifier of his own actions, and saddles the progress of all institutions with his rationalization. In our town of twinkling lights there are a myriad of tasks to be performed, if it is to survive and prosper.

Opportunity to exchange expertise and time for monetary compensation which is then traded for the services and products one either needs, or desires, has been a successful formula for centuries. However, those tasks that do not earn monetary considerations have a more difficult time being accomplished. There must be some other consideration if a fiscal one does not exist. Some other carrot must be dangled in order to accomplish these charitable acts.

Many are motivated by a sense of obligation to society, and give generously of their time and talent to accomplish these tasks not given to monetary compensation, but the "justifiers" are by far in the majority. Society has progressed in spite of the "justifiers." Towns, cities, and nations have survived without their assistance, and so it will be in the future, however difficult their apathy drags on events. There will always be those who take up the slack, and do more than their share, but the dangers must not be ignored, nor the discomfort of only part of the team pulling the load be glossed over.

Our town is not totally self-sufficient, as no town or enterprise is. The construction of large buildings is beyond the ability and capacity of any of our local contractors. We have to rely on a contractor from across the mountain to accomplish the event when it comes up. Our town's traffic has become a problem, so we need assistance of someone to help us lay out a plan to solve this dilemma. Only if our town becomes a large city can we be expected to contain all the expertise, finances, and resources to cure and solve all our projects and problems. Even then we may run into some unexpected major calamity that will be beyond our financial and labor resources to correct.

No matter the size and self-sufficiency, there are situations that will dictate our willingness to accept help, and in return, we must be ever ready to assist the other fellow. Masonry is no different except that by its very nature, the membership should not contain "justifiers." Being a Mason is participating, contributing in an active and physical way, and setting an example for the entire world to see. Each and every Masonic Body cannot be expected to contain all the expertise within its membership. Some are outstanding in quality, but very small in membership; hence, they may have times that expertise and assistance is necessary, and welcome from the Brothers across the mountain.

It is not expected, nor productive to fulfill a duty for another forever. Assistance until such time as the recipients are able to take over for themselves is of much more value, and much more rewarding. Not only are Masons to assist and support each other, but also they are to be among the bright lights of the town. By its very nature, the fraternity is to furnish leadership in every walk of life, and no Mason should be a "justifier" as long as he is physically able to contribute to society, not for financial compensation, but as a sincere desire to be a part of progress, assistance, and contribution to that beacon of light shining in the darkness between the mountains.

Yes, "It takes a lot of lights to make a city," and a lot of lights to make a Masonic Body.

How is your light? If it's off, turn it on! If it's on, turn it up!

To the reader: You never know what events will stir you to contemplation on a subject, in a different light than previously considered. Most take pride in doing good ritual work, and pleased to be recognized as a good ritualist. An evening of again witnessing rather poor work brought the writer to study the matter from a new prospective.

Chapter XXII
The Show

Nineteen Hundred and Fifty Four marked a singular year in my life, or so I thought.

Six years later my travel brought again, an event that matched the thrill of nineteen hundred and fifty four.

For many years sports were a big part of my life. No doubt the most success was realized in bowling, at which I spent a lot of time, perhaps too much; but it brought its share of thrills and recognition. Over a twenty five year career I managed to record twenty nine perfect games, five three game totals over 800, the highest being 855 which included thirty two strikes in a row; ten West Virginia titles; two time qualifier for the Masters; seven time qualifier for the National Individual Match Game Championships; and invited to the World's Invitational all five years it existed; comprises a part of the list. Through bowling I met Harold Lloyd, the movie comedian; Jesse Owens, Olympic Champion; Roger Ward, Winner at Indy; Rocky Marciano, arguably the greatest heavyweight champion; Roy Rogers, star of Hollywood and TV; and personal friends with most of the well known bowling stars. The Centennial Commission of West Virginia named me a West Virginia Sports great.

247

However, sports had absolutely nothing to do with 1954 and 1960. In 1954, Nelson Lodge #30, A. F. & A. M. looked favorably on my application, and in May, the Worshipful Master, my father, raised me to the Sublime Degree of Master Mason. In 1960, I worked my way through the York Rite Degrees, and was knighted in Wheeling Commandery No. 1. While these two occasions were significant, the excitement derived from the manner in which the events were presented.

On both occasions, everybody knew what, when, where, who, and why. Prompting was nonexistent. Missteps, miscues, and misplaced were not a part of any of those evenings. The whole experience on both occasions was more than impressive. There was no doubt, these men believed wholeheartedly in what they were doing. These were not evenings just to be out, nor were they some sort of lark to be enjoyed as a lighthearted escapade. These men were sincere, dedicated, and talented.

Material content can make or break a presentation, This is a view held by many; but in my opinion, this is a judgment error. The manner of execution can enhance poor script into an enjoyable event. Combine outstanding material with outstanding staging and delivery, and a memorable happening has been created. This was the case on those evenings in 1954 and 1960.

As all things are cyclical, officers become hard to find, and the presentation of work suffers. A bright spot is seen here and there, but the overall picture stirs up concerns, whatever the endeavor. Somehow the best things in life usually survive because they are rediscovered. Some things of great value fall into disuse, and are lost in the dust of eternity, much to the disrepute of those who permit it to do so. It becomes a question of responsibility.

For a moment, imagine that you have bought a ticket to a stage production - a ticket that has cost you a hundred and fifty, or two hundred dollars. Arrival at the theater is accomplished with anticipation. Excitement stirs as the orchestra blends its talents in a stirring overture. The curtain opens, and for the next two, or two and a half hours, a scene ensues consisting of what might be good material, if one could connect it into a coherent whole.

Some of the participants on stage are reading their parts; some have to be shown where to go and what to do. Props are missing and have to be located. Some speak with adequate volume, but there is no feeling, merely a monotone recitation. Others mumble, and prompts are necessary. The curtain comes down on the first act, and there is a delay long enough to convince one that the whole stage is being rebuilt. At last the curtain rises, and we see that a few props have been changed, but nothing that could warrant the interminable delay, and what's more, it hasn't gotten any better. More of the same. Mercifully the evening finally ends. We can now say that we were there, and carry the ticket stub in our pocket to prove the assertion, should we be questioned.

While we voluntarily made the decision to buy the ticket and attend this fiasco, we are now being urged to buy more tickets to see more of these poorly presented shows, being assured that these additional ticket stubs will further enhance our knowledge of the first show.

Good grief! Would one not be justified in asking for one's money back? Had this show no producer, no director, no stage manager, nor stagehands? Were not competent people sought to participate in the show? How can this cast continue in their ineptitude and expect to build a following?

Since 1954 and 1960, I have been witness to this scenario on too many occasions. Do we not have a responsibility, nay an obligation, to exert every effort to make the candidate's night one he will always remember as a highlight in his life, just as those Brothers did for me in 1954 and 1960?

Anything, other than arranging for truly "The Greatest Show in Earth" is unacceptable and counter productive. Growing up we are often reminded by parents, and other adults, that first impressions are of extreme importance and long lasting. In the instance of Masonry, the candidate appears at the lodge hall because of his impression of the institution. It is now within our power to confirm his opinion, or to destroy it by the manner in which he is received. Attention to courtesies previous to his arrival, and the attention and treatment he experiences previous to his degree work begins the process of confirming his decision to be there.

Embarking on new and unfamiliar exercises are most usually approached with some trepidation, and to begin the event alone creates an anxiety. How grateful we are in such a circumstance to be attended, made welcome, and assured in a positive direction. No doubt most candidates are accompanied to the Lodge Hall by an acquaintance. Someone was the recipient of his intentions and desires, else he would not be a candidate. So, we begin his experience with a friendly face, but it is imperative that he arrive early enough to be met and fussed over by the other members of the Lodge. Not a mere hello, nice to meet you, but a sincere interest in getting acquainted, and seeing to his comfort. Proficient and orderly preparations for the candidate's reception are vital to this, his first impression. He knows not what to expect, and may even have some preconceived notion that the evening will be a traumatic one. These concerns need to be kept uppermost in mind that our candidate is now beginning a long journey; one of mystery to him. One in which he will need assistance all along the path, and one that will be filled with new wonders. He must be convinced that he is not alone, and that he will be cared for, assisted, and accompanied with expertise all the way.

Soon the journey begins both for the candidate, and for those who have the responsibility to guide and teach him the remarkable lessons and truths of Masonry. The evening does not begin and end at the door. Nor does it end with the completion of the work. Our candidate may be distracted by apprehension. and only a proficient and knowledgeable performance of the work will tend to alleviate those concerns. It serves no purpose to see how quickly the work can be completed. Mere recitation of those words committed to memory accomplishes nothing other than to confuse the reason we are in attendance. Proficiency does not begin or end with a thorough knowledge of the work. It does begin with the thought that there is a responsibility to teach. Certainly exposure to an event carries some benefit, and with continued attendance, eventually it will be assumed, but it does not inspire a thirst for more. Exposure not understood creates a concern and an apprehension that one will be inundated with more confusing exposure that will also not be comprehended.

Responsibility for the evening rests not only with those charged with performance of the work. It rests with all who are in attendance. Distractions by whispers and movements on the sidelines are unacceptable, and create an atmosphere not conversant with teamwork.

All focus, all concern, all attention must be on the candidate, and the thrust of teaching him the objectives of the evening. All too often our new Brother loses the feeling of being a part of the whole, once the evening is over. His journey has just begun, and hopefully, he is inspired and thrilled with his decision to be a part of the Craft. His first impression had been good, and he looks forward to continuance of the journey. Now comes the most dangerous part of our new candidates Masonic travels.

Most, perhaps all, will say we conform to the general thrust of what has been here said, and we pride ourselves on the quality of reception of candidates., both in personal attention, and in the performance of the ritual. If so, the task is not yet complete. Our new Masonic traveler has much to learn, much to do, and our efforts must not diminish. The show must go on, and it must continue to be excellent in its presentation, and in the attention to our traveler.

Time, effort, and attention, will carry our traveler through the Blue Lodge, and now the efforts of the Brethren need to be redoubled. Our traveler must never feel that now that they have my money, they are on to something else. No, the big show is just beginning. He must be taken into the inner circle of brotherhood, and become a part of the show in some manner. If our work has been done well, we will have a lifelong worker in our vineyards. If our work has not been done well, and is not inspirational, then we have taken money and accepted a candidate under false pretenses. He will not return to be an active member, nor will he, or the Lodge, derive benefit from his membership. It has been said that many only seek the door of Masonry to attain access in other places. It matters not whether this is truth, or fiction, and is not a consideration in the thrust of our efforts. It is our responsibility, and our duty, to present the Lodge and its work in a friendly and proficient manner, make the new member feel welcome, and find a duty commensurate with his expertise to solidify his attention on what he has just experienced

Let us enumerate some suggestions regarding our discussion:

First, the notification of a favorable response to a petitioner's request for consideration for membership provides the initial opportunity to operate in an impressive manner. A phone call is not suitable, nor acceptable. A formal notification from the Secretary is appropriate; or perhaps some may prefer a formal notice signed by the presiding officer. This formal notice very well might be something suitable for framing, and saving by the recipient. If so, then a letter from the Secretary must attend giving all the appropriate instructions. Most definitely a copy of the Secretary's letter should be sent to the first line signer of the petition. The first line signer should also be apprised that it is his responsibility to contact the candidate, congratulate him, and make arrangements to accompany him to the meeting. place.

Upon arrival, the first line signer is to introduce the Secretary to the candidate, and stay with him until he is taken over by those whose responsibility it is to prepare the candidate for whatever is to follow. The first line signer is to make every effort to acquaint the candidate with as many of the members as convenient, and to see to his comfort of both body and mind. Once the candidate enters the area of ceremony, it is incumbent upon absolutely everyone in the room to be attentive, quiet, and respectful of what is being presented.

It is incumbent upon those actively participating in the presentation to be in the proper place and properly prepared. It is incumbent upon those responsible for equipment and staging to see that everything is in the proper place and properly prepared. A Director of Work has properly arranged and prepared those responsible for the presentation, and every effort has been made to make the best presentation possible by the membership to the candidate.

Once the evening is completed, I am one of those who think it inappropriate to request a candidate to make some sort of speech. This very well may be the imposed trauma that will encourage him not to come back. It is possible that he is a good extemporaneous speaker, and has no qualms about being called up. But those who would do anything to avoid such an event constitute an extremely heavy majority.

Let us presume that to this point everything has been accomplished in a manner worthy of our admiration. Our work has just begun. We cannot abandon our new member with simple congratulations at the end of the evening. Hopefully, we are able to provide some refreshments after closing our meeting, and see that our new member is accompanied to the refreshment table. There he should have the opportunity to converse with the older members in small groups. The members need to find out all they can about the new member, and from these conversations begin to formulate some plans in regard to where he can be assigned duties in line with his experience and expertise. Our new member needs to feel the warmth of fellowship, and experience a new chapter in his life. He needs to become aware that his decision has been a good one, and he needs to realize that not only has his future been impacted in a positive way, but that his family also benefits in an indirect manner. From the moment a petition is looked on favorably, the petitioner, to the end of his days, must feel the warmth, friendly attention, and genuine concern due him as a member of the Craft. He also needs to know that his wife and children have also been taken into the concerns of his new Brethren.

With each new petition comes a marvelous opportunity for the petitioner to enter into a time honored brotherhood resplendent with friendship, concern, and mutual respect. If the petition is looked on favorably, the membership is charged with the full acceptance of the petitioner, and all that connotes. There is nothing more exciting than a new birth, a new opportunity being brought into this world full of trouble and tribulation; but also a world full of wonder and excitement. The acceptance of a petitioner is appropriately likened to the decision to bring a new life into the world. We undertake the responsibility to feed, clothe, train, provide for, and educate the result of our decision. Our responsibility to a new member of the Craft is no less that the responsibility to our new child. The only difference is that the petitioner selected us of his own free will and volition, whereas the little baby had no choice in the matter.

No amount of time is too much to dedicate to the preparation for the arrival of our new member, and no amount of time is too much to see to his comfort, his education, and his future with, and in, the Craft.

To the reader: This paper was not prepared for the purpose of making a Masonic point of some sort. It was prepared as an assignment in the workplace. We could easily change a word here and there, and it would then appear as if presented at a Masonic function. That has not been done. It will be up to the reader to apply his own word changes, and make the connections that makes this paper equally appropriate in both Masonry and industry.

Chapter XXIII
Roles & Responsibilities

Roles are customarily either defined or presumed. In those cases where they are defined, the company executes a job description which is a nom de plume considered by some as interchangeable with the term role. Most usually the description is loosely, or ambiguously, worded so that the originator feels covered in any eventuality. A common concluding phrase is, "The preceding is not intended to include all responsibilities, nor to preclude additional assignments." Additionally, some of the same items are found on the job description of more than one job category that leads to confusion. This investigator considers the first consideration is whether, "Roles and Responsibilities" are synonymous terms. If they are, then we are engaged in redundancy by connecting them with an ampersand. In fact, it is here proposed that they are not synonymous, but that often, one follows the other.

In any company, or endeavor, the "role" of each and everyone involved is to exert his, or her, very best effort to support and carry out the company's policy statement. "Roles" are no more, and no less.

"Responsibilities" are how management determines to best divide and assign tasks that will bring

256

policy to fruition. Hence, it may be a misnomer, or misleading, to head an investigation with such a heading. The "role" for all has been established, and is not in question. The division, and the application of "responsibilities" is the area that demands our attention. Let us investigate the division and determination of responsibilities.

First, this division and determination must make some sense to all. Without a buy-in by those involved, the premise is doomed to failure. Therefore, to be successful, the determination and direction of responsibilities, and the way they are necessarily interwoven into smooth and efficient operation, requires consideration and input from all who will be involved.

Next, we hope for an hourly unit that is knowledgeable, efficient, and interested in the success of our endeavor. If they are not involved, if they have no input, or if they do not understand the fabric of what is being proposed, they cannot be expected to do any more than what is necessary to seemingly maintain their job, and collect their check. Industry and business recognize the preceding, and usually make an effort to include the hourly on committees, request information from them, and endeavor to make the hourly feel involved. A failure occurs when these requests are strewn out like chicken feed in the barnyard, and only the most aggressive, or perhaps those who feel this is an opportunity to avoid some of the daily chores, pick it up. It is here suggested that many of the best minds in the hourly unit are not tapped, and that is a loss that is too costly.

Additionally, many of these agendas are so broad that they are of little interest to those whose area is very small when considered against the big picture. It should be remembered that the paintings of the great

Masters were done one brush stroke at a time. Would it not be better to address each small area and discipline of the big picture? Would it not be better to consult not just the complainers, but also those who never seem to have anything to say? Do they perhaps have a major contribution to make, given the right forum? At the same time, such an endeavor cannot be undertaken without a bona fide feeling by the interviewee that the whole scenario is not just more smoke! How are the hourly to feel secure in their effort to make a contribution when their supervisors are really non-persons?

What is a non-person? That is one who has no authority, no latitude to make decisions, and is subject to criticism and pressures from both directions. This does not go unnoticed by the hourly, and indeed prompts some to turn down the opportunity to enter into supervision.

This atmosphere is of serious concern and should be seriously addressed. In the first line level of supervision, as well as the second line, the makeup of personnel is employees who were once hourly. In all cases, they were thrown into the water to sink or swim. There is some merit to the old custom of throwing the youngster into the lake to sink or swim, but in this case, there are sharks in the water! What's more, the company should not be satisfied with waiting for supervisors to learn the ropes the hard way. Nowhere in society should a person be required to make such a change of venue without appropriate, suitable, and extensive training. One of the issues of "Plant Services" states that many companies are now requiring 150 to 200 hours of training of supervisors during their first year. Additionally, the company pays for off site classes that are required of their supervisors.

What are the reasons an employee agrees to accepting a supervisor position?

First, they may feel that they can make a difference. They see flaws, and they see a way, they believe, they can improve the system. They quickly learn that they were mistaken. In these instances, the company is a big loser, for they stumbled onto a valuable resource, but ignored it, and thus took an excellent hourly employee, and in time turned him into a disgruntled, and perhaps inefficient supervisor.

Another reason the promotion may have been accepted, may be that the hourly employee feels that he can handle a Supervisor's position, given the latitude; and seized upon an opportunity to make a better wage without spending extra time in the plant. These individuals sometimes regret the decision, but are unwilling to swallow their pride and return to the bargaining unit. If indeed the employee accepting the promotion was correct in his self examination, again the company has lost the use of a valuable asset.

Possible scenarios go on, but in each case the end result is that valuable assets are either misused, or overlooked. What's more, the question arises regarding the advancement of these assets. On how many occasions have hourly employees progressed to first line, second line, and then, because of their ability and expertise, been advanced further? Have any ever reached the position of Assistant Plant Manager?

It certainly goes without saying that the company brings on board very competent, well educated management people; but does that mean that the company is incapable of handling personnel of long standing to the degree that they are capable of more responsibility?

Let's move on up the ladder. What are the responsibilities of what is commonly termed, upper management? That answer has already been given in the paragraphs that precede. It is their responsibility to make it happen. So what is the point regarding, "Roles & Responsibilities.?"

From birth everyone plays one role or another. Much as an actor either accepts, or is assigned, a role to play. All the background and directions are supplied. It is a matter of following the script. However, when the position consists of being given a common goal without scripted and rigid directions, then the assignment is one of "Responsibility." Everyone's role is to make the company policy statement a fact. The responsibility of management is to plan, do, and evaluate; and to remove the obstacles to productivity. In that regard, everyone employed is a manger, or is at least in the "role."

Progress comes when "Responsibilities" are assigned, accepted, and effectively carried out. There is much that should be done, and collectively the expertise is available; but a better approach must be established one brush stroke at a time until the masterpiece is completed.

To the reader: Many words in language that have been translated from ancient writings, perhaps, have been somewhat distorted. This occurs when a language does not have a word that exactly matches the one being translated. While the translator comes very close, occasionally Society, over the years, does not fully comprehend the intent of the original author. This chapter explores just such an instance.

Chapter XXIV
Faith, Democracy, & Masonry

Faith is revered in religious circles as an objective to be attained through an understanding and belief in that which is not seen. It is not a mere acceptance of theories, nor a tacit withdrawal of opposition to that which is not apparent. It is rooted in a consuming passion for a symmetry and order in life, and an inherent desire to be part of an unconquerable sprit of all that is peaceful and proper.

Properly considered, faith cannot be viewed only from a religious perspective. It's influence in the history of man, and his events, has not been restricted to issues of the relationship between God and man. Faith has been the determining factor in the advancement of civilization, and yet at the same time, has led humanity into unwarranted calamity.

A child has faith that it will be fed, clothed, sheltered, and protected. It knows not what difficulties, or sacrifices, might be encountered in accomplishment of those ends, nor does it care. The little one puts faith in its guardian, and expects that faith to be well founded. If that faith is shaken, the child is inadvertently taught that faith is a dangerous thing.

Dependence on faith in society does not disappear with maturity. Trust is placed in our educators, our civil authorities, our government, our employer, our spouses, etc., etc. Life experiences gradually eat away at that faith until some become cynical and distrusting of society in general. Only religious faith remains unsullied.

A military unit has faith in its leadership, and its ability to guide it in accordance with an overall plan that will lead to victory. This faith establishes a willingness to follow orders even though their purpose is not understood. If adversity is consistently encountered in following those orders, faith will be lost, and the military unit will be ineffective.

Faith governs every facet of our daily lives in some manner. The alarm will go off, the doorknob will open the door, the car will start, we will arrive safely at the workplace, etc.

Oh yes, we are occasionally disappointed, but we will staunchly refuse to suffer our faith being betrayed. If the alarm does not work dependably, out it goes, and the same goes for the doorknob, the car, and anything else that lets us down.

Things mechanical do not have to falter for us to lose our faith in them. Their age and/or appearance can lead us to discard that which has been faithful in favor of a newer model.

In some instances, our faith is the victim of our expectations of others. We engage in some relationship that falls too far short of perfection, in our view, to be continued. Seldom is an open minded inquiry made to determine where the shortfall lies. Our reaction is that the other party, or parties, were undeserving of our faith, and therefore the relationship must be terminated. The instruments of termination have been many over the ages: the headsman's axe, the guillotine, the divorce court, and the ballot box, are just a few; but they relate to the disfavor of an individual. Much more calamitous is the event that disillusions a broad spectrum of people. This opens the door for dictators, despots, and all manner of unsavory characters preaching new philosophies for their own aggrandizement.

In the overall picture of this discussion, let us be mindful that in this context, faith, belief, and trust are interchangeable. On our currency is the motto, "In God We Trust." It works just as well to say, In God We Believe, or, In God We Have Faith.

We now arrive at the point of this treatise. Faith is a noun that can be the subject, or object, of a verb, or object of a preposition. Biblically, the word is used as a noun to describe a religious conviction. In transcribing the Bible into English, it is the best that could be done; however, the Greek word used in this context in original Scriptures, is a verb, denoting action, or something you do. By adding an "e" to the end, and formulating a word that rhymes with "bathe," we communicate a more correct sense of Scripture by indicating that it is not a matter of something you have, but rather something you do.

To use the word "Faith" indicates that work and study will bring us to an accomplishment of fact. With culmination, work and study are expedient; however, by using the verb "Faithe," we indicate a continuing action. To "faithe" becomes a daily task of building a firm foundation upon which unrevealed trusts can be distinguished and accepted.

The point is here made that the Bible apparently did not intend for followers to arrive at a point where they now had "Faith," and so the journey finished and completed. As the original word was a verb, it was intended that the action be a continuing one. An action of "faitheing" on a daily basis is a dedication to continuing performance, and thereby, a progressive attainment.

The second part of our consideration, is that form of government consistent with a people's right to self government. The United States is not unique in its use of Democracy as its form of government by the people, either directly, or by their elected representatives. There are several examples of Democratic Government during the past few hundred years of history, but most of them required special qualifications of the voters. Our founding fathers placed restrictions on the voting franchise that were later abandoned.

The basic tenet of Democracy is participation by all the people. No person is to be denied his, or her, inalienable rights, but the will of the majority is to prevail in all things not contrary to those rights. Difficulty arises when the people do not participate in an active and constructive manner. All too many avoid the ballot box, and thereby undermine the strength of the institution. To vote is a privilege, and a right for all citizens, but unfortunately, is optional.

Democracy works superbly when everyone participates. When a significant portion does not participate, control is left to the influence of money, special interests, and personal agendas. When citizens avoid the ballot box as well as public debate, the exercise does not result in dictatorship, but certainly becomes a down the road neighbor.

Democracy, like faith, is a noun, and again, indicates something you have. If you have it, you don't need to work for it. If you have it, you are successful, and your goal has been achieved, and therefore no reason for concern...or is there!

First, we are always subject to losing something

we have.

Second, something we have might be stolen.

Further, it might be the agenda of some person, or agencies, to alter, or in some way change what we have.

Last, what we have cannot be merely placed on a shelf and forgotten. At the very least it will need some dusting or cleaning. At the most it will need constant care, attention, maintenance, and repair.

All our possessions exist somewhere between these two parameters. outside those parameters they will be either lost, or destroyed.

We are involved in the same dilemma as with Faith. Neither Faith, nor Democracy, are reasonably maintained if considered in the noun form. Both are subject to degradation from a cavalier, or a fait accompli attitude, as well as regular attacks by contrasting ideologies. To preserve these valuable human assets, it is imperative that they receive daily attention, care, and nurturing. The effort cannot be half-hearted, nor irregular, as the attempts to denigrate these basic tenets never cease. Instead of claiming we have Faith, we need to Faithe, which we have already discussed. Instead of merely observing that we live in a Democracy, it is important that we democratize ourselves, and those around us. Like faithe, democratize is a transitive verb, and means to democratize. In so doing on a daily basis, Faith and Democracy will remain alive and strong throughout the land.

Our third consideration is Masonry, and all the word implies. The applicant's request is looked favorably, is received, and learns the lessons of an Entered Apprentice. In time he is raised a Master Mason, and perhaps pursues the York Rite, the Scottish Rite, the Shrine, and perhaps the Grotto, or other appendant bodies. However much time and money our exemplar may spend is unimportant for our study. His being a Master Mason is our first interest. We'll address his other memberships later.

Our exemplar is very proud of his membership and purchases a nice Masonic ring to wear, and a pin for his lapel. He attends two or three lodge meetings, and then his attendance becomes sporadic. After two or three years, he never attends again. Some sixteen, or seventeen years later his oldest son petitions the Lodge and is accepted. Our exemplar is now in a quandary because he doesn't remember the form of a lodge, and is afraid he will embarrass himself. He inquires of a Masonic friend, and acquires the needed information so that he can be present as his eldest son receives his work. Having been raised a Master Mason, the son quickly adopts his Father's attendance habits. There are two more sons, but having reached maturity, they express no interest in the Masonic Lodge. Finally, our exemplar questions the two younger siblings, and learns that they could care less about Masonry.

Let us examine our results so far. We had four male members of the community, the oldest expressing an interest in Masonry. The relationship of the three younger males to the oldest is such that they should be looking to him for leadership and example. Over a period of time, the lodge should be the recipient of four additional members at each meeting to assist with the work, help with the props, or assist with the festive board. Instead the Lodge picked up a few dollars from two new members who are of absolutely no benefit to the Craft. The two younger sons feel that their older brother and father must be a little vain in that the only benefit visible from their Masonic membership is their ability to wear a ring that doesn't really seem to count for much. Father and eldest son have very little Masonic knowledge, and are unaware of what it means to be a Mason…but they are!

Should our exemplar and his son spend their time and money to gain membership in all the other facets of Masonry? The only gain by the Craft will be a few more dollars scattered around in some other bank accounts. The Craft is no better off, society is no better off, and the family is no better off.

As far back as recorded history addresses the construction of edifices, it has reported the knowledge and expertise of the persons attendant to the event. The architect, the supervision, and the workmen spent several years absorbing the knowledge and skills necessary to perform their functions. They spent the rest of their lives perfecting it, which resulted in their profession being better off, society being better off, and the families being better off. In all history that has not changed.

Masonry, like Faith and Democracy, is subject to failure if looked upon as something you have rather than a lifelong endeavor of investigation, practice, and perfection. None of the three are sustained, or strengthened, by mere card carrying members, or those whose only interest is a right to wear the label. Society is neither benefited, nor progresses, by inactive attention to our three considerations.

It is beyond the expertise of this practitioner of the English language, to take either the word Mason, or the work Masonry, and ascribe, or substitute, a transitive verb as we did with Faith and Democracy. However, Masonry conveniently supplies an applicable verb in its ceremonies when it calls the Craft from refreshment to labor. Only from the proper engagement of labor has mankind improved his lot. It is the vehicle that gives hope of reaching self ascribed goals for our families, our society, and ourselves. Attainment limits through individual and collective labor have not been reached, nor are they known.

September 3, 1938, Fritz Oakes, Tulanes's veteran track coach was interviewed and asked how far he felt the pole vault record could be pushed. His reply, for what seemed valid reasons, was sixteen feet was the absolute limit it would ever go. The pole vault record today is over twenty feet.

In the late thirties, Buck Rogers, and Flash Gordon received a lot of attention from youngsters. Their parents said that men flying around in space was ridiculous fantasy, and we shouldn't fill out heads with such nonsense. Man has consistently turned fiction into fact, through his persevering labor. Our concern for this examination is whether there is some concept that will enhance the present stature of Masonry so that it will benefit families and society.

Faith, Democracy, and Masonry have outlived all their disciples except those walking the land this day. Our considerations are then to see that they are strengthened and preserved for those that follow.

Any, and all, inheritances diminish and disappear, if not properly managed, and descendants are deprived of the comfort and security of those valuable treasures constructed so painstakingly by their ancestors. Time will cover and hide the fact that the treasures ever existed, and the descendants are sentenced to beginning all over again, if they are so minded and inspired.

How are we to mange our inheritance of Faith, Democracy, and Masonry? How do we insure that our progeny will benefit from what has been constructed by those who went before us ? How can we not only return, but also add to, that which we have enjoyed?

How do we inspire our children to the importance of concerns?

"A long journey begins with a single step." Life begins with a single heartbeat; but if the heartbeats stop, the life ends, and if the steps are ceased, the journey ends. Our dedication must be deep and unfaltering. We must Faithe, Democratize, and Labor without respite to the end of our days.

The task is not only worthwhile, but is most enjoyable, self satisfying, and extremely productive.

To the reader: Much has been said, and much has been written regarding Masonry. Many have endeavored to define the institution; however, since all do not totally agree, we may presume that the efforts probably fall into the category of theories. Perhaps it is a matter of what it means to, and how each individual interprets it. Having studied several of these "Theories" prompted the following examination.

Chapter XXV
Theories

Masonry is not without its theories. It would seem at this date that all the possible theories of Masonry would have been explored and a conclusion reached. The skill and assiduity of many Masonic scholars has been, and is, of outstanding quality. Their research and study is extensive and seems to have examined every possibility without venturing in realms of over-speculation. Indeed, much circumstantial evidence by Masonic scholars has been discarded in many instances because it could not be verified with concrete, and cross checked information. There is much upon which there is agreement, and some that is not, However the question remains whether a venue has been established from which there is a reluctance to wander.

From the brilliant mind of Dr. Albert Galatin Mackey, comes the following: "The very spirit of all our lectures proves conclusively that when they were formulated, they were designed to teach pure Christianity, and while the Jewish Scriptures did forecast the intermediary of a Christos, as all the ancient heathen mysteries did also, yet Jesus Christ as shown and demonstrated in the writings of the New Testament, was not understood by the Jewish writers of the Old Testament, nor by but very few of that faith since. The first three degrees taken in connection with the Holy Royal Arch, as they have always been with our Brethren of England, certainly show pure Christianity, as taught throughout the writings of the New Testament Scriptures." This poses an interesting theory of the background and meaning of the first three degrees. Is it correct? Perhaps…perhaps not!

Ecclesiastes 12 is an Old Testament Scripture familiar to many, and a common interpretation by William Adrian Brown follows:

*"Remember now thy Creator in the days of
thy youth, while the evil days come not."*

It is the lucky youth who can look to God while he is still young enough to work hard in the vineyard of the Lord before old age comes.

*"Nor the years draw nigh, when thou
shalt say, I have no pleasure in them."*

As we age, we lose the vitality of youth to do the things which, when we were young we most desired. We become too tired to enjoy pleasures of life.

*"While the sun or the light, or the moon,
or the stars, be not darkened, nor the clouds
return after the rain."*

Refers to the earliest signs of changing eyesight.

*"In the day when the keepers of
the house shall tremble."*

The keepers of the house are the arms, shoulders, and hands. The trembling comes with the feebleness of old age.

*"And the strong men
shall bow themselves."*

The strongest of men cannot escape the inevitable; old age weakens everything, nothing can stand against it.

*"And the grinders cease
because they are few."*

In reference to the teeth, the chewing stops as we start to lose our molars. Often they do not meet the ones that are left.

*"And those that look out of
the windows be darkened."*

The windows are the eyes. Failing sight is common to old age.

*"And the doors shall be shut
in the streets, when the sound
of the grinding is low."*

The doors are the lips; the streets are the mouth by which nourishment enters; and the sound of the grinding is the human voice. In old age, when the teeth are lost, mumbling is a very common attribute.

*"And he shall rise up at
the voice of the bird."*

The bird is the crowing cock. In old age, mankind is more restless in his slumbers and early rising is a habit with many.

"And all the daughters of
music shall be brought low."

The daughters of music are the ears. The voice loses its strength and hearing becomes less acute in old age.

"Also when they shall be afraid
of that which is high."

In the declining years men fear to scale the heights that in their prime they ascended with ease and grace.

"And fear shall be in the way."

Timidity is a common fault of older people. They are filled with apprehension at the first sign of danger.

"And the almond tree shall flourish,"

Refers to the white flower of that tree, significance to old age when the hair of the head shall become white.

"And the grasshopper shall be a burden."

Again, to the weakness of old age. Even the weight of so small a thing as a grasshopper is a burden.

273

"And desire shall fail."

The appetites and desires of youth cease in the declining years.

"Because man goeth to his long home,"

Literally, to his grave as a final house for the body, or to that undiscovered country from whose bourne no traveler returns.

"And the mourners go about the streets."

To the Oriental custom of official mourners who walk in the streets and publicly lament the passing of one to the other world.

"Or ever the silver cord be loosed."

The spinal column with the silver marrow inside. This statement should be brought together with the following.

"Or the golden bowl be broken,"

The golden bowl is the brain. Its yellow color and shape; with death both the silver cord and the golden bowl break down completely.

"Or the pitcher be broken at the fountain"

The pitcher is the great vein carrying blood to the ventricle, here referred to as the fountain.

"Or the wheel broken at the cistern"

Refers to the great network of arteries that receive blood from the left ventricle of cistern and distributes blood over the body.

> *"Then shall the dust return*
> *to the earth as it was, and the spirit*
> *shall return unto God who gave it."*

This interpretation fits like a glove. It would appear that there is no doubt concerning the correctness of that which has been put forth. Perhaps…perhaps not!

More than one Masonic scholar has pointed out that Dr. Anderson and Dr. Desaugliers both being Christian ministers, and they being to a great extent responsible for the ritual, no doubt assembled the ritual in a manner that closely paralleled Christian Doctrine. Perhaps…perhaps not !

It has been said that those who assembled the ritual for the Third Degree used the Hiramic Legend to indicate the immortality of the soul and conquering of the grave by the Savior. Perhaps…perhaps not!

Another theory is that John the Baptist, in his act of Baptism was symbolizing the raising of one into a new way of life. A sort of washing off the old to take on a new identity. perhaps…perhaps not !

And so, the list goes on and on regarding interpretations of Masonic ritual, its symbols, and its philosophy; none with the authority to say this is so. It would be well if we investigate with an open mind, and a preconceived determination to look for that which most benefits the Craft.

There has been much effort to connect the Craft with the Christian Religion, and certainly the explanations are clearly defined as well as tenable. However,

Masonry, at the same time claims to be open to all who maintain a belief in one Supreme Being with no other philosophical stipulations. If the ritual and symbols are rooted in Christianity, is the Masonic Experience then really acceptable to those who do not espouse the Christian belief? Obviously not. As Christian ministers, would Dr. Anderson and Dr. Saguliers have developed the ritual in such a way, and with a predisposition to limit the focus of Masonry to Christian Principles? If it were their intent to evolve Masonry into some sort of secret Christian Society, then perhaps they would have embarked on such an effort. But what would be the purpose? Why would there be a need for such a reform? What advantage, or clotured agenda would be served? It is difficult to think of one, unless these two historic individuals had some bigger purpose than simply that of serving the Craft in general. Certainly the historic background of Freemasonry held no disposition toward any Religious Belief, other than the belief in one Supreme Being.

To believe these two men were of any such mind serves no purpose, nor benefits the Craft in any way. To assign then such a disposition seems to this writer, to establish an unwarranted cynicism.

There is a phrase which will not be new to the reader, nor revolutionary in its concept, It is: "Masonry is a search for Truth."

If we consider the operative origin of Masonry, it is consistent to state that the workmen searched for the true manner in which to erect an edifice. Engineering is based on proven facts. The architect makes his designs based on known engineering truths. Therefore, does it not follow that when the Craft becomes speculative in nature, it is based and founded on facts, or truths? A structure not erected on the truths of engineering will

276

not survive. Does it not follow that Masonry, both operative and speculative, is based on truths, or it would not have survived for several hundred years?

Engineering and architecture have historically continued to seek new facts, or truths. Modern materials have added to the scope within which these engineers and architects are able to work and design. Advancement in technology opens new fields of discovery in engineering and architecture, and thus the engineer and architect continue to seek new truths. What was once deemed impossible has, in many instances, become commonplace.

So the theory here propounded is that the basis of Freemasonry is very simple, a search for the Truth, whether one considers it in the parameters of operative masonry, or within the parameters of Speculative Masonry.

For the remainder of this discussion, rather than attempting to examine the myriad of theories relating to Freemasonry to some sort of religion, which this writer deems inappropriate, let us attempt to put this concept of Masonry being a search for Truth to the test.

First, it is imperative that we recognize that wisdom comes from truth, and truth from fact. Our everyday life is governed by what we know to be fact, or truth, and that which we do not know, we seek. Much is learned in school, but what is there absorbed will not suffice to make out lives complete. School answers a few basic questions, but opens the door to many other questions which some attempt to answer through investigation and experience. Of course, there are those who stumble through life with nothing more than what we call a formal education, never realizing that what they received in the institutions of learning was merely a key. The doors to wisdom, and there are many, can be unlocked with the keys of learning, but the door must be kicked open, entry made, and what is beyond assembled in proper fashion in order to obtain true wisdom.

Our attitude must be tempered with belief. While there is a need to operate on fact, we cannot obtain facts without beginning with a belief. Those beliefs steer us in a certain direction that we believe to be a correct avenue down which to proceed. Time may prove our belief to be fact, or it may indicate that we have taken a wrong turn somewhere necessitating a reevaluation of our belief in this particular venue. Such a setback does not mean failure, nor that we should surrender the field. It really means that we have been successful in that we have proven this particular belief to be in error, and that it needs corrected. Often it takes many failures to bring about progress.

It is time to put this theory to some sort of test. It will not be here attempted to cover the length and breadth of Freemasonry, but only to touch upon a few areas to make a preliminary review to see if we can readily discount our premise, or if it bears continued pursuit.

Earlier we referred to Ecclesiastes 12, and the interpretation that has been attached by one scholar. Let us substitute a theory that the Biblical Chapter refers to "Truth."

Previous to the Twelfth Chapter, the book of Ecclesiastes speaks to the vanity of pleasure and the necessity for fruitful labor. It warns against the rashness of words, and the vanity of riches without use. In this reflection upon the vanity of riches, Ecclesiastes points out that wisdom is indeed riches, more so than material things. Hence, it does not stretch our theory when we relate truth to the Twelfth Chapter as wisdom comes only from knowledge of the truth.

With these thoughts in mind, let's see what we can do with the Twelfth Chapter of the Book of Ecclesiastes:

*"Remember now thy Creator in the days of
thy youth, while the evil days come not,"*

It is imperative that young people be dedicated to the search for truth, before temptations of life lure then into false and evil thoughts; thereby dishonoring their Creator.

*"Nor the years draw nigh, when thou
shalt say, I have no pleasure in them,"*

For if truth is not pursued, the passage of time will bring discomfort rather than joy.

*"While the sun, or the light, or the moon,
or the stars, be not darkened, nor the clouds
return after the rain."*

Only in truth is there light, and only in its pursuit can man walk in the light. The pursuit must not be abandoned even when tempted to be disheartened.

*"In the days when the keepers of
the house shall become frightened."*

Without truth, even the leaders of men shall become frightened.

*"And the strong men
shall bow themselves,"*

And the bravest of men shall know fear.

"And the grinders cease
because they are few,"

Those who produce will become few because of the despair in not understanding life, and finally even the few will cease their operations.

"And those who look out of
the windows be darkened,"

Those who are not producers, but rather witnesses of events will discontinue their watch as all seems of no purpose.

"And the door shall be shut
in the streets, when the sound
of the grinding is low."

As work diminishes, so will interaction between people.

"And he shall rise up at
the voice of the bird,"

Fear and despair will be such that even the voice of a bird will startle the quiet over the land.

"And all the daughters of
music shall be brought low."

There will be no harmony.

"Also when they shall be afraid

of that which is high,"

Man with no perception of wisdom, and in his ignorance will be frightened of the Deity which he does not understand.

"And fear shall be in the way,"

His fear will prevent him for searching for the path of truth.

"And the almond tree shall flourish,"

The staples of nature upon which man depends will flourish and take over the land.

"And the grasshopper shall be a burden,"

There will be nothing left for man except pestilence and discord.

"And desire shall fail,"

Man will have no ambition, no desires, and no goals.

"Because man goeth to his long home,"

The future of mankind becomes terminal.

"And the mourners go about the streets."

Too late, all will be sorrowful for ignoring the pursuit of truth.

281

"Or ever the silver cord be loosed,"

The umbilical cord between man and the Deity is of the purest silver, but that cord may be loosed by the Creator, if man refuses to function as intended.

"Or the golden bowl be broken,"

He may dash the Golden container of Manna, or grace, if man refuses to seek the truth.

"Or the pitcher be broken at the fountain,:"

The container to dip from the fountain of truth may be broken from disuse.

"Then shall the dust return
to the earth as it was, and the spirit
shall return unto God who gave it."

If man does not seek the truth, and thereby obtain wisdom, then he will regress to an unproductive creature in the terms of wisdom and understanding. At that point the Creator will return man's body to the dust, and reclaim the spirit. Thence man will not have the favor of walking the earth any more.

Does the preceding make any sense? Perhaps… perhaps not!

Is the preceding correct? Perhaps…perhaps not!

Could Dr. Mackay have been misled when he determined that the lectures indicated the Chirstian trinitarian theory? Perhaps the trinitarian theory is that of the eclectic Platonists and Neo-Platonists. The trini-

282

tarian theory is defined by Numenius of Apamea as The Supreme God, Logic, and the World. The rationale being that God's connection with the World is through logic…Perhaps…Perhaps not!

Let us move on to the Hiramic Legend. Previously we said that many feel that the legend is used to illustrate the immortality of the soul and conquering of the grave by the Savior. If that is so, is not Masonry taking some sort of religious view beyond the belief in one Supreme Being? While many believe in Christ as the Savior, there are those who have different views on the subject. It has been this writer's understanding that it is not the intent of Masonry to promote any particular religious theories, but rather to keep the door of Masonry prepared for any who knock and who believe in one Supreme Being.

Let us substitute "Truth" into the Hiramic legend.

Truth is a divine attribute and the foundation of every virtue. Further, all the progress of mankind in every field has been through the discovery of the truths that pertain to that particular endeavor; whether that effort be in the field of human relations, science, business, politics, or any of a myriad of others. The pursuit of truth must be along an appropriate path step by step. There is no shortcut to revelations of any kind. If we persist in bypassing the appropriate in order to realize the mother lode, we will end up losing the ability to reach our goal. Thereby, the destination will be lost, the entire effort subjugated by impatience and greed, and we are restricted from success. Is the truth then lost forever? No, the truth still exists, but it is hidden from our eyes until such time as we can understand our error, reconstruct how it is was lost, and proceed along the proper path to resurrect it. Is this a correct interpretation of the Hiramic Legend? Perhaps...perhaps not!

John the Baptist, in his baptizing is said by some theologians to symbolize the raising of the baptized into a new life. His act a sort of washing off of the old to take on a new identity.

Indeed, according to the Biblical Book of St. Luke, Chapter 3, John was baptizing people because they had attained a new way of life. It was the "Baptism of Repentance," or a public declaration of having learned truths regarding proper conduct, and then proper relationships between people, and between people and their Creator. Masonry, through the ballot box, exhibits its confidence in the petitioner's pursuit through his youth, of these Truths regarding proper conduct between people, and his belief in a Supreme Being.

An attempt as has here been made to touch on a couple of points that will stir the reader to make his own investigation. To this writer, Freemasonry is indeed a search for the Truth about all things. Further, Freemasonry is an effort to communicate those discovered Truths by example throughout society in general, and one's community in particular. The candidate in Masonry is given certain keys with which to work, but he is not, nor will he ever be an infallible authority in the endeavor upon which he has embarked. If the neophyte Brother feels that learning the words, the symbols, and the explanations is the intent of his Masonic education, then we have failed him. It is for him to join in the never ending search for wisdom and truth. It is for all Masonic Brethren to share what we feel we have discovered with others, not as a statement of fact, but as an additional building stone on the great edifice of Truth.

The theory of this writer is as follows:

The great message of Masonry is that men can work together in peace and harmony toward the discovery of the great Truths of life, judging none in the way he chooses to worship the Supreme Being, but conducting himself in a charitable manner admirable both to the Craft in particular, and to Society in general.

To the reader: As time passes, more and more discoveries are made that astonishes us with the knowledge and expertise of those ancestors of man who seemed to have abilities and wisdom far beyond what seems reasonable. The following is the result of research into the knowledge of our ancient ancestors, and an attempt to discover the background of their mental abilities.

Chapter XXVI
Origins of Knowledge

This paper has been advertised as being the Origins of Masonry; however, the theme agreed upon was the Origins of Knowledge. Perhaps we shall discover a connection between the two, or at least some tangential evidence that promotes a gestalt not before considered.

Knowledge is not restricted to man, but is central to the existence of all living creatures. Without it, a species would be unable to provide for itself, or to propagate itself. In many instances we would consider this ability an instinct rather than true knowledge; but many species not only have the ability to provide for themselves, propagate themselves, and survive; they also have the ability to reason to some limited degree, and also to communicate with one another.

The difference between man and the creatures of this environment lies not in the size of man's brain, for the elephant, the whale, and the porpoise all have larger brains than man; however, man seems to be the only one that has almost limitless reasoning powers, and thence the ability to rationalize and invent that which he feels will be to the betterment of his lot in life.

The beaver seems content with the dam he builds, and as the generations pass, the beaver continues to build his dam in the same manner with no attempt to improve on the design of his parents. Man has never been content with his way of life, or with his inventions. No matter how useful and beneficial a device might be, man will try to improve it. No matter the superb station of man's life, he will continue to press forward in an effort to make it better.

Perhaps in man' zeal. he overlooks the obvious, for a great many of his improvements in life have ominous side effects. He discovered and made use of fire with which he proceeded to burn himself at the stake. He invented the wheel with which he ran over himself and his fellow creatures. The rope became indispensable to a good hanging, and without electricity, he would have been at a loss with his electric chair. The invention of iron gave us mace and spear, and steel provided knives and guns, all of which have been very valuable in man's destruction of himself.

Not content with the limited abilities of these items, man has developed the automobile and the airplane so that he can destroy himself in larger numbers, and in an innocent manner, as the use of the other items seemed intentional and barbaric. At last, man reached the ultimate. Through long and difficult research man has at last developed a power that enables him to destroy all of his fellow creatures as well as himself in just a few minutes. However, I hasten to point out that man has not given up. He continues to try to improve even on that which seems to be the ultimate. With the ability in hand to destroy himself in just a few minutes, man continues to research and develop ways to do it with a smaller and more devastating gadget.

Let us suppose for a moment that man attempted to destroy himself and failed because a few survived the holocaust. Those survivors would find themselves hard pressed to put this world back together as it was. They would not possess all the technology, nor the expertise, nor the facilities to accomplish such a task. No doubt they would begin again the best they could, and would spend evenings telling their children how it used to be. As time passed, the stories would be passed on from generation to generation, getting more distorted with each telling perhaps; but would the time not come as civilization grew that much of the old technology would be discovered again? Is it possible that man might foresee this holocaust and would record his knowledge for the benefit of those that might possibly survive? Is it possible that under such circumstances, the technology might take a different direction, and might the instincts of this new birth of man be channeled in a different direction? Is it possible that they would be concerned with the quality of life as relates to human relations rather than relates to human pleasures? Might they be more interested in agriculture, horticulture, and things of the spirit as relates to their maker and to each other? This would not be inconsistent with man's present preoccupation with more and more of better and better.

The instinct would be the same, but channeled in a different direction. Or conversely, perhaps man was concerned with the sprit before, and those few who survived the cataclysm, to a great extent abandoned the spiritual in favor of the material. Is it possible? Well, anything is possible, perhaps, but more important, is it likely?

Let us suppose that we have a cataclysm, rather than a man made holocaust. Is it then likely that the survivor's attention to progress would have a different direction? If either a cataclysm, or a holocaust, were to occur, and if there were survivors, what effect would

288

the event have on the minds of the survivors? Can we. with assurance, predict man's reaction in such a situation?

History teaches us that the human species seizes the first opportunity to divest itself from that which causes him discomfort, either in mind or body. Further, the human species takes the steps it reasons to be necessary to see that the discomfort does not happen again. Lastly, history shows that having experienced calamity, man takes the precautions he deems necessary to prevent recurrence, or to keep the results within tolerable limits, should he be unable to completely insure himself against the event. Should he deem the event inevitable, he strikes off in a different direction that indicates he is attempting to disregard the approaching reality.

All the foregoing is to establish background upon which we may base our premise as to the Origins of Knowledge. That knowledge that is inherent in the birds of the air, animals of the field, and the fish in the sea. That knowledge which gave man the foundation upon which to develop his mind and to invent and produce that which he desired. Perhaps some feel that it is the inquisitive nature of man that ultimately leads him to progress, but I submit that there is nothing more inquisitive than a raccoon, but he certainly has not made any great strides over the centuries. No, there has to be something much deeper that has enabled man.

Ignoring all the recent invention and additions to technology, let us jump back in time to the edge of recognition of sophisticated knowledge. Let us go back at least to 2600 B. C., and perhaps further back. Let us explore knowledge at a time when most men believed the world to be flat, a time when he thought the Mediterranean area was the extent of the earth, and centuries before the events found in the Holy Bible in the Book of Exodus. Reference is here made to the Great Pyramid of Gizeh.

Time, and consideration for your patience will not permit us to make an extensive study of this structure, but it is essential that we grasp a clear understanding of what is entailed and represented in this ancient edifice. There is no comparison between the other pyramids, and the Great Pyramid of Gizeh. The others have not the size, the perfect construction, nor the intriguing mathematics involved.

The Great Pyramid is massive, a forty story building rising from a 13 acre base. The length of one side of its base is more than two and one half football fields. Each sloping side covers five acres. The casing stones were quarried and transported across the Nile. They were 100 inches thick, and weighed fifteen tons each. They were fitted with an optician's precision, having less than one fiftieth of an inch between blocks. The cement boggles the mind of today's contractors, as it will take stone with it rather than be separated from it.

Its construction is stated variously by different researchers, to have occurred from 73,000 years ago to 2600 B. C. Evidence establishes the most likely date at 2623 B. C. However, this date must be established as the very latest date that can be considered, and it is difficult to debate with those who claim an earlier construction date. Another very likely date for its construction, other than the one mentioned is 3999 B. C. The date of construction is not particularly important, other than to understand that it is impossible for the Great Pyramid to have been constructed later than 2623 B. C.

The Pyramid is oriented exactly to true North, being off only three minutes of one degree, if one checked today. This very slight deviation has been found by archeologists and scientists to be caused by a slight subsidence of the structure because of earthquakes. The closest man was ever to come to establishing true North with his fancy instruments was 6 minutes of one degree variation. The technology of satellites has given us the ability to make these calculations with definitive accuracy today.

Long before Pythagoras, the 47th Problem of Euclid was used in the construction of the Pyramid, as well as 3.14159, the value of Pi. The huge Cathedrals of Milan, Florence, St. Paul's Basilica in Rome, and Westminister Abbey could all be placed in the base at one time. If one were to grind the stone contained in the Pyramid, and make a roadbed a foot thick and eighteen feet wide, beginning in New York City, it would reach to Salt Lake City.

The core Masonry is made up of 2.3 million stones, the smallest weighing nearly three tons, and the largest fifteen tons.

The complexities of gravitational astronomy were known by the Pyramid Builders, as well as accurate interpretations from the complex study of astrology. Both of these bodies of knowledge required thousands of years to verify, and both require mathematics that are very complicated. We are asked to believe that some time between 5000 B. C. and 2623 B. C., man stepped out of the Stone Age and into the Bronze Age with the knowledge of the Earth's orbit around the sun, the size and shape of the Earth, and the fact that our planet wobbles as it revolves around the Sun, all of which were known by the Pyramid Builders. Three thousand years later, men would be confined to prison for even suggesting such things. We think of ancient man as ignorant, but we do not live today on a planet with peoples that are ignorant. Could not some fantastic intelligence have coexisted with Cro-Magnon and Neanderthal? Let us pursue the matter a little farther.

The Pyramid is built according to the Pyramid inch. A Pyramid inch is exactly one five hundred millionth of the diameter of the Earth from North to South Pole. It differs from the present day English, and American inch by the width of one half of a human hair. The great Pyramid designer thus calculated the diameter of the Earth at 7,899.31 miles. Herschel and Colonel Clark of the British Ordinance Department calculated it at 7,899.23 miles, and astronomer R. S. Ball, later calculated it at 7,899.42 miles. Today our orbiting satellites tell us the distance is 7,899.8 miles. Fact is the Great Pyramid was right on the nose because the difference from the Pyramid to the satellite calculations reflects the accumulation of polar ice in that length of time.

In the Great Pyramid, the year circle has a circumference of 36,524.22 inches. That number is exactly the number of days in a Solar year multiplied by one hundred, or the number of Solar days in a century. Each side of the base has a hollowed in factor. When measurements are taken along the hollowed in side, rather than a straight line from corner to corner, it measures 365.256 pyramid cubits, or precisely the number of days in a sidereal, or star time year. This year is determined by the length of time it takes Earth to orbit the Sun in relation to a fixed star. There is a deeper hollowing in factor at the center of each base. When this is taken into account, it measures 365.259 pyramid cubits, which is precisely the number of days in the anomalistic year, which is the time it takes for the Earth to travel from perihelion to perihelion (the closest point to the Sun). When an arc is drawn along the hollowed in side of the pyramid base, it is exactly the curvature of the Earth.

The entrance to the Pyramid was covered in its construction; hence when the Arabs under Al Mamum tried to enter the Pyramid in search of riches, they had no idea where to start. They decided on the North face in the center. They began to dig and hammer their way into the structure. Eventually, hearing something fall off to one side, they found that the entrance passage off to the left of center by 286.1 inches. Remember that in history, the left has always been considered sinister.

The Egyptian Chronological Lists of Kings uses the Pyramid to establish and rationalize the ascension to the throne. Davidson disproved this theory when he predicted that when the rubbish was removed from around the base of the Pyramid, they would find it short of the Egyptian numeral list by exactly 286.1 inches. Indeed, this is exactly what happened. The builders apparently built this displacement factor into the Pyramid for a purpose. When the Pyramid reached the top, and the builders were ready to place the stone which was to be the "head of the corner," it was 286.1 inches too big, and hence was rejected.

Along with the entry being offset to the left by 286.1 inches, the center of the King's Chamber is offset from the East - West axis of the monument by exactly 286.1 inches. The difference in the height of the ascending passage called the "Hall of Truth in Darkness," and the "Grand Gallery," which is called the "Hall of Truth in Light," is exactly 286.1 inches. Your attention is directed to the human gestation period which is ideally 286.1 days.

The entrance passage descends according to geometric calculations. It also descends in line with a certain star that during the nearly 26,000 years it takes for the North Pole of the Earth to complete its wobble as the Earth rotates, it becomes the star we use for the North Star for a period of 1290 years during that time. On exactly the Equinox during the 1290 years, of one particular year, it has been calculated that the light from that certain star shines down the passage all the way to the bottom. On exactly that same Equinox a bench mark about thirty feet down the passage points to another star. The star that becomes the North Star is Thumen in the constellation Alpha Draconis, and the star in line with the benchmark at the same time is Alcyone in the constellation Pleiades, which is between the horns of Taurus the Bull. The last time these two stars lined up with the Pyramid was at midnight on the autumnal equinox 2623. B. C.

Moving down the passage, you come to an ascending passage that has been blocked. That passage goes upward, and is called the Hall of Truth in Darkness. The juncture of this ascending passage occurs at benchmark 1453 B. C., the established time of the Exodus from Egypt by the Children of Israel. The next juncture is the point where the floor level strikes a perpendicular to our chronograph. The floor of the Queen's Chamber drops a couple of feet without apparent reason. When this drop is extended out to meet the juncture of the Hall of Truth in Darkness, at a point the Egyptians call the "new birth." it marks the date, September 29, 4 B. C., the date of Christ's birth. Further up our chronograph, the narrow Hall of Truth in Darkness opens brilliantly into the Grand Gallery, or Hall of Truth in Light, and as previously mentioned, it opens by 286.1 inches. This marks the date April 3, 33 A. D.

In 1973, a professor from the University of Tennessee used a computer, and worked the moon cycles back in time to determine that the Crucifixion actually took place on Thursday, April 3, 33 A. D. These two points indicating the life of Christ on Earth, and the line of the floor of the Queens' Chamber combine to form a triangle on 260 plus. When this triangle is set on a rhumb line of the Pyramid, it points directly along a line that passes through the Red Sea at a place called the Sea of Reeds, the place where the Children of Israel passed through the parted Red Sea. The line passes directly through Bethlehem and on to the Jordan River at exactly the point where the Children of Israel entered the Promised Land. Further, the distance from Bethlehem to the Great Pyramid along that line is 2,159 furlongs, the accepted measure of long distance in ancient times. The distance from the Pyramid to the City of Bethlehem is the same number as the years till the birth of Christ in that city in 4 B. C.

From the foot of the great step which coincides on the original year chronograph to January 1844 which was the discovery date of the last Chapter of Acts in Constantinople, to the top of the great step, we obtain a starting time for a special chronology in which a pyramid inch equals 30 days. The Book of the Master of the Egyptians is still our allegorical authority; the actual construction remains unchanged, and our starting point has been taken off the original scale, which was determined by geometry and astronomy.

The dates roll on and on, such as the mark of the beginning of World War I, and the mark on the exact day of its end, the Great Depression, and so forth. The information and dates here presented touch only a few highlights, and therefore are confusing and hard to follow, but the intent was to impress the wealth of scientific knowledge that someone had accumulated from some source long, long ago.

There are those who scoff at the Great Pyramid and judge the information is mere coincidence and/or invention. One of those in said category was Davidson, who after retirement at an early age as a barrister in England, undertook to disprove all the "invention" surrounding the Great Pyramid. He went to Egypt, and after much research and investigation became a firm believer in the Pyramid. He wrote five volumes on the subject, and had material for another volume which he did not publish. He found a benchmark that he thought was the last one. He reasoned that by the time his volume was published, there would be no one left to read it, as he presumed the benchmark to indicate the end of the Earth. His erroneous prediction fed the naysayers. Looking back, we can see that the benchmark Davidson mistakenly thought to be the last one actually indicated the date of the pact between Hitler and Mussolini that opened the door of aggression for Hitler.

The next benchmark you wonder? It was 1952 which turned out to be the beginning of the Age of Aquarius. The next one you ask? The next one marks the year 2001[1]. We'll see!

Referring you to Isaiah 19: 19 and 20 which in part states. "In that day shall there be an altar to the Lord in the midst of the Land of Egypt, and a pillar at the border thereof to the Lord." The Great Pyramid is in the midst of Egypt, and on the border between Upper and Lower Egypt.

The Hebrew language did not contain numbers, as does our language. They used letters for numbers as well as for words. If you assign the numerical quantity to each letter in the preceding noted verses of scrip-

---

1 *This paper was presented a couple times during the 1970's. The Pyramid was correct. 2001 was indeed a year of note in history.*

ture, and total those numbers, you arrive at a total of 5,449. That is the exact height of the Pyramid.

Within the King's Chamber there lies a coffer. The dimensions of the coffer are exactly correct to house the Ark of the Covenant, according to the dimensions stated in the Holy Bible. And so the remarkable prophecy contained in the Pyramid goes on and on, and also the remarkable accuracy in which the Pyramid relates all the facts about our Earth as well as correct astronomy. The mathematics are really unbelievable when the time of the construction of the Pyramid is considered.

The Great Pyramid of Gizeh is the oldest structure on the face of the Earth, and at the same time it reflects an intelligence and a knowledge that was not matched until the last twenty-five to thirty years; and even so, there is still much about the Pyramid that we do not understand.

Obviously in relation to our question, the Origins of Knowledge predate the Great Pyramid. That is to say that highly technical knowledge and skills existed previous to 2623 B.C., but apparently they were somehow lost. One possibility for this loss is the fire that destroyed the Library at Alexandria. The claim of some historians is that said fire set the World back approximately 2000 years as all knowledge, inventions, and information were stored at Alexandria.

To trace origins previous to the construction of the Pyramid is not possible if one is required to prove his points in a court of law. If one is to accept circumstantial evidence, and to piece together what might appear to be unrelated items, it is possible to arrive at a gestalt that answers many questions, including our own.

Let us then proceed with a theory that fits together very nicely. After the Edenic state was brought to a close, man's fist civilization began on a huge continent that is now almost entirely submerged beneath the Pacific Ocean. The dawning of this first civilization took place about 78,000 years ago, and though people did not strive to attain the technological heights we have reached in modern times, they far surpassed us in the ability of society to help citizens generate purpose, peace, prosperity, and character growth. Some time prior to the time this civilization, often called Lemuria, was destroyed by a cataclysmic shift in the Earth's crust, migrants developed a civilization on a large group of islands that are now beneath the Atlantic Ocean. This was the beginning of the legendary civilization of Atlantis.

Other civilizations also developed. One was called Osiris and existed in what is now the floor of the Mediterranean, and the other was called Rama and existed in India. These latter civilizations, especially Atlantis, developed a sophisticated technology with equipment that would amaze us today.

The continent of Mu, another name for Lemuria, in the Pacific was destroyed by a major cataclysm about 26,000 years ago. The sinking of the huge land mass lowered the world's water level considerably and joined the island of the Posied Archipelago into a continent situated in the present day Atlantic. This continent was itself submerged in two minor cataclysms and disappeared beneath the ocean about 11,000 years ago.

If these truly existed, where is the proof? It lies beneath the ocean under rocks, and lava, and mud. Most of the evidence of previous civilizations was swallowed by cataclysms, but there is an outstanding amount of evidence that such civilizations indeed existed. In the Pacific Islands alone there is enough evidence of previous civilizations to obliterate the theory that the cradle of civilization was the Middle East. Geologically speaking, the continent of Mu, or Lemuria, is clearly outlined. The Tectonis Plate of Mu from North America, South America, and Asia encircles the vast area that includes all of Australia, New Zealand, the Philippines, Oceania, and part of North America. That California and Australia are part of the same continent seems borne out by matching soils and flora. The Eucalyptus and Acacia are native only to Australia and California. The story that the Eucalyptus trees were imported from Australia to California is widely circulated, and it is true of some species, especially those grown for use as power poles. However, there are Eucalyptus trees found along the central coast that are hundreds of years old and are definitely indigenous to California.

Within the Ring of Fire, the islands of Ocenia are dotted with the ruins of some ancient and generally unexplained culture. The island peoples living there today, obviously did not build those same ruins of the Lemurian Society. On Poape, one of the Caroline Islands, there are ruins of a city that could conceivably have housed more than a million people. Today there are less than 50,000 inhabitants on all of the Caroline Islands.

It is pointed out in the book, "The Ultimate Frontier," by Eklal Kueshana, that this ancient city is called Metlanim, and the ruins contain stones weighing up to fifteen tons apiece. The stone used is not found on the islands today. Referring to Metalanim, the Author of "The Ultimate Frontier;' says: "Artificial waterways capable of passing a modern battleship intersect the city." Metalanim is remarkable for its architecture and engineering excellence, and is not at all like the primitive works one associates with the natives of Oceania. This city was apparently built by the people of Lemuria of rock, hewn from now submerged islands.

In Mexico, and in South America, pyramids exist in remote areas today which gives further credence to the thought that some ancient civilization existed that was far advanced in technology and engineering, and that they indeed appeared in several places in the Western World.

Egyptian histories in referring to the Great Pyramid of Gizeh, refer to a people called the Hyksos, also referred to as the Shepherd Kings. These people arrived in Egypt in a peaceful manner, and without violence took over the country through their superior intellect. They organized the workmen and were responsible for the engineering and knowledge to construct the Great Pyramid. They also were able to cause the Egyptians and their Priests to abandon their heathen worship practices, and introduced devotions to just one God. After some time the Hyksos moved on, and the Egyptians returned to their previous Religious practices, and to their Pharaoh Man-Gods to lead them. They retained none of the knowledge of the Hyksos in reference to technology as none had been imparted to them. The Pharaohs tried to imitate the structure of the Pyramid to build tombs for themselves, as they believed the Great Pyramid to be a divine edifice.

One more item of interest to our exploration and search for the Origins of Knowledge comes from very recent archeological finds that are called the Celtic Cauldron. Archeologists believe they show and prove that Noah was a Mongol rather than a Caucasian as previously surmised. Putting all this information together, we arrive at the following theory:

Noah and his family being Mongols were in-

300

habitants of a land far to the East of the Mediterranean area. That land was situated in the Pacific, and was called Mu, or Lemuria. Being apprised by the Great Architect of the approaching cataclysm, they constructed the Ark according to instructions. When the Ark floated on the deluge, it took a westerly course that would be consistent with the wind and the tides. Following the deluge, they found themselves in a new land that is now the Middle East. The Hyksos, or Shepherd Kings, also came from a land far east of Egypt, according to Egyptian writings, and therefore, it is entirely possible that they were the descendants of Noah, or other survivors of the cataclysm, depending on the time frame involved. Certainly from the Bible, and the Lost Books of the Bible, we know that Shem had great knowledge, and that many very knowledgeable men gleaned their wisdom at the knee of Shem.

The Hyksos, and/or, the descendants of Noah, were not only extremely far advanced in engineering and astronomy, but they also held the wisdom of divine prophecy. In constructing the Pyramid, they erected an edifice that contained not only the knowledge of a previous civilization, but correctly conveyed the divine wisdom for civilizations to follow.

In assembling all of these pieces of information and discoveries, and in carefully studying the almost stunning revelations of the Great Pyramid, we arrive at the thought that knowledge comes from only one source and that is from the Great Creator. It might be thought that man has the ability to discover and invent, but he certainly does not have the ability to make divine prophecies. Those who constructed the Pyramid had both; hence, it must be deduced that along with the divine revelations made to them, they were also given the knowledge of geometry and astronomy necessary to erect the Great Pyramid, and preserve those divine revelations.

While the preceding might be deemed interesting, one might inquire as to what all this has to do with Masonry. Well, let us examine the Land of Mu. When referred to as Mu rather than Lemuria, the inhabitants would be know as Musons. Let us not forget that the character for the letter "U" in ancient Hebrew is also the character for "O" and "A"; so, it is entirely possible that rather than Musons, the people might have been known as Mosons, or Masons.

WOW! Is that grasping at straws, but would it not be consistent with the character of the Craft for ancient engineers to possess the knowledge to construct a magnificent edifice in peace and harmony, and then to move on? Is it not consistent with the character of the Craft to keep inviolate the knowledge it possesses? Is it not consistent with the character of the Craft to have the ability to organize, assign tasks, and accomplish great things in society without violence and discord, even among the uninitiated?

The theoretical conclusion is then here presented that the Origins of Knowledge lie with the Great Creator, and that he conveyed the knowledge to set forth prophecy and knowledge in the Great Pyramid to a people who existed long before recorded history, in a land that does not now exist, and who either were the forerunners of Freemasons, or who were very much like the latter day Craft. If man developed an interest in peace and harmony with himself, and the world around him, and then was nearly wiped out by a cataclysm, would he then perhaps, be inclined to concentrate his efforts on material items of pleasure? Is it possible that over time, he has come to view fact as some distorted theory? Has he developed a callous, and unbelieving attitude toward the possible?

One final point to make before closing this treatise. Alongside the Great Pyramid of Gizeh lies the Sphinx. What is the background and history of this remarkable stone so close to the Great Pyramid." There have been some opinions on the Sphinx, but none that seem to particularly relate to the Great Pyramid itself.

Permit me to put forth my own determination. It has long been presumed that the Sphinx is part man, and part lion. We have no photographs, or records, to indicate that the presumption is correct. The face has been partially disfigured. The headdress worn by the Sphinx was commonly worn by both men and women of nobility in ancient Egypt. My thought is that the Sphinx is part lion, and part woman!

If our premise is true, then we have represented, Virgo and Leo, which in ancient times were the first sign of the year and the last sign of the year. If true, then perhaps the Sphinx is stating that here to my left (the sinister side) is Alpha and Omega, the beginning and the end!

Ignore what is here presented to you at your own peril!

Is this present exercise a whole lot of hogwash… maybe…but it's interesting!

To the reader: A number of years ago, I was asked to speak at a Masonic event regarding the relationship between the Order of DeMolay for young men, and the Masonic Fraternity. The story of circumstances surrounding the origin of DeMolay in Kansas City, Missouri, by Frank S. Land in 1919 is an interesting one. However, at the time, my decision was to attempt to make a point regarding the importance of DeMolay not only to the Craft, but also to society.

Chapter XXVII
Responsibility, Our Heritage

In the life of a man there may occur a few truly great moments, but for many an individual an entire lifetime flits by without the passing of a single episode worthy of note. The young men of DeMolay, on the night of their initiation, experience a memorable and auspicious occasion in their lives when they take upon themselves the obligation of the Order.

They were caused to realize that they must begin now to prepare for the responsibilities that are their heritage. Responsibilities that have been passed from father to son since time immemorial, and that are just as vital to the security of posterity as the continued blessing of our Divine Creator. Responsibilities that have been instilled in mankind by the Supreme Grand Master of Heaven and Earth, and that are inherent in each and every one of us.

Through the ages, many men and women have recognized a duty to posterity and accepted, cultivated, and worked diligently to perform more than their fair share of the responsibilities of scientific advancement. social compatibility, and religious conviction and faith. Some however, for one reason or another, have lacked either the ability, or the opportunity to perform what might be considered their due portion of the labor of the moment. But in view of their devoted effort in the face of obscurity, I am confident that although their names may never appear in our history books, or their likeness be exhibited in marble, they are, nevertheless, dearly beloved by their descendants, and have secured an ineffable and eternal happiness in the world to come. Surely, no man or woman could ask more than this.

Down through the ages man has striven to improve his knowledge, his way of life, and his relationship with his fellow man. Many have contributed their small share to the great forward movement of civilization, until there has now been forged a tremendous chain that links us closely with our forefathers, and shackles us to the future of mankind on God's Good Earth.

Nothing remotely approaches the importance of our responsibility to mankind. Without it our very existence today would take on a meaningless atmosphere that is frightening to the imagination. History plainly outlines the strength and conviction with which our forefathers accepted and carried out the task of promoting the general welfare of their contemporaries. Their efforts on behalf of civilization have been such that we can count it one of our many blessings to have been placed on this earth by our Creator in these modern times. The countless conveniences that we take for granted are the result of sweat from the brows of those who have gone before, and it is not only our dream, but also our responsibility that we make the world even more pleasurable and safe for our children.

But we must keep foremost in our minds that the material things of life are just as capable of corrupting our civilization as enhancing it. The resultant good of any of our scientific advancement depends on the verve with which we have accepted from our ancestors the responsibility of following the precepts and ideals that should animate us all.

We must work diligently and actively on the development of the intangibles of our everyday life. Early man was concerned only with food, shelter, and the propagation of his own kind, but as the generations passed, man increasingly realized his responsibility to his children and to his children's children. He strove to improve his mind and his thoughts that he might pass on to his children, through education, the tools of the mind that would enhance their lives.

Through the years, man has, through trial and error, solidified his moral precepts and ideologies so that today we are blessed with the enrichment of our lives by an all-encompassing conviction of religious belief and faith. Our forefathers gave of their life's blood that we might be afforded the peace of mind and an immeasurable security that is our inheritance from them.

For us to ignore our responsibility of continuous everyday effort toward a world united in the just fear and worship of our Divine Creator would be blasphemous and tragic.

Moral precepts such as are taught and illustrated in DeMolay ceremonies are as chaff in the violent wind of hypocrisy and its resulting degradation, unless we unite in actively living the lives and setting the examples we fervently desire our children to follow.

The God of our Fathers has blessed each one of us with varying talents, but he has fashioned us all with one common denominator...a chain of responsibility to our children forged with the indestructible steel of

306

devout conviction not only to emulate the teachings set forth by Him, but also to work and strive actively and diligently to cement in the minds of our youth the moral precepts and religious ideologies without which the world would sink into chaos.

However, if we sow the seeds of morality and social conformity without the fertilizer of resolute purpose, we will have plagued future generations with a weakness that will destroy them.

We, of DeMolay, urge every man and woman to join with us as we stoke the furnace of posterity with the fuel of responsibility. Roll up your sleeves and help us as we pick up the hammer of righteous morals and forge an indestructible link in the responsive chain of human relations, As we work together, never be discouraged because we meet with indifference from those around us even though our purposes are commendable. For though our capabilities can never approach the hallowed example, we nevertheless are inspired, and our efforts ignited by the fact that the most successful and most enduring endeavor ever undertaken on this Earth, was accomplished by a carpenter from Nazareth, and just eleven loyal disciples.

Each of us has inherited the responsibilities of world direction and management. Each of us has inherited the responsibility of preparing the next generation for the day they claim their rightful inheritance. And each of us has inherited the conscience and the conviction that stimulates us not only to the acceptance of these tasks, but also to an abiding determination that we shall not fail.

To the reader: A number of years ago this writer was a partner in a camp, deep in the mountains of West Virginia. While trout fishing, a beautiful waterfall was encountered. Lunch was enjoyed more than once at that wonder of nature. In the fall and winter that same waterfall was encountered while rabbit hunting, and again, lunch was partaken. The writer sat at the base of the falls, and was somewhat mesmerized watching the water. Contemplation on those two events gave rise to the following paper.

Chapter XXVIII
Beyond the Waterfall

Water, life's liquid, is encountered daily, and when questioned, all attest to its precious necessity. The very word triggers mental pictures of manmade fountains standing amid a square of resplendent architecture; or the pleasurable vision of a lake, or reservoir, framed with the greenery of summer, or the euphony of color on a bright autumn day. Or perhaps one recalls the imposing scene of the giant wonder of nature, Niagara Falls, with its overwhelming display of strength and power. But none of these visions relate to water in its true perspective.

To absorb all that life's elixir has to give, and teach, the student must make two trips. The first cannot be dictated by planned itinerary. It can only be timed by selecting a lovely spring day when the weather is clear and comfortable, and life is springing again into nature. Trees have budded and leafed, flowers are blooming; birds are busy with their songs and tending to their nesting. The day must be one that epitomizes the rebirth of life with the inherent promise of a continuation of that which has been.

Anywhere in the majestic hills of West Virginia

will do for the origination of our journey with no preference given to general direction. Arriving at a starting point, simply work your way into a convenient hollow with a good stream of water. Then work your way upstream noticing the aforementioned awakening of nature along the way until you reach your objective - a waterfall.

As you draw near the fall, the change in sound draws your attention. At first, the meandering stream seems lazy and quiet, moving through the forest effortlessly, and with a dignified grace. As you work your way upstream, you begin to hear restlessness in the water from up ahead, with the rush of sound becoming more pronounced as you near the falls.

Having reached your goal, let us examine and contemplate; but first, let us refresh ourselves. Finding a suitable rock at the foot of the waterfall, make yourself comfortable, and off with the shoes and socks, up come the pant legs and into the water go our lower appendages for rest and relaxation. Now…out of your pocket with a peanut butter and jelly sandwich, or whatever your favorite might be, along with a piece of your favorite fruit. One item you purposely do not bring…a thermos. When it becomes necessary to assist the dissolution of our sandwich with liquid, we have nature's own cool, clear, life giving liquid right in front of us. However, it would not be appropriate to bring a cup, or any other sort of contrivance to bring the liquid refreshment to our lips. You must go to it.

Lie down, brace yourself on a couple of convenient rocks, and lower yourself down to that cool refreshing stream. Remember to tilt your head so that your nose does not encounter the water before your lips. Having reached the proper position, purse your lips like Grandma used to do when she kissed you, and draw in the delicious refreshment, being careful not to close your eyes. It is important to the psyche of the moment to observe yourself in nature's mirror during this most pleasant enterprise.

Now that you are refreshed, it is time to explore our subject - beyond the waterfall! You recall working your way upstream, so to direct your attention back downstream is to view that which is known, that which is past. We observed the rocks, the eddies, the riffles, and the pools. We saw the trees, the flowers, and all the things that these little droplets of water in front of us will encounter and pass on their journey downstream. That which lies ahead of the water is to us, in our view, unknown to the water, We contemplate it has no idea whether the route ahead will be such that nature's elixir will be dashed and tossed, churning it into a turbulence of spray; or perhaps what lies ahead will be peaceful and calm with pools and lazy eddies and only an occasional little riffle. We feel the water knows not, but that we know, for we have been there.

Are we then superior to the water by reason of knowledge of what lies ahead, and it does not? As we watch the tumbling and thrashing before us at the foot of the fall, can we so inflate our ego with the ability to admonish the water of what lies ahead? Are we able to advise and prepare it for its future?

Hardly, for indeed we are not superior to the water, for we know not what is beyond the waterfall, but the water does for it has been there. Well, perhaps we can journey farther, but we will never reach the water's source. We will be eventually dead ended by a spring, a run off, or some similar barrier to our knowledge. The water will always know something that we do not!

It will be best if we are content to sit by the waterfall and listen to the wisdom of the water. As it tumbles and churns over the rocks, it talks to us of all that it has seen - the beauty, the wonders, and the rebirth of nature. It tells of the life it has fostered within itself as well as that along its banks. If one is patient, the water will explain that we are incorrect in our assumption that we can apprise it of what lies ahead, for it has been there many times before.

Yes, it passed this way before, was picked up at some point by a squall at sea, or perhaps evaporated in the heat of a southern clime, but in any event, was carried aloft, moved by the winds and eventually deposited again on Mother Earth to make its way downstream after furnishing nature with a shower and a cool drink. In reality, with all our knowledge there is nothing we can tell the water, but there is much it can communicate to us if we will but listen.

The water has traveled the mountain streams, moved along creek beds, flowed majestically in great rivers, and stretched farther than the eye can see in the great oceans of the world. It has been carried aloft and traveled the heavens only to return again and repeat its journey. Open your mind, clear it of preconceived notions, and listen carefully as you gaze into the waterfall and the stream. Be patient and attentive, and it will enlighten you.

But we spoke of two trips. What is the destination and objective of the second?

The destination is that same waterfall, and the objective is to seek more knowledge. However, the timing is different. This trip must occur in the fall when the animals are storing up for the approaching winter. The leaves have turned their brilliant hues, and are one by one drifting lazily to earth.

Our goal having been reached, we noticed along

the way that everything to be seen is preparing for the long cold days ahead; or is preparing for the apparent dissolution brought on by winter's chill. Refreshing ourselves as before, it is time to again hearken to the water as it tumbles and churns ever the falls. Are those indeed the exact same droplets that we observed in the spring? They very well may be, but if not, there certainly is no distinguishing them from the ones to which we previously listened. Again, one must clear the mind, observe, and listen intently to the water. It tells of its travels since last we saw it. That while the world is changing, at the same time, it remains the same. We learn of the successes, the living things sustained, the crops grown, the earth cleansed and refreshed except in those places where the water was not properly appreciated; those places where it was abused, and amongst those people who listened not to the water, but rather tried to impress it with tales of what lie ahead. In those cases, the water returned not, but favored its life giving elixirs to whom and where it was respected.

As we listen, the water warns that with the coming winter, there are those who will charge that all is lost for everything is dying. Even the water will freeze over, and discontinue its activities, they will assert. Those faint of heart wander off aimlessly overlooking that which is right in front of them, ignoring the obvious because they began to preach, and cease to listen. We who listen are reminded that under the ice, the water continues its journey; that the snows of winter are a more appropriate manner for the water to replenish the springs that feed the ground. We are thus informed that winter is not a dying, not a pause, but simply continued progress and nourishment in a different form.

And so it is with Masonry. We must make

the effort to go to an appropriate place to listen and to learn. It is not for others to lead us there, but for each in his own heart to seek out knowledge. It is not for us to tell Masonry where it is going, for it knows whence it travels, and from whence it came. The true voice of Masonry comes not only from the ritual, but also from its history, and most especially from those whose hair has turned white at the edges, and whose step has shortened and slowed. They made those trips where contemplation taught the neophyte, and are the living connection to that which has been found productive, as well as that which has been found wanting. Sit down, rest and refresh yourself at the stream of Masonry. Be Attentive, and listen to the voice of Masonry. It will instruct the younger with the lessons of life, and assure them of continued sustenance as long as they appreciate and do not mistreat the stream of Masonry. As the water keeps the earth fresh, clean, and healthy, so Masonry will do for its society of members. But woe unto those who ignore and abuse, for they are doomed to a symbolic dust and parched spirit.

As water at the fall assures us that winter is appropriate for some of its chores, so is the wizened Masonic senior citizen admonished. Masonry comforts him by pointing to the evergreen as a sign of the continuance of life into the following spring. While the coming of winter inflicts thoughts of termination and dissolution, if we will but listen to the water along with its ally, the evergreen, we will learn that contrary to our thoughts, the wintertime of age is rather the beginning of rebirth, and an ultimate promise of continuance.

For those who will listen, those who will adhere to and respect what is heard, there is much to be learned about life and Masonry - Beyond the Waterfall!

To the reader: The following paper was written after reading the book, "Van Loon's Lives." The book stirred many thoughts, but the chapter recalled in the paper brought rise to what this writer thought provoking.

Chapter XXIX
Would he, would they?

Simon and Schuster published a book in 1942 titled, "Van Loon's Lives." It was written and illustrated by Hendrik Willem Van Loon, and it is here most heartily recommended to you. The premise of the book is that Van Loon and his friend, are able to leave a note under the old lion statue by the town hall requesting notables of history to honor them with their presence for dinner. For example, Mozart, Hans Christian Anderson, and St. Francis of Assisi, attended one of their dinners. One of the oddities is that at the stroke of midnight, the visitors suddenly disappear.

On the evening in question, after dinner and some enjoyable conversation, Mozart was intrigued by the sounds of his music being played on a phonograph record by a modern orchestra. At a quarter to twelve, Mozart said that was enough music, and suggested that Anderson tell one of his stories, and suggested that he tell one that he remembered, but had never told when he was alive. Anderson replied that indeed he had such a story, lit his pipe, and began. What follows is from that chapter of "Van Loon's Lives."

Anderson began, "Once upon a time, the good Lord decided that He had been just a little lax in the attention He had paid to the human race, and that He ought to go on a short tour of inspection. So, He went to St. Peter to ask him the best method of reaching Earth for there had been so many changes in the course of the planets since He had last visited that particular part of the stellar system, that He was afraid He might lose His way or get hurt, and He wanted to refresh His memory. To His great surprise, He found St. Peter none too enthusiastic about the idea, and He asked him what was on his mind that he offered so many objections. 'Dear Lord,' good St. Peter answered, 'it is, after all none of my business what You do, or don't do. I only work here, and You are the boss, as I used to say to James and John in the olden days when I worked for them on the Sea of Galilee. But will You allow me to ask You a question?

'Of course, I will,' the good Lord replied. 'Well then, You remember, when You created that particular planet You called Earth, how You said it was going to be your 'great experiment' and how You meant to make it as beautiful and lovely as You could and how You were going to create a new kind of being - You meant to call him man - and he and his fellow men were not only going to be given full possession of that delightful garden in which You intended that they should spend their days, but You were going to do something You had never done before. These so-called men were going to be endowed with a will of their own - ' free will' was the expression You used, I think - and they were not going to be bound by any hard and fast rules, but they were going to be allowed to act according to what they themselves thought the right way to act. Of course, all that was long before my time, but You often told me about it when I came here first, and when You seemed very much depressed, and said that You had just experienced the worst disappointment of all eternity.'

315

'You are perfectly correct, my dear Peter,' the Lord answered, 'All that is exactly as you say.' Saint Peter stroked his long white beard a couple of times before he was ready to go on. 'Well then, dear Lord,' he continued, 'here is the question I always wanted to ask You, but I never had a chance before. It might have seemed an impertinence on my part, but this gives me good excuse.'

The good Lord had not the slightest idea what His faithful old gatekeeper was driving at, but as He always had felt a very warm liking for this plain-spoken old fisherman, He told him, 'Go ahead, beloved friend, go ahead and ask Me anything you want.' Once more St. Peter ran his hand down his beard, and then he asked his question. 'Dear Lord,' he said, 'we have known each other for a great many years now, and when one loves a person as I love You, one comes to know a great many things about him he never thinks you have even guessed at, for everybody is always sure that he can hide his thoughts by frowning or looking solemn or smiling or something.'

'I know,' the Lord replied, 'that was one of my cleverest ideas, and I am very proud of it - that ability I bestowed upon people to hide their thoughts.' 'And You think, Lord, that You Yourself are any good at it?' asked Peter, who had not been born to be a yes man. 'Yes, I rather do,' the Lord replied. 'Well then, I am afraid, Lord, that You have another guess coming, which, of course, is not the way I should talk to You, but that is what I feel.' 'Forget it,' said the Lord, 'We are old friends. We can speak our minds. Forget it and ask your question. What is it? 'Well then, good Lord, since You insist. I know what great hopes You had set on that famous experiment of Yours on that little planet, and how You were full of hope for the future, for

316

now at last You had created a being after Your own image and had given him a fine place of residence and an abundance of free will. That was a combination that must succeed - that could not possibly go wrong.'

This time it was the turn of the Lord to stroke His beard. 'I remember,' He answered. 'Well then, what I have always wanted to ask You, but never had a chance to do so until now, when You want to go back there..."Yes, Yes" the Lord interrupted him. 'What is it?' 'What I wanted to ask You is this. If You had to do it all over again - this experiment with this strange bi-ped created after Your own image and endowed with a will of his own which he could use for either good or evil - would You do it Again?"

Hans Christian paused. I used the opportunity to look at my wristwatch - one more minute!
Go on, I begged him. Tell us the rest. Yes, but my pipe has gone out, and I lost my little tindersticks. I lit a match and held it over his pipe in such a hurry that I almost burned his long nose. Hans Christian was a very deliberate fellow when it came to lighting his pipe. Finally, it was done, He took a deep puff.

'Please go on,' I told him, 'what did the Lord answer? Go on - we have only a few seconds.' One more pull - a minute before midnight. Then he said, 'The Lord took quite a while, for this was a very important question - the most important one He had ever been asked - then He answered, You ask Me whether I would do it again - create an animate being after my own image and endowed with that freedom of choice between evil and good which is part of my own omniscience, but without that wisdom and experience which I have acquired during an eternity of thoughtful contemplation and practical application.'

Two more seconds to go. "It is very difficult to

give you a direct yes or no" ...one more second..."but on the whole, I feel inclined to say that..."

Bong said the clock outside. The room was plunged into darkness and our guests were gone!

This ends the particular chapter from "Van Loon's Lives." That is an intriguing question. Would not all of us like to know what the Lord would answer to such a inquiry?

Certainly God cannot be pleased with the results of His great experiment. Through the centuries man has worked diligently to promote his own personal welfare, primarily without regard to the consequent impact on his environment. He has repeatedly exhibited an insatiable appetite for creature comforts and literally raped the Earth and its atmosphere in the process. But the most distressing realization is man's intolerance for himself. With few exceptions he has, and continues, to exhibit greed, jealousy, and arrogance that contradicts the basic premise of civilization. He has repeatedly used his talents and abilities to create a world of technology that is advancing faster then the mind can encompass. But with it all he has not yet learned to live with himself, nor to truly enjoy God's most precious gifts.

From the dawn of recorded history man has slaughtered himself in the name of politics, in the name of religion, and for reasons of greed and jealousy. Most were never satisfied with what they had, but coveted their neighbors success. While smiling and complimenting their neighbor, underneath they were envious. The Creator laid down his text and guidelines for happiness and enjoyment clearly and concisely in his Great Book. His Book is not a mystery, nor some coded work that needs deciphered, but the world is replete with those who feel compelled to interpret it for us, and tell us what it really means. There are a myriad of Bible teachers who are sincere in their work, and are a blessing in leading us in the worship and praise of God's glory. They are effective in leading us in our study of God's great works, and we give thanks for them. However, there are those who interpret, decipher, and try to lead us to believe that we cannot follow God's Book without their wise counsel. They are easily recognized, for all their protestations, it is obvious that they are obsessed with the accumulation of wealth through Religion..

Despite man's innate intelligence, he often seems to lack the wisdom to concentrate his best efforts in learning how to live in harmony with himself. He is obviously more concerned with inventing a new toy, or some new way to either slaughter himself, or ruin his environment. And the most amazing thing about all this is that when each is questioned, he agrees that something must be done along these lines. He states that he is all for it, and will be glad to freely do his part, but that it is the other fellow that is the problem and that it is hopeless.

Observation has taught the writer that in the area of human relations, man can, at times, be totally and helplessly stupid. This nation is over two hundred years old, and yet we still are changing and adding to our laws because many of our citizens keep diligently working on how to do the other fellow in without breaking existing laws. If the citizens would only quit this endeavor, there would be no need for most of the laws we now have, and no need to add continually complex clarifications to the body of law in our society. What is wrong with this country - ask around! The poor man says the rich man sucks up everything and consequently there is little left for him. The rich man says the poor man won't work and wants everything given to him as his right, and without any accompanying responsibility.

Ask the man in the middle, and he says they are both right.

Ask a Republican what is wrong with the country, and he will give you a lesson on the failed policies of the Democrats. The Democrat states that Republicans do not understand what the common people really need and want; hence, the trouble with the country is the responsibility of failed Republican policies.

A great deal of industry in the United States is in trouble, and the problem is that we do not have one single business in this country that is run properly - ask any of the employees! Management emphatically asserts that the sole root problem of American Industry is the lack of production by the employees. The employees are only interested in picking and complaining. They have been raised in the economic scale to unprecedented heights, but are never satisfied. Well, the examples go into every facet of life on this planet; countries, religious denominations, races, etc, etc.

My submission to the examination of this topic is that while man has indeed learned to communicate almost to distraction, he has not learned to listen, nor has he learned to say what is in his heart. Man says, and does, what he believes will be the most advantageous to himself.

Permit me to present the following example from personal experience.

While advancing through the line of the Grand Commandery of West Virginia, it is required that Grand Officers inspect two or three constituent Commanderies each year; thus, when reaching the office of Grand Commander, it is presumed that you will have visited each of the Commanderies in the state. In the early years of my travels, the Commander of a Commandery, which I had been assigned to inspect, called to ask by what route I would be entering his city. He asked that I arrive by a certain time previous to the meeting, and that he would meet me at a prearranged location. Upon arriving at the appointed spot, he took me to his home for some tea and pastries. While enjoying the repast, he asked that I listen to his Commander's ritual work. I listened carefully, and upon conclusion complemented him on his preparation, assuring him that he would be excellent in his presentation later that evening. He informed me that he had just wanted me to know that he was proficient in his work, but that he would not be doing it that evening. He explained that one of the Past Commanders always performed the work of the Commander, and that the Commandery was reluctant to refuse him. This Past Commander had been, and continued to be, a dedicated Templar, and he obviously felt disposed to do the Commander's ritual work. The Sir Knights did not want to hurt his feelings

At the lodge hall, I stood in the hallway exchanging pleasantries with the Sir Knights, and soon the Past Commander in question made his appearance. He and I were talking when the current Commander and a couple of other officers approached and asked the Past Commander if he was going to do the work that evening. He replied that he guessed so.

After they left, he turned to me and said that he sure wished these officers would learn their own work. He said he was tired of having to keep sharp on the ritual when it was their responsibility to do so. I suggested to the Past Commander that when the evening was over, he go to the officers and inform them that he had enjoyed doing the work over the years, but that tonight was the last time. There would be plenty of time before the next presentation and they should be prepared to be on their own as he would not even be in attendance on the next occasion of ritual work to ensure that they would do the work themselves. Such was done, the Past Commander remained active, and the officers did their own work.

The previous story might be interpreted by some as a good example of a lack of communication. I submit that it was a case of not letting the other fellow do his job, and further that the Sir Knights did not listen when they talked to that Past Commander. They felt it was something he wanted to do, but it was obvious to me that it was not ,from the tone and manner of his conversation with them. We must listen to the other fellow, and we must permit others to do their job. Not only does man complain that the other guy doesn't do his job properly, but he insists that he can do it better. The world is full of experts on what the other fellow is doing wrong. Each time we denigrate someone else, or what we perceive is another category of people, no doubt much worse is being said about us. I have known a few people in my time that I never heard make a derogatory remark about a fellow human being. If confronted with someone who failed, they expressed the opinion that no doubt he had done his best, and that the present circumstance would be a learning experience, and would thereby add to the proficiency of the next attempt.

I said a few…I can count them on one hand, and the truth and beauty of the matter is that I never heard anyone say anything derogatory about those few. Truly, you reap what you sow.

So, would God do it again, given the question ?

The final results are not yet in, and I like to think that he would hold his answer for further developments.

Let us take the question to another premise. Let us presume that a referendum were to be held on each of us. Two ballots are to be held. In the one case, a communication of our Blue Lodge is to consider the matter of our membership, There are no charges brought of misconduct…simply a review of our membership in the Craft. Everyone with whom we have come in contact in Masonry is to be in attendance, and each is to be given the opportunity to ballot in secret concerning our activity and stewardship as a Mason. The question propounded is whether this Brother has dedicated himself to the principles of Masonry, and lent of his time and talent in service to the Craft?

The second ballot is to be convened amongst those with whom we have come in contact in our lives that are not members of the Craft. Men, women, and children, are all to have the opportunity to ballot on whether we stand out in the community as an exemplary person…one who personifies all the best of virtues, and one who inspires an admiration for the Masonic Craft. Think Brother! Thank hard and be honest! Do you think you could pass such a test, without a dissenting vote in either ballot?

Perhaps it is within the scope of only a few to reach such heights of respect, but it should not be so. Everyday is crowded with many decisions reflecting upon our conduct. It has been said that to "err is human." To err where relations with our fellow man is concerned is not a human fault, it is a result of thoughtlessness.

Consideration should here be given to another statement, "Act in haste, repent in leisure." There is a certain amount of merit to that statement, but is also true in reverse, "Act in leisure, repent in haste."

The world at large should benefit from the example of Masons taking the time to consider their actions and their words. Those words and actions should reflect the guidelines established in God's great Book, and they should reflect that consideration which would bring mankind closer to living in harmony one with another. Is that not the objective of Freemasonry? We must disassociate ourselves from the gripers, the complainers, and the militants. If we are adamant in our determination to engage in productive and proper conduct, giving each to another that respect he wishes for himself. and keep ourselves above the pettiness that has ruled the world since the beginning of man... the gripers, the complainers, and the militants will lose their audience, and maybe see a better way of life through our example.

Would God do it again" The results are not yet in. Would Masonry do it again, where we are concerned? The final results are not yet in...There is still time to assure ourselves of an affirmative answer in both instances.

To the reader: Those with a firm belief in a Supreme Being, seem to have little difficulty accepting the miracles outlined in their Holy Book. However, there seems to be a tendency to indicate that there must be a logical explanation for any event, or occurrence that occurs today. Perhaps it is a feeling that miracles, or intervention by an unseen power, only happened during the early years of civilization. Of all the myriad facets of life and relationships this writer has been most focused on a desire to be consistent. If one states that Divine intervention occurred only in Biblical times, and not today, then a dichotomy is created with which the writer is not comfortable. The following paper was presented at a Masonic gathering with no other intent than to accurately relate the facts. The reader is free to make his own interpretations, The writer has his.

Chapter XXX
One Never Knows

In the fall of '84, the Grand Royal Arch Chapter of West Virginia honored this poor soul by electing him Grand High Priest. Going in, I made a resolution to spend my time in office within the confines of our great Mountain State, attempting to provide what leadership and encouragement I could to our constituent Chapters. Perhaps it is well for Grand High Priests to visit other jurisdictions, but at the time, it seemed more important to spend as much time as possible at the stated convocations of our Chapters, finding out what they needed, or wanted, and giving them a pat on the back, and a word of encouragement.

One dark night that winter found this poor soul on a lonely stretch of Route 7, south of Clarington, Ohio. It was one of those nights when Mother Nature seemed out of sorts and disgusted with the world, and determined to vent her anger in a most forceful way. The snow the day before had been a general one, blanketing the state, and closing secondary roads. The drive that Sunday morning from Wheeling south had been slow going and treacherous. My family had expressed concern about traveling in such weather, but I was determined to be in attendance at the gathering of the Companions that afternoon in Kenova for a school of instruction. My oldest son urged me to use his four wheel drive Bronco, and my wife insisted that I take a woolen scarf, which she produced with the warning to be careful and to stay bundled up.

Driving slowly south that morning I passed through New Matamoras, Ohio, and in a yard alongside the road I saw the most beautiful snowman. He was formed to perfection, and was properly outfitted with arms, eyes, nose, mouth, ears, and a hat cocked just a little to one side. The snowman had a rather jaunty air about him, and gave the impression of being well pleased with the weather, and presided over the wintry scene with obvious self satisfaction.

The snowman brought pleasure and cheerful thoughts to mind at a time when I desperately needed encouragement and support. Because of personal problems, I had suggested passing up the opportunity to be Grand High Priest, but a couple of Past Grands prevailed upon me to continue my service to the Grand Chapter. In any event, the snowman brought a warm feeling, and much to my surprise, I realized I had pulled over to the side of the road. What I was about to do was a complete new experience for me, and one that seemed silly in a way, for my finances were as low as my morale. Nonetheless, I marched back to the yard, up the sidewalk, onto the porch, and knocked on the door. A very bright young man of about five opened the door, and I asked if he was responsible for the snowman in the yard. He was hesitant, but replied that indeed he had helped with the project the previous evening.

In my very best manner I tried to convey to the young man what the snowman meant to me, and presented him with a dollar. Retracing my steps to the car, the snowman seemed to be watching as I passed, and it certainly looked as though his smile was a little broader, and it appeared that the lumps of coal through which he watched, had a sparkle that had not been there before.

Continuing the journey south, I crossed the Ohio River to the West Virginia side at St. Mary's, and just south on Route 2, I came across a lady and two small children in a station wagon in a snow bank just north of Belmont, West Virginia The road had been plowed, but she had gotten too close to the piled up snow in passing another car, and she would soon be late for Sunday School. Remembering I had seen a tow chain in the back of the Bronco, she and her two children were soon away in what she said would be time enough to make Sunday School.

The trip south was not without further incident. West of Charleston, West Virginia, on Interstate 64, a motorist was sitting in his car alongside the road. In these times, it is not considered prudent, perhaps, to stop to pick up riders, or to offer help along the way. You often read of untoward happenings, but even so, I stopped to inquire if he needed assistance. His car, he explained, had quit running, no doubt the fuel line had frozen, for the temperature was below zero. We made our way to the next exit, where I left him with a service station attendant, who promised of take care of his needs.

The Chapter gathering at Kenova was productive and informative, and my spirits were again raised as I was pleased with the camaraderie, and the obvious interest the Companions exhibited in the work of the day.

Upon leaving, I discovered that the Bronco had developed a flat tire which some of the Companions graciously changed for me, and after fortifying me with a fine meal, they took me to a service station and filled the Bronco with gasoline. They bade me God speed, cautioned me to be careful on the drive home, and I was on my way north to home, hearth, and family. At about ten o-clock that night I found myself on a deserted stretch of road south of Clarington, Ohio. The Bronco began to sputter, and protested my efforts to keep it running. It coughed and chugged, nearly stopped, then fired up and ran another fifty yards rather smoothly.

Just as I was congratulating myself, it took a turn for the worse, and sputtered to a stop. Despite my best efforts, it stubbornly refused to start, and it was time for careful consideration of my situation. One possibility was to remain in the car, and hope that some motorist would happen along with a disposition to stop and give me assistance. An alternative was to leave the car, and begin walking until a house with the lights shining through the windows as a beacon of safety and aid. We have all heard the admonition to remain with your car when in trouble, but I reasoned that I was dressed warmly with a very heavy overcoat; further, I had the woolen scarf my wife insisted I take along, and I had serious doubts about any traffic at night along that particular road. Reasoning that Clarington was still about two miles ahead, and believing that I had seen a house about a mile back, I wrapped the scarf around my neck, locked the Bronco, and headed down the road in the direction from which I had come.

The night was very dark, and there was a brisk breeze along the Ohio River. I later learned that the temperature was eighteen below zero! After making my way about a hundred yards, I began to have some doubts about my decision to leave the vehicle, but determined to go on. After a quarter of a mile, I could feel the cold wind through to the bone. The feeling was as if my clothing had disappeared, the flesh had been stripped away, and Mother Nature was blowing her bitter cold breath across my bare bones, no doubt in retribution for all the times I had ignored her, or ignored her handiwork.

I stopped and looked back, trying to decide whether to turn and go back to the Bronco. It seemed as though my thought processes had slowed, and it was difficult to think clearly. At that moment, a very small car came from behind me, from the direction where my car was alongside the road. I was not aware of the car until I heard a voice yelling at me from just ahead, and across the road. It was the voice of a young man, and he was repeating himself, Finally the words came through, "Hey Mister, are you alright?"

It seemed I was answering him, but then realized that he had hold of me and was repeating the question again. I assured him I was okay, but he didn't seem convinced. He asked if that was not my Bronco alongside the road, to which I replied in the affirmative. The young man helped me across the road, and put me in the back of the little car. There was another young man at the wheel, and he asked his companion if I was all right, to which he got a rather tentative reply. The little car seemed as though it was warm, for I could feel the heat on my face, and though I no longer felt the wind was whistling through my rib cage;

nonetheless, my bones felt as if they had been fast frozen. The driver revved up the little car and headed down the road while the passenger who had helped me across the road leaned over the seat trying to assess by condition.

As I slowly warmed up, I told them that if they could get me to Bellaire, Ohio, I knew that one of my sons would come and get me. They readily agreed and turned the car around and headed for Bellaire, passing the forlorn Bronco on the way. They explained that they had determined to get their car out and give it a run to make sure it would be in condition to take them to work in the morning. They also told me that if they had not seen my vehicle first, and then determined that I was in trouble walking along that road, they would not have stopped. Living in that area, they knew that picking up pedestrians along that deserted stretch was a no-no.

After several minutes in the car, my thought processes begun to work a little better, and the danger I had been in began to come through. I also began to notice that the young men were smoking, and they had only one cigarette between them that they were holding with some sort of funny little holder. Each would take a puff or two, and then pass it to the other. Believe me, I had never encountered a cigarette that had such a strange and awful aroma. Cigars and pipe are my forte, and in my time I have tackled the best and the worst, but I had never smelled tobacco as offensive as that cigarette. In my situation, whatever they were smoking was all right with me!

When I was warm enough to converse intelligently, I asked the two how much further I would have walked before finding a house along the road. I stated that I thought I had seen a light about a mile before the

330

Bronco quit running. They replied that I had been mistaken about seeing any house closer than about two miles from where they found me. They also said that the official temperature according to the weather bureau was 18 degrees below zero!

The two young men dropped me off at the City Restaurant in Bellaire, a fine restaurant that, at that time, was always open. Reaching in my pocket, I found some loose change, and a ten dollar bill. The ten spot had been to buy gas for the return trip, but as the Companions in Kenova had graciously filled my tank, I was able to reward my young rescuers with a very fine likeness of Andrew Jackson. Perhaps they would be able to use it to buy something of a better quality to smoke, and would not have to share. These thoughts went through my mind as I gave them the ten with my sincere thanks; but in appreciation, I did not express them aloud.

In the restaurant, I used the loose change to call home, and in about forty five minutes my youngest son, and his wife appeared and rode me home to safety in style, concluding my adventure on a bitter cold winter's night.

As we pulled up our driveway, I was silently recounting my adventure. The motorist alongside the road that I gave a lift, the lady and her two children stranded on the way to Sunday School, and the snowman. I reflected on my miraculous good fortune along that lonely stretch of road. The two young men choosing that particular time to take their car out for a drive on such a bitter and ominous might, and the fact that I had chosen to walk in a direction that the young men saw the stranded vehicle first, and surmising that I was in trouble, stopped to help.

One hears of people who claim that God has

spoken to them, and if some person of ancient history makes that claim, we tend to believe it. If one who walks the Earth with us today makes the claim, perhaps we have serious reservations. Most certainly, I have never heard directly from the Supreme Being, and am afraid I can see no reason for Him ever to take that much personal interest to favor me in such a manner. But as I climbed the porch steps of my home, I was thinking again of the snowman…did he smile at me?…was he watching me?…did his eyes have a special sparkle as I walked past him back to the car?…I wonder!

As I opened the kitchen door to the safety and warmth of my home and wife, I heard no voices, I saw no unexplained lights, but very clearly and distinctly, the words flashed though my mind…"Ophir, we're even !"

One never knows!

To the reader: Writers begin with an idea, a point, a philosophy, or some event. They make an outline, and determine the direction of their treatise. Perhaps extensive research is needed to prove the premise, or perhaps the entire matter is one of opinion derived from experience.

All of the previous chapters in this effort have been nothing more than a collection of papers previously written. What follows was compiled solely for this book. It was inspired by a personal event where this writer came all too close to the final chapter of his life.

The circumstance was sudden in nature, occurred late at night, and while traveling alone in a remote area, and is not the adventure related in the previous chapter. This one was a much closer brush with the final dissolution.

Later, the writer deliberated on the circumstances of that night. He found himself pondering, "What will be the last thing I see?" So, what follows was not originated in the usual manner, but was written as the mind considered the quoted question.

Chapter XXXI
The Last Thing I See

When writer and reader meet on the printed page, the writer has the advantage of determining the direction the relationship will take; however, the reader holds the ultimate weapon, for he, or she, decides whether to remain in concert to the end, or to terminate the relationship at some point. A consolation to the writer is that he continues in the aura of his self esteem, believing his work has brought enjoyment and enlightenment to the world. He is completely unaware that some reader has abruptly ended the union in disinterest.

Those who put thought to paper usually approach study and typewriter with an idea and an outline in mind. It has been my custom to jot down a phrase I hear that languished on the ear and resonated in the mind. Often times, the phrase arises from something seen, or something read. Invariably, it gives the promise of stirring reflective thought in a particular direction, upon a particular matter, or on a person. These notes are kept in a steno pad, and gradually an outline takes shape in the mind. When the outline and direction have taken shape, it is time to turn paper around the platen and reduce the matter to print.

In the present instance, this writer has no advantage, as he hasn't a clue of the direction of this relationship. Further, he has only the phrase from which no outline has permeated his thoughts. Indeed, the only rationale to this endeavor, is that the subject is intriguing to the writer.

Hence we begin. In what direction, or to what end, we will discover together as we go along.

At some point in every person's life, he becomes truly aware of his mortality. Sometimes a grave illness from which he escapes makes him cognizant of the fact that he is not indestructible. Occasionally some event startles him to that realization, and very often the passage of time slowly convinces him of the inevitable. The inescapable flaw in man's persona is his inability to listen. Not just the polite keeping still when someone else is talking, but also the intelligent taking to heart the other fellow relating his knowledge and experiences. Oh, we listen when we pay. We listen to the professional for whose services we pay; but, we seldom listen to the one whose professional knowledge and skill are being offered to us for free.

How many times have we been cautioned to spend our time wisely, for it is priceless? Ever heard the old saying, "Enjoy yourself, for these are the good old days you are going to talk about twenty years from now." Have you not been encouraged to save your money, invest it wisely, and thus be secure on a rainy day? All these things and more, we have all heard time and time again, but from whom?

Without exception, every time we have been lectured about time, money, education, morals, etc., it has been by a professional. In this instance, a professional is someone who is older. Perhaps you have a different experience, but this writer has never been lectured by someone who is tender in years. Why is that? It appears that the young are not as interested in time, as it appears unending to them. However, to the senior person, time seems fleeting and precious. How can the seasoned professional on the passage of time cause the neophyte to listen and take the lessons to heart…it would appear that charging for the advice is perhaps the only solution.

These thoughts on time have led this writer to the subject of this treatise…"The Last Thing I See." Like all young people, the passage of time seemed slow and unending. There would always be time for those things I had not yet done, but now it becomes painfully obvious that many of those items on the list of things to do in life will never be accomplished. For that situation, there is now no solution. But what of the end of the road? When the time comes, I wonder what will be the last thing I see?

My paternal grandfather passed on long before I was born. He was a Methodist Minister in Southeast Tennessee, but never accepted money for doing the Lord's work. Whenever he heard of a small church in the mountains that had lost their Minister, he would ride horseback to that community and preach either on Saturday night, or Sunday afternoon. He would permit members of the congregation to put him up over night, if he preached on Saturday evening, and to furnish him a meal; but he would accept no other compensation, nor did he accept compensation from his regular congregation in Copper Hill.

To take care of his needs, and his family of wife and seven children, he worked in the copper mine as a foreman. When conducting a marriage ceremony, he would not accept pay either. He would ask the new couple to call him when they were ready to build their first house, and permit him to lay up the fireplace and chimney for them as his wedding present. It is my understanding that at one time the area was full of chimneys that the Reverend had laid up. You can understand that it is with much pride that I cherish his trowel. Though well worn, to me his trowel exudes love and respect.

Grandfather was also the Chaplain of his Masonic Lodge for many years, and was a highly loved and respected individual. The story of his death related to me by my grandmother many years ago applies to the matter under consideration.

Copper mines in Tennessee are shaft mines, rather than slope. An elevator cage goes straight down into the ground that carries the men to their work. My grandfather was coming up on the elevator with a new man, and as the cage neared level with the top of the ground, the new man jumped out, but Grandfather waited for the floor of the elevator to reach equity, and for the elevator to stop moving. It never made it. The cables slipped, and the elevator went to the bottom, terminally injuring my grandfather. His wife was summoned, and she sat by his side, as he lay unconscious. As she watched over him, he opened his eyes briefly and saw her. He spoke to her gently and said, "Mary, do not be concerned for me. I have seen where I am going, and it is more beautiful than I can describe...I love you Mary." And with that, he gave up the ghost.

As I ponder with you, the story of my grandfather touches me. The last thing that he saw on this earth was his wife, who had served him faithfully, and whom he loved very much.

My feelings are the same, and most certainly it is my desire to convey my love and appreciation to my wife before I pass this veil of tears. I want her to know that her love and devotion have not been casually accepted, or taken for granted, and that her many sacrifices for our children and me, are far beyond my poor ability to repay. Most importantly, I would want her to understand that she is not to grieve for me, for my love for her continues no matter my dissolution.

Although I have not seen where I am going, like my grandfather did, it is my desire to see and say those things that are important to my wife. To wait for the proper time might be poor judgment. Perhaps what I see today is among the last things that I will see. No doubt it is important to convey these things to my wife now, and then update then periodically.

My father lived a full and useful life, and was vibrant and strong at the time of his death in his eightieth year. He was home in his living room on New Year's Eve. Being from Tennessee, he had a warm spot in his heart for the University of Tennessee football team. On that evening, following supper, he took a nap that was his custom, but asked my stepmother to wake him for the Orange Bowl Parade. He wanted to see the parade, and then wanted to watch the Bluebonnet Bowl, for the Volunteers of Tennessee were to play in it.

He was awakened from his nap on time, and watched the parade until time for the ball game. During the first half, with Tennessee playing well, and in the lead, he pitched forward from his rocking chair and was gone. Dad was at work that day in his store. He had no hobbies, but lived and breathed the store he had started and run for fifty six years. He enjoyed sports as a spectator, and always rooted for the Tennessee football team. And so, he spent his last day doing what he liked best, waiting on customers in his store, and passed out of this world with his team in the lead. He never knew that they lost the game in the second half.

Yes, I want to add those items to my formula also. My last day, given the chance, I want to spend doing something I enjoy. My pursuits are much broader than my father's were, and I have many interests. I have no preference, so any of them will do, and most certainly I hope to go out with my team in the lead. I can't help them after I'm gone, but it is my desire to keep them on top while I am here.

Life is indeed fragile, and we know not what tomorrow may bring. The young fellow might not take that to heart, but this writer is old enough to give it careful consideration.

So, it behooves me to make sure that henceforth, I do something every day that brings me joy and comfort. Everyday must bring some activity to my life that I enjoy and look forward to doing. This will, of course, take some planning, but as I think about it, it will make life more pleasant. How nice to look forward to the joys each day will bring. At the same time, I must see that those teams in which I am interested - and I am not referring to sports - are always on top. Everyone should be on some "team" or other, and it is important that you always do your best to keep your "team" on top. You have no knowledge of when they will be deprived of your assistance in perpetuity.

My father-in-law fits this same category. All his life he was an ardent fisherman. He would plan his trips over and over. He would gather night crawlers, tend to them, and see they were in fit condition for the trip. His gear and tackle received special attention, and was carefully packed and double checked well in advance. No one ever left on a fishing trip with as much careful preparation as "Pop." He was active in his church choir and enjoyed it. He belonged to the York Rite, and while not a regular attendee, we spent many an enjoyable evening together in Lodge. He never failed to be present when someone he knew was receiving work. But with it all, fishing was his passion.

His wife fell ill, and he missed his annual trip to Kentucky with his son, nephews-in-law, and friends. This had become an annual trip and they had named themselves the "Dallas Pike Fishing Club" but his wife's illness made foregoing the trip necessary, While in the hospital, she made him promise that he would take his son, son-in-law, and the four grandsons on a fishing trip to Kentucky, and that he would pay all expenses. This was to be accomplished as soon as she was either well, or gone. A short time later she left us, a very great lady in my opinion, which we all still miss. My father-in-law informed all of us of the pledge he had made, and that as soon as all the legal matters were finished he would make the arrangements and set the date.

And so, we all went to Kentucky. "Pop" rented a houseboat, and we had the most glorious time. He reveled in the grandsons, and he also had some private time with his son, and importantly to me, "Pop" and I had some private time together also.

On leaving the houseboat on a Thursday, I asked Pop, his son, and his grandsons to line up on the back of the boat while I took a picture. I always had taken the camera on trips, but had never taken any pictures. The camera had to be found, then film located, and finally I got the snapshot. Everyone now has a copy of that photo. On Sunday following, Pop made the comment that he had his fishing trip in and was now ready to go and be with Midge (his wife). On the following Thursday morning, the shop where he worked part time after his retirement called and reported he had not shown up that morning. My wife and sister-in-law found him in bed...he had his fishing trip in, and was now with Midge.

Fishing is also one of my passions, but I have not done any for a number of years now. My eldest son and I made a pact to go on a trip every year. We had hoped the other boys would go with us, and they did for a couple of years, but it evolved down to the oldest and myself. I envy "Pop," he got his fishing trip in. A project to get back to that trip every year with my oldest son seems in order, considering the present discussion.

I first met a very good Masonic friend in the bowling alleys. I know, they call them lanes now, but to me, they will always be bowling alleys. It was in bowling alleys where I staked my claim to fame in the sports world, and I am not about to rewrite history by saying they were lanes.

At any rate, my friend and Brother was very active in the Commandery, and was one of the best Commanders Wheeling Commandery ever had. He was a tireless worker, and a very organized individual. When the Prelate of some twenty five years plus stepped out, my friend accepted election to the post, and was an outstanding Prelate. His expertise not only covered excellent ritual work, but he was very adept at formulating successful programs. At the same time, he was not one to claim the spotlight. When another Past Commander expressed an interest in the Prelate position, my friend stepped aside over the objection of the membership. He wanted to keep as many as possible active in the work. It was his way.

One evening while I was on a fishing trip, the Commandery was conferring the Order of the Temple. The new Prelate was doing a very competent job, and my friend was serving in the Prelate's escort. Following obligation of the candidate, my friend left the escort and went to the sidelines. Others went to him with concern, and he reported that he didn't feel very well, and with that joined the escort that services the Captain of our Salvation. I knew him well. I worked with him in Commandery for years. It is my belief that he would have been pleased with the obligation of a new Sir Knight into Templary as the last thing he saw.

That is not an unworthy thought, to see a new Masonic life created as one ends, but impossible to arrange. But continued activity in the affairs of the Craft will ensure that Masonic events will be among the last things one sees.

The last thing President Abraham Lincoln saw was a play. Some say that Lincoln enjoyed the theater. That evening at Ford's Theater he was watching a popular nineteenth century comedy with which he was familiar. The President had a great sense of humor, and no doubt enjoyed at least a few laughs before John Wilkes Booth's fateful entrance into the President's box.

George Armstrong Custer's last view was of more Indians than he cared to see, as they were both unwelcome and unfriendly. Given the choice, would Custer have made some other selection of the last thing he was to see? Perhaps, given the manner of his life, he would have chosen to go down in a blaze of glory as a military hero.

The last thing Colin Kelly saw in World War II was a Japanese ship as he dove his damaged plane into it. He gave the last full measure of devotion to his country, and his final thoughts, and the final thing he saw, were of his choosing.

Do we not owe it to ourselves to so conduct ourselves, and plan our lives, so that the last thing we see will be enjoyable, or of which we would be proud? Do we not have a responsibility to plan our lives to ensure that our last activities will be either pleasant or productive?

There will be no opportunity to plead for just a little more time so that we can say those things others deserve to hear from our lips. No postponements are available to offer additional time to catch that last fish, or hit that last golf ball. No exchange of tickets for the next scheduled transportation, so that we can attend the Lodge meeting we have been putting off. No pleas for probation so that we might make some contribution to society. Once the decision is made on high, no man can avoid the decree. Each must judiciously program his life, and schedule his time, so that he is productive and happy in his activities.

Perhaps no one can truly answer the question of what he would select as the last thing to see. There are so many from which to choose, and the list of each would be different. The importance is to be aware of the priceless value of each second of time. Do not waste it, and do not waste that of others. Nothing can be done about that which has already been wasted, but to mourn over the loss, which is an additional waste of time. My Brother, be of good cheer. Let us, you and I, here determine that we will so live, and so relate to others, that we will find joy and pleasure in whatever happens to be…The Last Thing We See !

Epilogue

Masonry is not a one time a week, nor a one time a month undertaking. Neither is it a carry the card in your pocket, look what I am identifier. Masonry is a dedication to all that is good in life.

It is imperative that every Mason be exemplary in the performance of every duty, both within and without the Lodge, and actively support his community in a way that brings honor to the fraternity.

It appears that the Craft is again at a crossroads in its history. If so, the corrections must be made in each village, town, and city, as Masonry's real strength is in the recognition of immediate acceptance between Brothers, and between Lodges. It derives its progress from the willingness to strengthen and support each other across geographical lines.

At one time it could be said that Masons were leaders, and leaders were Masons. Hopefully, it can still be said in your area, but perhaps not. The Craft structure is such that it attracts the attention of those with the attributes of leadership, concerns for one another, faithful pursuits of personable interaction, and respect for institutions of right thinking people. If persons of those qualities are no longer seeking Masonry, it is not the fault of changing times, nor the advent of technology. It lies in the lack of devotion to keeping the perception of the Craft at the level it has customarily held over the centuries.

Paying dues and carrying cards makes no contribution to the continuance of the institution of Freemasonry. Permitting the organization's financial stature to languish in the economy of yesterday's history denigrates the perception. Masonic leaders who are not prepared, nor willing to dedicate the time and effort necessary for success, hinder, rather than help.

Many issues need to be studied and reviewed in order to return Masonry to its rightful place, and such work begins with each of us in our daily deliberations. Even if you disagree with the premise that Masonry has lost ground in the last thirty years or so, due to the lack of proper adjustment and correction, it is still imperative that all matters be constantly reviewed and evaluated.

It would be highly unusual if nothing could be located that could not be improved with some proper attention. Everyone should study, learn, and investigate, to come to those conclusions that make him a better man, and add a little something both to society, and to the Craft. If just one Brother is encouraged to rededicate himself to the virtues of friendship and Brotherly love, then your efforts and mine will have been successful.

Before leaving you on this occasion, permit me to quote from two works.

The first is from something called, "Streams in the Desert," whose author is unknown to this writer. The second is from the Bible...

> "Be quiet!
> Why this anxious heed.
> About thy tangled ways?
> God knows them all.
> He giveth speed
> And he allows delays.
> Tis good for thee to walk by faith
> And not by sight.
> Take it on trust a little while
> Soon shalt thou read the mystery aright
> In the full sunshine of His smile."

And from Corinthians II:

"Finally brethren, farewell.
Be perfect, be of good comfort,
be of one mind, live in peace:
and the God of Love and Peace
shall be with you."

It is here hoped that we meet sometime again upon the printed page, either yours, or mine.

To obtain a copy of this title for College or University Library archive purposes, please send letters of request on official letterhead to:

Dragonfly Press Publishing
PO Box 830635
Ocala, Florida 34483-0635

Or email us at:
sales@dragonflypresspublishing.com
Subject line "Freemasonry - Vellenoweth"

Please direct emails to the author to:
author@dragonflypresspublishing.com
Subject line "Vellenoweth"

Visit us online at:
www.dragonflypresspublishing.com

www.ingramcontent.com/pod-product-compliance
Lightning Source LLC
Chambersburg PA
CBHW051724260326
41914CB00031B/1732/J